A SECOND SELF

A SECOND SELF

The Letters of
Harriet Granville

1810 – 1845

EDITED BY

VIRGINIA SURTEES

MICHAEL RUSSELL

Editorial matter © Virginia Surtees 1990

First published in Great Britain 1990
by Michael Russell (Publishing) Ltd
The Chantry, Wilton, Salisbury, Wiltshire

Typeset in Sabon by The Spartan Press Ltd
Lymington, Hampshire
Printed and bound in Great Britain
by Biddles Ltd, Guildford and King's Lynn

ISBN 0 85955 165 2

Contents

Acknowledgements

I wish to thank Lord Granville for his kind permission to allow me to quote from unpublished letters in which he holds the copyright, and the Howard Family of Castle Howard for access to this material.

I am very much indebted to the Hon. Betty Askwith for her contribution in handing over to me her papers and notes for *Piety & Wit* (a biography of the writer of these present letters) and for the help she has given me in many ways. Also to Mrs Noel Blakiston, great-granddaughter of Lord and Lady Granville, for her assistance in elucidating family concerns and for her sympathetic encouragement. I have benefited from welcome advice from Mr John Cornforth, Mr Oliver Davies, Mr Eeyan Hartley, archivist at Castle Howard, Mr Burnet Pavitt, and Miss J. Ramkalawon. Lady Gladwyn's *The Paris Embassy* has been close at hand for the Paris years, while to Mr James Lees-Milne I am grateful for a lively and enlightening correspondence at a time when he had started on his forthcoming biography of the 6th Duke of Devonshire, the much-loved brother of Harriet Granville.

Author's Note

From the earlier two-volume edition of these letters edited in 1894 by the Granvilles' youngest son, the Hon. F. Leveson Gower, much has been omitted or cut to make a more commodious book; some unpublished letters have been added. The original editor, obliged to reduce to two volumes the vast extent of his mother's correspondence, took occasional liberties with the text by interpolating passages from one letter to another. His datings are sometimes faulty and ill-defined. Those now given may be slightly more conclusive, though it has been a perplexing pursuit since Lady Granville cared nothing for such niceties; besides, she was in almost daily, sometimes twice daily, communication with her sister. In this I have been liberally helped by a complete and carefully annotated typescript of the correspondence from 1810 to 1819 made in 1940 by the late Iris Leveson Gower, granddaughter of the original editor.

The use of French in this correspondence was as natural as breathing to the writer – as it would have been to all her contemporaries – and it has therefore seemed advisable, for the convenience of the reader, to exclude italics from the text where a foreign tongue is used. Her spelling has been preserved throughout; capitals and ampersands have been modified; marks of omission in the letters have not been introduced. The French practice of lower case for titles has not been adopted. Since in almost every case the letters begin: 'Dearest G' and are signed: 'H.L. Gower' or H. Leveson Gower', occasionally 'Harriet Leveson Gower', and later with a change in circumstance simply 'H.G.', these forms of salutation and farewell have been omitted.

A superior b after a proper name (the first time it appears) implies that he or she is included in the Biographical Index. I have distinguished between explanatory footnotes, found at the foot of the page, and bibliographical glosses or source notes, marked with superior figures and found on pp. 293–7.

Introduction

Until her marriage to Lord Granville Leveson Gower[b] in December 1809, the life of the Duke of Devonshire's[b] youngest daughter, Lady Harriet Cavendish[b] ('Hah-yet Can'dish' as it was pronounced),[1] had not been altogether an easy one. After her mother's death and sister's marriage she found it impossible to live at Devonshire House, Piccadilly, where her father's mistress, Lady Elizabeth Foster,[b] took upon herself the role of hostess which should rightly have fallen to Harriet. Also at Devonshire House lived Augustus Clifford[b] and Caroline St Jules,[b] the illegitimate offspring of the Duke and Lady Elizabeth, who as a widow with two sons of an earlier marriage had been a most dear friend and confidante of the late Duchess Georgiana,[b] the legendary 'beautiful Duchess'. This *ménage à trois* had succeeded surprisingly well. But with the likelihood of the Duke marrying Lady Elizabeth it became of paramount importance that Harriet, who disliked her, should have an establishment of her own. Marriage would solve the problem.

Her aunt, Countess of Bessborough,[b] chose her own adored Granville for her niece. She had borne him two children, Harriette[b] and George Stewart,[b] and had loved him passionately for seventeen years but was aware that he must now settle down and marry. Whilst for her the sacrifice must have been extreme, to Granville, at thirty-six, it was the natural course.[2] A member of Parliament for Staffordshire, prominent in society and half-brother of the Marquess of Stafford[b] (later the 1st Duke of Sutherland), it was time to get married. His exceptional good looks and the '*occhi azzuri*',[3] 'those eyes where I have looked my life away', as Lady Bessborough remembered,[4] made him irresistibly attractive to many women. He had had several love affairs but his long-standing and once ardent liaison with Lady Bessborough seems not to have been a hindrance to proposing matrimony to her niece. He was an habitué of the Devonshire

House set and his marriage to the daughter of the house was regarded with satisfaction though the couple were not well off and the Duke was less generous in the matter of a marriage settlement than he had been to his eldest daughter, Lady Georgiana Morpeth,[b] the 'dearest G' of these letters. His family were devoted to him, Harriet adored him. It was the perfect marriage.

Harriet Cavendish was born in 1785 into a society of all that was brilliant, political, cultivated and good-mannered in the world of fashion, of which Devonshire House was the centre. In 1802 at the age of seventeen Georgiana had married Lord Morpeth, the eldest son of the 5th Earl of Carlisle[b] whose wife was Granville's half-sister. Their London house was in Park Street but they made their home mostly at Castle Howard with the Carlisles. During adolescence and the awkwardness of living at Devonshire House, Harriet had turned to her sister for guidance and support and had stayed in Yorkshire for prolonged visits. Her love for 'G' (which was reciprocated) was one of the strongest affections of her life. To her younger brother, Lord Hartington (soon to succeed as 6th Duke of Devonshire[b] on their father's death in 1811), she was almost equally attached. Her maternal grandmother, now the Dowager Countess Spencer, and her governess Miss Trimmer, whom Harriet had known since infancy, had provided a steadying influence and a predisposition for religion which would be a mainstay of her mature years.

She had not inherited her mother's looks; she spoke in 'the bleating drawl of the Devonshire House set';[5] like her sister she was inclined to be anxious about her health, though nothing like to the same degree, for the elder suffered from a nervous constitution and imaginary fears to which twelve pregnancies no doubt contributed. But Harriet had intelligence and understanding, a lively wit and a great fund of enjoyment as well as a down-to-earth common sense.[6]

These letters, written (with some exceptions) to her sister, start in August 1810 after Georgiana Morpeth's departure to Castle Howard. They had seen each other constantly in London ever since the Leveson Gower marriage seven months previously and now Harriet was pregnant.

In this correspondence – and there are surely no other letters comparable for sheer entertainment – she reveals little interest in politics until later years. Brought up in a Whig stronghold, she had married a middle-of-the-road Tory with a lifelong friendship for George Canning,[b] but what we do receive is an alluring portrayal of the times in which she lived. By their sharp observation – and Harriet never lost her sense of the ridiculous – they provide an entertaining peepshow into the manners, habits and morals of that much-intermarried section of aristocratic nineteenth-century society which also embraced the dandies, wits and beaux. Until Granville was appointed Ambassador to Paris in 1824 he and Harriet spent a large part of the year in perpetual motion, moving from one great house to the next on the long round of country house visits which made up the pattern of fashionable life, or else they entertained at home. They had a town house, first in Stanhope Street, later in Bruton Street, which they often let. They rented Tixal, in Staffordshire, in 1811 for eight years and Wherstead in Suffolk from 1819 to 1824.

Eliminations in the letters include bilious attacks, births and deaths of little interest, the ever-debatable question of the integrity of the childrens' governess, the efficacy of diet, the weather, and a rather over-generous proportion of parties and drums. But much remains of what must have diverted Georgiana, the dearest of sisters, living in the Yorkshire splendour of Castle Howard.

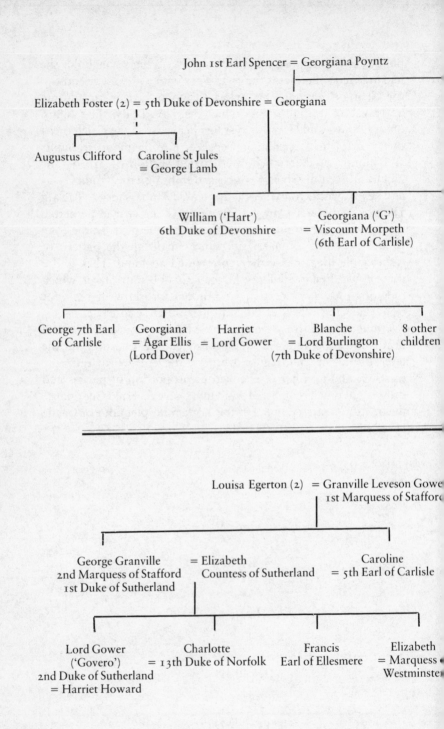

John 1st Earl Spencer = Georgiana Poyntz

Elizabeth Foster (2) = 5th Duke of Devonshire = Georgiana

Augustus Clifford   Caroline St Jules
= George Lamb

William ('Hart')
6th Duke of Devonshire

Georgiana ('G')
= Viscount Morpeth
(6th Earl of Carlisle)

George 7th Earl
of Carlisle

Georgiana
= Agar Ellis
(Lord Dover)

Harriet
= Lord Gower

Blanche
= Lord Burlington
(7th Duke of Devonshire)

8 other
children

Louisa Egerton (2) = Granville Leveson Gower
1st Marquess of Stafford

George Granville
2nd Marquess of Stafford
1st Duke of Sutherland

= Elizabeth
Countess of Sutherland

Caroline
= 5th Earl of Carlisle

Lord Gower
('Govero')
2nd Duke of Sutherland
= Harriet Howard

Charlotte
= 13th Duke of Norfolk

Francis
Earl of Ellesmere

Elizabeth
= Marquess
Westminster

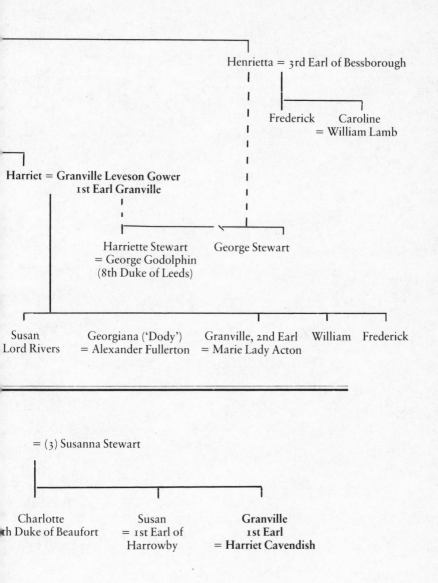

Henrietta = 3rd Earl of Bessborough

Frederick   Caroline
               = William Lamb

Harriet = Granville Leveson Gower
          1st Earl Granville

Harriette Stewart   George Stewart
= George Godolphin
(8th Duke of Leeds)

Susan   Georgiana ('Dody')   Granville, 2nd Earl   William   Frederick
Lord Rivers   = Alexander Fullerton   = Marie Lady Acton

= (3) Susanna Stewart

Charlotte   Susan   Granville
th Duke of Beaufort   = 1st Earl of   1st Earl
                 Harrowby   = Harriet Cavendish

SIMPLIFIED FAMILY TREE
SHOWING MOST OF HARRIET'S RELATIONS
MENTIONED IN THE TEXT

The Letters

The Leveson Gowers were about to start for the country on a round of visits to include both of Granville's sisters, the Duchess of Beaufort[b] at Badminton and the Countess of Harrowby[b] at Sandon Hall in Staffordshire, where Hartington eventually joined them. From there they continued to Lilleshall in Shropshire, stopping for a night at Trentham, the Stafford property not far from the Harrowbys. Before leaving London Granville had a last fling at the gaming tables at Brooks's, a pursuit that worried Harriet for the considerable debts it incurred. Harriet's first cousin, Lady Caroline Lamb,[b] not yet of Byronic fame, came to dinner with her husband. Unpredictable she had always been, but her eccentricities would eventually degenerate into mental derangement. She was always known as 'Caroline William' (the name of her husband, William Lamb[b]) to distinguish her from her sister-in-law, once Caroline St Jules, who had married William's brother George,[b] and who in turn was called 'Caroline George'.

Harriet was due to lie in towards the end of October, in London, and for this she had engaged the services of Sir Richard Croft (later to mismanage Princess Charlotte's childbirth) and Farquhar, another well-known obstetrician.

Stanhope Street
Wednesday [1 August 1810]

I need hardly talk of my health now. I feel better and stronger every hour and we shall certainly begin our journey on Saturday. I long to be gone as I am rather en proie to the Duchess [of Devonshire] who comes in a white satin hood oftener than I could wish.

God bless you dearest. Granville says a great deal to you and

Lord M[orpeth]. He was prosperous again last night and we shall, I hope, leave town in triumphant circumstances.

Stanhope Street
Thursday [2 August 1810]

We have the whole Bessborough concern for dinner today. Duncannon and Caroline Lamb who is arrived without W[illiam] in a great alarm about a partial dropsy. They say she really has an odd swelling on her head, but I daresay she disturbs herself unnecessarily about it.

Granville went to Mr Arbuthnot's ball last night for a short time. He went from it to Brooks's and as you care about our affairs I must tell you that they go on prosperously. He has won eleven hundred £ in the last ten days and lost therefore not quite six hundred by the year.

Stanhope Street
Friday [3 August 1810]

I get up early and walk in the Park and feel so strong and active that I can hardly believe myself to be with child, certainly for the first time these six months. I really have not felt so well since my marriage as I do now.

Granville won 130£ last night. You are very kind to think about it. Caroline [William] Lamb dined with us yesterday and I never saw her so rational, 'like another' and agreeable. They do not appear to have any uneasiness about her complaint, though it certainly is an odd one – she suffers no pain and her general health seems remarkably good, but the whole skin of her head is raised in lumps containing water. She says it has the appearance of a ploughed field, but that she belives it is only the exuberance of her fancy which has mounted there.

Croft took leave of me yesterday stuttering out all sorts of directions, any one of which it would kill me to follow. I have taken the management of my health entirely into my own hands, having bullied Sir Walter [Farquhar] into the most perfect acquiescence.

Granville is trying shooting-ponies up and down Stanhope Street. Does not that sound rural?

Stanhope Street
Saturday morning [4 August 1810]

Miss Berry[b] was with me yesterday looking wretchedly and talking in the most melancholy way of her own existence and prospects.

Lady Oxford and Caro Wm Lamb have been engaged in a correspondence. The subject, whether learning Greek purifies or inflames the passions. Caro seems to have more faith in theory than in practice, at least to judge by those she consults as to these nice points of morality. The letter she repeats as having received from Lady Oxford is almost too good to be true; after a great many maxims and instances, she ends, 'all the illiterate women of Athens were bad but what does my sweet friend think of the virtuous Aspasia?'

[Badminton]
[9 August 1810]

Dearest but own sister. The journey was great happiness with that angel of kindness and goodness, my husband. We arrived here to dinner. They are quite alone. I felt a sort of Badminton horror come over me for the first five minutes. It went as soon and I feel nothing but the contrast and a sort of pining to see your dear face.

Badminton
Friday morng [10 August 1810]

The last four days have been perfectly delightful to me. We had time enough to travel only between the showers and to be quite at home at all the inns. I feel my happiness more and more every hour and Granville's affection and angelick kindness make me the happiest of human beings. I look forward to this week with great pleasure – the Duchess [of Beaufort], Granville and I perfectly alone as the Duke, sons and tutors go this morning to

[19]

Monmouth. In spite of everything I long for October[*] and with it all its pleasures and pains.

There are eleven children here, little Eliots included. They make a little too much noise for my nerves and a great deal too much for Granville's.

I left Miss Long[b] refusing to right and left, the only news in town. Sheridan says he sat by Lady Catherine [Long] at supper and that she mouncht and mouncht plates full of sallad till he took her for an old sow and caught himself just going to say to the servant, 'Pray change this lady's trough.'

Badminton
Friday [10 August 1810]

I am happy to hear of Caroline [George]'s being with you as it must be so great a pleasure to both. If you could know the care of myself which I, partly by compulsion and partly by inclination take – early hours, gentle exercise, roast mutton and French beans. Nothing is such madness as to neglect health, as it does contribute so much to happiness. I hope I am sane for life upon the subject and 'as regular and temperate as Lady Leveson Gower' shall become proverbial.

A love affair between Mrs Charles Bagot and Captain Arthur Upton had become something of a scandal. In London the previous month the Persian envoy, while observing that her beauty was such that the 'beauties of paradise' must pay her homage, nevertheless disapproved strongly of her conduct.[7] Her husband, Charles Bagot,[b] acted the mari complaisant *despite her misdemeanours and her later unlawful pregnancy. She was known as 'The Fair Penitent', derived from the tragedy by N. Rowe (1703).*

Badminton
Sunday evening [12 August 1810]

Nothing can be more delightful and comfortable to me than the life we lead here. God bless the Duke and his Welsh concerns. I

---

*The month of her confinement.

have a terrible consciousness of the necessary dulness of my letters and my attention is taken up this morning with G's profile at chess. I never saw him in such beauty. He looks as if he was rouged and his long blue eyes[8] watching the pawns are quite irrestible. He is really more adorable than ever and his kindness, sense and sweetness make every hour passed with him happier than the one before it.

Mrs [Charles] Bagot is a prettier and more melancholy subject for scandal. I am told there never was anything so decided or undisguised as her flirtation with Arthur Upton and that upon both sides the liking seems most serious.

[Badminton]
[August 1810]

The Duchess, Granville and I are left here en trio. We have been talking, playing at chess and as for me it is quite amusement enough to look at his beautiful face. How angry it would look if he knew what I was writing. He is much handsomer than ever.

The thoughts of my début in London makes me laugh. Meek and resigned where other people would be fierce and jealous, associating with his old loves, admiring his new, patient and political, obedient in my actions, dependent in my ideas, governed and subdued, drinking soup and green tea! Are you prepared for a very dissipated career – if you could know how I hope for a great deal of home – of beautiful, comfortable, happy home.

Badminton
Wednesday [15 August 1810]

I forgot to tell you that the Dss has invited my grandmother to come here and I rather expect her today. The Duke's sons and tutors return tomorrow which diminishes my regret at leaving Badminton most considerably. The Dss read me a very entertaining letter from Lady Harrowby with a long description of breakfast at Kensington [Palace]. Mr Ward[b] flirting with the Princess [of Wales – Queen Caroline], Mrs Bagot looking à ravir, but affecting low spirits because A. Upton is obliged to attend the Duke of York to Brighton – nasty little wretch. Charles Bagot pink, erect in native dignity and, I hope, not valuing her a pinch of snuff.

[Badminton]
[August 1810]

The Duke is the most good humoured friendly honourable person in the world I am convinced, but body and soul a fox hunter which must narrow even wider intellects than his. He never is sleepy but 'his peevish hearers sometimes wish he was'. There is a sort of brisk intelligent alacrity with which he hunts all his foxes over again.

[Badminton]
Friday morning [17 August 1810]

Thank you for your letter, it is a delight to me to hear from you that I cannot describe. I had also a most amiable one from Caro [George] which really affected me from not expecting her to mention my situation and her doing it in a way the very kindness of which proved to me how much she feels her own disappointment.*

We set out tomorrow. The weather is beautiful and I look forward to the journey with the greatest pleasure. God bless you my own dearest love.

We shall be at Sandon, Litchfield (let me impress it), on Tuesday. For the first three days poor Granville will be obliged to set off at nine every morning for the assizes and, what is worse, to dine with the judges, but this last only once, I believe. My hope and prayer is that nothing will prevent our going to C[astle] H[oward] next year. I certainly admire it more than any place I ever saw and would not it be nice to be there together? I have a feel of health and spirits that I certainly have not had before since marriage. Early hours, mixed salts in eau tiède, roast meat and

---

*Her 'disappointment' was that she could not have children as her husband was impotent.

rice, Bohea tea, six bunches of currants for supper – but all this au pied de la lettre – will procure the same for any body and I think I try it hard; in my eighth month with a little Hercules kicking me till I really can at times hardly forebear screaming. When I arrived here a week ago I looked as if I was expecting to lay in every hour; the second day I was very unwell and bilious.

I sent for a ministering angel, a doctor, who gave me a good dose of calomel and ordered me the salts; ever since I have looked a Miss.

God bless you, my dear, dearest sister. Granville is putting up all his beautiful regular features and saying – 'Now do leave off – it is really too foolish, tiring yourself.'

What an angel he is eating buttered roll.

Badminton
Saturday [18 August 1810]

I write one line to you to tell you that we are setting out. The day is delightful, hot summer air. We do not go till two and then only to Gloucester. This mode of travelling enables us to be as much established at the different inns as at home. We dine regularly at six, walk, read Paley &c as if we were in Stanhope Street and to give you a still higher idea of the leisure of it, take mixed salts every morning -- joys that the bilious only know – and set off again in the same stately progress.

Sandon
Tuesday [21 August 1810]

I found two of your letters here, my dearest sister. You are much too good to like my letters and I am conscious of their real intrinsic dullness. (I do not mean to be modest but I really have latterly talked of nothing but fine weather and mixed salts.) I have some variety for you now; a new place and a most delightful one, with other men, other manners – though these are at present confined to Ld and Ldy Harrowby who are quite alone and 5 very amiable, quiet children.

Sandon is a very modern place with young plantations but the ground laying very prettily and the woods all well bestowed. Of

[23]

comforts and luxuries I never had an idea before – the rooms are so full of couches, arm chairs, flowers, books, footstools &c that ones only difficulty is where to settle in the midst of so much possibility of enjoyment. The flower garden to which every thing opens is beautiful, and a greenhouse with sofas in it, like some of the descriptions in the 'Castle of Indolence',* the very sight of which would make my grandmother and Miss Trimmer faint away. Lady Harrowby is perfectly kind and amiable, but I do not think her quite well – she is oppressed with her situation and I do think an eighth Ryder must incline one to sing à quoi bon. Lord Harrowby is blooming with health and spirits, the consequence of Tunbridge waters – and very agreeable. Granville is delightful and I am so healthy and happy that I think I must be a comfortable sight to the humane and charitable.

Sandon
Wednesday 22 [August 1810]

I have been enjoing this delicious day in this delicious place most thoroughly; walking, driving and sitting out of doors all through the hottest, sweetest, August longest day. The quiet independent liberty of Sandon, with the happiness of having Granville with me every moment, is not to be described. We are going next week to sleep one night at Trentham and soon after into Shropshire for three or four days.

I prefer the children here very much to those I have just left. The fathers tell in the comparative understandings and Lady Harrowby keeps hers in the most perfect order. The Duchess [of Beaufort] I think spoils hers; she suffers them to make incessant noise in the room with one and to be perpetually interrupting her when she is talking or reading, with questions or complaints. This either made my head ache or my temper boil half the day through, for I think the shrill loud voice of an indulged child cosa da morire. The little Ryders are perhaps too often checked, but it adds so much to the quiet and comfort of this place that I can only hope it is for their advantage as much as it is for ours.

*A poem by J. Thomson (1748).

[24]

Thursday [23 August 1810]

You have had a narrow escape of a most tremendous long letter from me today. A long visit from Lady Talbot took up the time I had destined for it and a morning made endless by Granville's being during the whole of it at the odious assizes, was originally to have been all prodigué upon you. Lady Talbot looked very handsome and was all over plum coloured silk, bluets and lace, which had its due effect contrasted with Lady H and myself rather dirty in great straw slouches. She seems a doleful sort of person, all full of grievances about children, house, land, health, &c.

Pray if you remember it remember me to the Duchess of Rutland.* I can conceive of being fond of her because I am fond of Granville's beautiful white horses and his fine bookcases, and she is like such things, handsome, goodnatured and perfectly inoffensive, but her silks and her bridling are discouraging to ones finer feelings.[9]

[Sandon]
Friday [24 August 1810]

You cannot think what these assizes are to me; I know it is no calamity and that if it was, it will all be over by four o'clock in the morng, but Granville's constant kindness and attention and his reading to me, driving me, &c make him so necessary to the enjoyment of every moment of my time, that I feel quite helpless without him and as if my hands, feet and understanding were all with him in the Town Hall at Stafford. I can as little describe the resource it is to me to write to you. Lord Morpeth must think it ridiculous as I see Granville does. Men so little understand the comfort of talking a great deal about nothing at all.

I shall never be easy till you have seen this place. It is really delicious, like iced water or strawberries and cream. Ld and Lady Harrowby are the two most independent people I know, which gives an aisance to ones existence beyond anything I ever met with. Society and comfort being the sentimental part of her character, I mean her highest idea of enjoyment, there is not an

*The Duchess was Lord Morpeth's sister.

inch of the house or garden that is not formed for both, and Granville and I spend our time like la Belle when she first got into la Bête's palace; at whatever hour we get up we find breakfast prepared in a room to ourselves, opening with great glass doors to a flower garden sweeter and more beautiful than anything but some of the descriptions in Ariosto and 'The Fairy Queen'. We might, I am convinced if we pleased, never see a human being, for my dressing room, which we are a good deal in later in the day I could be content to pass my life in – one continued couch and flower basket, but about four we all meet. Lady H drives me in a low chair; G., when he is here, walks with it.

God bless you dearest sis. I am in rude health and very much in love with my husband. Rousseau says the only two reasonable causes of suffering are remorse and bodily pain. He would therefore account me at the very pinnacle of human happiness, which is a truth worth all his paradoxes.

I said God bless you before and I say it again and again; I dare not look forward to the happiness I may feel the end of October – I dare not think I deserve it.

Sandon
Saturday [25 August 1810]

We called on Lady Talbot today in my finest laces, not to be outdone by the plum colour. She has a great deal of conversation and we get on very well together. Ingestre is a very fine old place, flat but with some uncommonly fine trees.

I have been writing to Hart to ask him here. I cannot fancy anybody being at this place and not enjoying it and I think he will particularly. It will be very good for him too in his recovering state and Granville is the only person here that ever tastes wines. He will consequently have no temptation to overheat or fatigue himself, which are clearly the things most to be apprehended for him. The Dss [of Devonshire] in her last letter hopes and believes Papa will go to Hardwick* in three weeks. He will as soon go to Japan.

We go to Trentham the day after tomorrow, Monday, for one night.

*Hardwick Hall in Derbyshire, which belonged to the Duke of Devonshire.

Tuesday 28 August [1810]

I am delighted with this place and I do not think its faults great enough to prevent me thinking it quite beautiful. We arrived here yesterday in time to drive over the greatest part of the Park and through the most beautiful wood I almost ever saw. The house is made very comfortable with two fine rooms but the new one built in the most extraordinary manner as to its effect on the outside, giving the same sort of appearance as to the house as if any body was to fasten a hump upon their back, and how Lord Stafford, with good taste always on his lips, should have contrived such a specimen of bad as this excresence I do not understand.

We fared sumptuously at the rich man's table, and I think the steward would have made a better marquis than monsieur mon beau-frère, though our reception has really been ridiculous. The dinner for us two was soup, fish, fricassée of chicken, cutlets, venison, veal, hare, vegetables of all kinds, stewed peas, tart, melon, pine apple, grapes of all sorts and sizes, peaches, nectarines, &c, &c, with wine, biscuits &c in proportion. Six servants to wait upon us, whom we did not dare to dispense with and a gentleman in waiting and fat old housekeeper constantly hovering round the door, to listen, I suppose, if we should chance to express a wish that could possibly remain unsatisfied. Before this sumptuous meal was well digested, that is about four hours after it, the doors opened and in was pushed a supper in the same proportion; in itself enough to have fed me for a week. I did not know quelle contenance faire, whether to laugh or cry; either would have been better than to do what I did – to begin again, in spite of system or sense, stuffing artichokes and grapes, with the prospect of a calomel pill tonight and redoubled abstemiousness for a week to come.

The house is full of portraits which amuse me more than all the rest; two of Ld Stafford, positive and important making a nose, three of her, one by Phillips, very fierce and foreign but none of them really good or like; three of Lady Carlisle, all very handsome but less so than I have always heard she was, as they are none of them glowing or brilliant, but drole to see her in pink attitudinizing with vases and Lord C's bust; poor dear Lady Louisa Macdonald, very pretty and very sentimental, leaning upon an anchor* and last but not least, Granville between three and four, dancing with all his might with his sisters,† and a drawing of him by Downman when he was seven and a half in a sky blue coat, making eyes and perfectly angelick and beautiful.‡

I am summoned to an immense cold collation; we breakfasted two hours ago.

[Sandon]
[August 1810]

You will grow sick of hearing me repeat that I am happier every day. It is the only subject that occurs to me. Granville's kindness is not to be described. I long to talk to you, my own, my dearest. I shall prefer finding you settled in town and independently of you have a sort of secret indescribable dread of returning to London.

This picture [portrait of Granville] is next to him what I adore. If I had not married the original I think I could have been well contented to pass my days in a gilt frame opposite the copy if I might spy.

Sandon
Wednesday 29 August [1810]

How could you ever imagine I would be a careless correspondent to you; writing to you and hearing from you are amongst my greatest pleasures and I am too selfish ever to neglect or forfeit them. You do not know how necessary your affection is to my happiness and there is nothing I look forward to without mixing the idea of it with every other that brings me real satisfaction. Today is my birthday and the first I have been away from you, I do, and have been all day thinking how triste it is not to see you. God bless you my beloved G and repay you for all your kindness to me. If you had loved me less I should have been a very unhappy and perhaps a very worthless person, my heart would have been

*The Family of the Earl of Gower, 1772, by Angelica Kauffmann RA is in the United States.

†Romney's painting of The Gower Family, 1776–7, is at Abbot Hall Art Gallery, Kendal.

‡The portrait of Granville aged seven, by J. Downman, is reproduced as the frontispiece in Lord Granville Leveson Gower, Private Correspondence, i, 1917.

shut against everything about me, the faults of my character would have been confirmed and I should have neither had fortitude or almost desire to struggle against a lot that without you would then have been almost a hopeless one. All this you saved me from and have in fact been the cause of all the happiness I have since felt. I do not exactly know what I say, but I know what I feel and I do feel love and gratitude to you very very hard to be expressed.

Lady Harrowby's eldest son is something too bad to be borne. I mean, poor fellow, as to manner and appearance. He is made like the extinguisher of a candle; his head the ball, his shoulders the point with a gradual swell to the broad basis below. He has a dreadful impediment in his speech like the hooping cough, as much detail as my aunt George [Lady George Cavendish]^b and a bustle and importance that are really odious. All the others are in different ways very nice children.

I had several letters from different quarters yesterday: from Caroline [George] enchanted with C H, Lord Carlisle's graciousness to her and having seen you more comfortable than she almost ever did before; from the Dss [of Devonshire] about my 'bel bambino', contriving to make even that subject dull; from my grandmother all kindness and satisfaction at having embarked me at last in a regular, docketted, numbered correspondence; from Samuel [footman] returning his 'respect and duty' to announce his being made footman to the Prince of Wales.

I daresay Lady Harrowby sends you her love but I am too lazy to go into her room to ascertain it; my suspicion is grounded upon the look of great satisfaction when I told her you sent her yours.

Sandon
Thursday 30 [August 1810]

I pity you for Lord Morpeth's absence with all my heart but your children must be such a resource upon such occasions, added to the pleasure of having such nice loves always about you, must console you for almost anything. You see by this how much I expect d'avance from my darling baby; now suppose he should come forth such a three-cornered thing as Dudley Ryder [the Harrowby's eldest son] should I be quite as well pleased or think à quoi bon the trouble of hatching such a chicken?

I received a long letter from F. Foster today; angry with me for all odd reasons, 'tu est tuoujours à pigger' (what a word!) 'et tu ne pigge jamais.' He complains of being at 'cette éternelle Chiswick' where it is my opinion that my father will remain, for I hear no more of Derbyshire and I think if he had really ever seriously intended going, Hartington would have waited for him.

I heard a story the other day which amused me very much. Lord Harrowby reads family prayers every Sunday evening. When the Chief Baron and Lady Louisa [Macdonald] were here she thought when they were announced it was supper and walked in saying in her loud shrill voice, 'Well, just for the form's sake.' The Chief Baron, under the same mistake, hollowing out from the other end of the room, 'Never mind me, begin, begin; I'll follow soon.'

The Bessboroughs are going to Brighton. There is something drole to me when that concern is put in motion which I cannot explain – my uncle with his little drawing books, full of firs and poplars, my aunt en victime, Sally and Thomas [servants], Rolla [dog], and even the unfortunate harness, traces and pole, never in preservation for two miles together, are to me quite a caricature. She writes really very entertaining letters, so much more so than her conversation, much more variety and *vigour* in them and not all the little tricks and egotisms that make her so heavy in hand in a tête-à-tête. Then the want of authenticity is not so much felt in a correspondence when one has not to face the relater with an obligation to look like a dupe or a convert to some downright qui dab.

Sandon
Friday 31 August [1810]

We go to Lilleshall tomorrow. I shall enjoy it most excessively as I always do being alone at any place with him, and I have another reason for liking to leave Sandon for a week just at this time – Lord Harrowby's sister, Miss Elizabeth Ryder, is expected and we shall by our expedition, miss her today. To account for my satisfaction I must tell you that she has passed many years of her life with Doctor Willis;[*] I believe there never was so unjustifiable a thing

---

[*]Dr Francis Willis and his two sons, Drs John and Robert, are known chiefly for their treatment of George III during his periods of mental affliction. They ran a mental home in Lincolnshire.

done as sending her there and he said when she was placed under his care, that she was no case for him; in short, I believe she was no madder than the generality, but her father and her were always quarrelling about peculiarities in her conduct, owing to her having a weak mind in a sickly body. For instance, he could not prevail upon her to eat roast mutton and potatoes, (how fond he would have been of me) and in the hottest, deepest days of summer she would walk out in pattens and a shawl tied under her chin. The variance upon these points grew to a pitch of irritation in him and obstinacy in her, that in my mind make it a moot point which of the two was fitted for a mad house, but it was easiest to send her, which they consequently did sans peur et sans reproche. This measure, oftener adopted, would make many families more harmonious and almost more comfortable, but I confess that reflexion does not reconcile me to the practice. Since her father's death she has lived either with her brothers or more distant relations, as sane as need be, but yet I do not wish to cultivate her acquaintance. She looks no bigger when she gets off the chair than when she is seated, owing to the unequal distribution of parts; she consequently moves her head quick from one side to the other, a sharp eye looking at one rapidly out of the very corner of the lids. 'Elle n'est pas une folle, mais elle a vécu avec eux' would, I confess, never be out of my mind.

We are at this moment returned from our visits, where we found Lady Anson. She is worn to the bone, which with her immense eyes and her rapidity of utterance, makes her look half wild. Lord Anson, who as Lady Harrowby says, looks like a large turbot, seems the most good humoured and obliging of people. Peggy [Hunloke][b] seems doomed to live with great talkers, which must be a daily penance to her, unless the sort of contest there must be and the occasional triumphs enhance the pleasure.

Lilleshall
Monday 3 September [1810]
I am delighted with this place and could pass months here with the greatest delight. The house is an enlarged farm, with good substantial airy rooms, large beds and a commanding view (to talk like a tourist) of a very fine rich country. Lord Stafford's

magnifique mâitre d'hôtel nous comblant de ses bienfaits and making us live upon venison, game and the produce of all the Trentham hot houses.

Granville is like any steward all day at business and accounts till I wish there was no such thing as coal[*] or a sixpence in the world, and today he is gone out to shoot which I bear with still less resignation. In a chariot and pair I am going to set out for Lilleshall Hill to superintend the sport. You cannot think how strong and degna di te in these matters I am grown.

George Howard, the Morpeths' eldest son, now eight years old, was a great favourite with his aunt and although she was devoted to all Georgiana's children, George, 'the greatest love', came first in her affections.

Lilleshall
Tuesday evening [4 September 1810]

The post is terrible here, and our letters are sent by *opportunities* to the post town; nothing is so difficult as to avail oneself of an opportunity. I ought not to complain of it in one way as it brought me last night George's delightful Tragedy. Clever pompous darling.

Today I had only time to write to George which I could not resist, as my morning was entirely taken up with going all over the Iron works and making the agreeable to Lady Caroline Wrottesley,[b] who came thirteen miles to pay us a morning visit and staid with us in proportion, looking so like the Bennets that she bored me more in imagination than reality, for she has much more conversation and is less heavy in hand than any of them. Of all created things she is to me the ugliest, and you may see her as well as I did today if you will but fancy Lord O [ssulton] grown enormously fat, les larmes aux yeux, a very red nose, with hands and feet like large cream cheeses, in a pink cap and feather, sash and shoes.

The Dean [of Lichfield] seems to me a most delightful person. He is beautiful per commenciare and what one should have painted

---

[*]Granville had inherited earlier some small coal-mining property in Staffordshire.

for a Dean before the purity of one's ideas upon the subject had been corrupted by a sight of Mr Edward Legge in that capacity. He is very tall and thin and graceful in his look and manner beyond any person I ever saw. ('A gentleman indeed', as Walker [maid] observed upon his opening a door for her to pass and taking off his hat, but she would have thought Parson Legge an Apollo Belvidere en pareil cas), immense brown eyes with perfectly straight black eyebrows, a very regular profile and the finest, whitest teeth that ever pressure preserved. His wife is only very ugly, very stingy and very faithful, but I shall not see her till next Tuesday when the Races begin and we are to take up our abode at the Deanery. The Dean is bilious! A strong tie between us – especially as he eats no butter, dines upon fish without sauce, meat without sallad and artichokes with salt, has not touched fruit for years. He does not eat eggs and potatoes, but otherwise the sympathy is striking. My diet is become so known that I could not commit the slightest debauch if I was ever so inclined to it. Nobody thinks of me till they see roast mutton or beef and the servants bring me my boiled rice and glass of water as if I was doing penance upon it for some crime.

Goodnight, dearest sis.

Lilleshall
Wednesday [5 September 1810]
You should have seen us last night. The Dean reading George's Tragedy out loud in a tragic tone according to the directions. I believe Granville has read it half a dozen times and I really know it by heart. He is shooting this morning and I submit to his absence with a very good grace, for he comes home so radiant in health and beauty and seems to thrive upon it so much that I cannot find it in my heart to be selfish about it. I really think I am happier every hour. There never was anything so angelick as his kindness, so adorable as he is in every way. I have enjoyed being here more than any where else; it is such perfect quiet and *monopoly* of him.

God bless you dearest sister. What with dim ink and cross posts it is most probable that you will not see this prodigious performance at all.

[33]

Sandon

Monday 17 [September 1810]

This is Hartington's last night, I must therefore put you off with a line till tomorrow and defer my account of my Litchfield gaieties, which luckily are of a nature to do just as well stale as fresh.

On Wednesday begins our journey which will take us five or six days. We shall be at Roehampton, I believe, till near the time you arrive and then, what I think would be pleasantest, would be to establish ourselves at Chiswick till the first twinges. Might not we borrow it of Papa even if he was gone? Oh, how I long to see you, my own dearest sister and how I shall enjoy being with you all day long.

Sandon

Wednesday [19 September 1810]

Indeed we are happy and your happiness has the advantage of being confirmed by time and safe labours! There are sorrows in life. The harvest bugs bite; one loses one's needles, breaks one's thread in hemstitch, but I bear them like a man.

Mr and Mrs Macdonald came today; she does very well, is very intelligent, animated and good humoured and I do not know why I feel that I never could, if hanging was the alternative, like her one bit better than I do – and the same about her person. Her hair is grown dark, her complexion brilliant, her features fined down, her figure faite à peindre, and yet I cannot think her the least pretty – no, not even with the help of yellow sattin and cairn gorams. He or his taylor make his coats &c too tight, which is my chief criticism sur son compte – but as they seem delighted with each other, my sentiments upon the subject are not of much importance.

We all go to Shugborough,* Ld Anson's tomorrow morning for two days. I am quite stout but you must not delay an hour after the time originally fixed.

*Family seat in Staffordshire of 1st Viscount Anson.

[34]

Shugborough
Thursday [20 September 1810]
We go tomorrow to Blithfield to meet the Fair Penitent.

I send you to amuse you the Dss [of Devonshire]'s letters. Amuse is not the word, for it is a slow poison which makes the subject of it more *her* victim than any one else's. What false reasoning, ill judged views and what a ridiculous style of writing. I have written her one of my moral essays in reply. Like it she won't, but lump it she will.

Shugborough
Friday [21 September 1810]
I wish I could give you a sketch of the room I am now in – the biggest I ever saw; square, long, magnificent, all lustres, blue sattin and or moulu. In a remote corner of it at a small, round table commanding the whole prospect, General Pigot (a little, smug, serious, good sort of man) and I writing our letter; a little way from us, Granville and John Talbot, Lord and Lady Anson at whist. Mrs Macdonald in the middle of the room, her very best appearance on, in pink sattin, deep lace and curled like a new wax doll; beyond a round game, Mr, Mrs, 2 Misses and Master Cook, in deep pink crape with fine complexions, chignons and thick throats; Mrs Pigot, who I am convinced if she settled upon one would sting; Peggy Hunloke in a frock, sash and neat hair, looking like a fat girl of fifteen though Hart swears she is forty-one; two Mr Ansons, undersized turbots, Macdonald who cheats, I understand, and has such a reputation in consequence that some people will hardly speak to him, and dear, good, overgrown Lord Talbot.

Granville is a talisman to preserve me from every evil in life, great and small and the very consciousness of belonging to him makes me independent of circumstances.

The General has done, is desoeuvré and peeps into my letter; yet Pigot is an honourable little man. Lady Anson is a very estimable delightful person, full of sense and good qualities; she talks too loud and is too much devoted to a life of representation, but these are not even errors and I know of nothing else against her.

[35]

God bless my own sister. I am grown very big and my child really quite impetuous in his movement. You must not delay.

Saturday [22 September 1810]
It is now three o'clock and from having made a general breakfast, spent quite a morning at Ld Anson's and travelled here, I feel as if this day had been a week and was to last another. My letter last night was written under very different circumstances, for the noise and bustle of Shugborough, to which I have been so little accustomed of late, had put me in a fever and I felt all the time I passed there like someone walking in a high wind, carried on by a foreign impulse and quite satisfied to go where it blew. I sometimes think of *the* event with the greatest philosophy, and sometimes with the greatest terror; when the last I cannot persuade myself that you have passé par là and I long to have it confirmed by your own solemn assurances of it. Like all sceptics I am not easily persuaded and the seven [G's confinements] which would to most minds appear sufficient proof, do not just now act upon my mind as such. Lady Anson has undergone twelve and makes very light of it, as far as talking goes.

Peggy Hunloke's eloquence is mastered in a great degree by the rapidity of Lady Anson's matter of fact, but if she has the field for five minutes she is very good.

I have enjoyed myself so particularly lately in Granville's almost uninterrupted society and Zia [Lady Bessborough] seems by her letters to be in her most plaintive and exigeante mood.[10]

Sandon
Sunday 23 [September 1810]
We shall be in town the last day of the month and find my grandmother probably arrived in Jermyn Street, the Bessboroughs returned to Roehampton and Papa I suspect still at Chiswick, for the Duchess still hopes about the Derbyshire expedition.

I have just finished working my baby a cap which I look at as if it was the perfect thing itself. Leave Cholmondeleys to the Earl [of

Carlisle] and come to me. I am quite unreasonable I know, about it, feeling as I do the very great kindness it is in you and Lord Morpeth to come to town at all at this time of the year.

My letters from town are dull. The poor Dss building castles in the air, instead of going to one. Lady B writes very entertaining accounts of Brighton;[11] she is living with the Grevilles, Mrs Villiers and a long et cetera in the same style. Think of poor William Lamb in the bosom of it all. When I think of him amongst all the petits soupers, musicks, and hypochondriacs, I feel a mixture of pity and admiration. I imagine my aunt doing very well amongst them all. There are no great passions to work with or upon and she may raise Charles Greville's[b] languid pulse and astonish the beaux and the belles with a little friction, with much success and the most perfect impunity.

Sandon
Monday 24 [September 1810]

Every now and then I am in a deuced fright. You know nothing of the danger of the operation [of version] which is the flooding afterwards (ne vous déplaise). It is there where Croft invariably fails, as it requires prodigious skill and one may die of it in five minutes if the pulse is not properly watched and the proper remedies instantly administered. All the people he has failed with have died of this, and he knows no more how to treat a woman who has it, than the man in the moon. The alternative therefore if attended by him is to live if one has not it, to die if one has it, and the danger is so sudden that assistance cannot be procured from any other quarter. I have thought of hiding Sir H. Halford and Thynne in the two wings of my wardrobe, like statues in niches, for I think of Croft and Farquhar much as I do of vapour and vixen, and I shall expire of the fright of being left at their mercy.

Coleshill
Thursday [27 September 1810]

Travelling is now quite a joke to me and I could fancy myself H. Cavendish on the North Road, if it was not for appearances which, in that case, would be rather against me.

[37]

We shall be in town Sunday or Monday. You must make haste. Lord C[arlisle] never was near nine months gone with child and must learn to make allowances.

Whilst Harriet was nervous of having her first confinement without her sister at hand, Lord Carlisle, who preferred to have his family about him, was finding every reason to delay the Morpeths' departure.

Stanhope Street
Monday [1 October 1810]

I am perfectly well and just going to take up our abode at Chiswick till they go which the Dss says is to be Friday or Saturday, Papa says he has not fixed a day. We meet the Bessboroughs, Duncannons there with F. Foster grown slim from a violent indigestion in a light pepper and salt coat.

Are you coming piece of perfection, friend, sister, midwive, physician? Oh G, G, you must not put it off – il sera bientôt consolé and I never should.

Chiswick
Thursday 4 [October 1810]

This is the state of the case. Croft gives me from 14th to 21st, putting the 21st, you see, as the latest. I may, however, as even Croft is a fallible being, go on for a week, or a fortnight, three months like Lady Bagot, or two years like the woman in the fable, but it may be the contrary way and I fairly own I should get very nervous without you if I thought there was a possibility of my 'going to bed' before your arrival.

We mean to remain here as long as we can. You know about as much of Papa's plans at C H as we do here. The Dss now says Monday. I am in hopes your coming may prevent it, though it would be high treason in her eyes to say a word against it, which is one reason for my fearing any further delay on her part.

The weather is June or July or what you please; my father in remarkably good spirits and quite talkative. Mr Sheridan is here very sober very entertaining and agreeable.

Stanhope Street
Friday [5 October 1810]

Here I am, dearest sister, dans la plus grande prosperité, having seen Sir Walter who is delighted with the state of my health and prudence in having constantly taken open medicine! oh shame where is thy blush! never in a physician's cheeks.

Mrs Griffith, who is one of those calm, comfortable looking people whose very appearance is a cordial; Mrs Hannon, with my pretty babe's things, beautiful and cheap; my grandmother and Miss Trimmer both all good humour and forgiveness for my idleness, which I did not expect.

The plans of all parties are as follows – my father has really authorised the Duchess to write to Hartington that they shall meet him at Hardwick, and Tuesday or Wednesday are the days now standing for their setting off; my grandmother leaves town again early tomorrow morning, principally to escape a meeting with the Duchess, and returns to Jermyn Street on the 13th. We return to Chiswick this morning and shall either stay on there till they go or join the Bessboroughs at Roehampton.

Chiswick
Saturday 6 [October 1810]

We returned here yesterday from a morning of midwives and wet nurses, to Papa, the Dss and William Spencer. They sat after dinner till eleven o'clock so that I had a long tête-à-tête with her; she is courteous, gracious, kind and useful beyond measure, and really if the Devil himself has as much inclination and as great a power of being useful to one as she has, it would be very difficult not to toad eat to him a little. She has begged me to have my baby left here whilst we are in Devonshire and was anxious to know if you would not wish your children to come and settle here, adding 'but of course when she comes she will do just as she likes about it.' This is really a convenient system for heads of families. My father still gives his silent consent to being taken into Derbyshire.

Chiswick
Wednesday 10 [October 1810]

I have this moment received your letter and am really in hopes that this will find you en famille at the George Inn, for my father intends sleeping there [Buckden, Great North Road] tomorrow night. We are setting out for Stanhope Street this morning.

You must dine with us on Friday. I cannot believe you are really coming and I assure it to every body I meet not having much faith myself in the fact. I never knew certainly how much I loved you, how necessary you are to my happiness, for no ties, however strong, no being engrossed (as I own myself to be with my adoration of Granville) has the power to make you less an object to me, and if I was isolée and unhappy in the garrets of D House, I could not look forward with greater feelings of delight to seeing you again than I do now.

My grandmother will not be in town till Monday, though she writes in a continual fever and her dear kind heart and imagination are entirely taken up with an idea that I am seized with a premature labour and her letters nothing but entreaties for a man and horse to be sent after her. I am going to write to her myself this morning, as I am in a state of calm, stupid security that I think must in some degree communicate itself to my correspondents.

Chiswick has been very pleasant, the weather delightful and my father particularly kind and amiable. I am afraid I have liked it better for being confined a good deal to my pretty dressing room. Nothing can be more essentially kind than the Dss or so invariably as my aunt, but their society does not particularly suit me or please me. When they are in spirits and obliged to be fond of each other they are so causante, playful, piquante and young that I lose l'esprit de mon âge and have the feeling described by so many old people of feeling myself, in spite of bonne volonté and exertion, a burthen and sort of check upon younger companions.

Miss Trimmer came to sleep here! We took out our hemstitch, laid the foundation for a most perfect system of education to be tried upon the Leveson Gower that shall be, and I felt for the first time since my return, a sympathy of age, tastes and occupation.

[40]

Oh, time has changed me since I saw you last; I am grown much thinner but only in the cheeks, throat and elbows, my face is narrow and yellow and I am universally reckoned a bad likeness of Hart. Bless you again and again.

Hartington was at Chiswick when Harriet had her operation of version, and Susan, the first of the Granvilles' five children, was born on 24 October.

[From the Marquess of Hartington]   [Chiswick]
                                                    [October 1810]
Harriet has happily made an end of her business and is none the worse and in high spirits. She did it five minutes after dinner and it was a providence that we had not all to leave her in possession of the dining room.

Bless you dear G. This is only a line to put you out of your suspense for it was not pleasant to think her unlike other people in her operations.

[In Harriet's hand:] Indeed my dear G, it is not at all unpleasant, a miniature of the great operation. How free we all are; after ages will find this in some old trunk and wonder over the profligacy of the times. Goodnight, very dearest sister, parent of countless babes. I must have done and pray write. Hart says what I have written looks as if I was jealous of your talent.

[To the Marquess of Hartington]   [No direction]
            [Endorsed in his writing: 'Harriet, Oct 25th 1810']
My little girl has begun dressing very fine; she is really beautiful with a presence like Lady Hertford;* she has a dimple in her cheek like Lady Holland,*b* to which I hope the resemblance will be confined. The servants all say to me 'C'est milord, c'est absolument milord', but I dare not yet be sanguine about it. Oh, if you could know how adorable milord has been – but I will not

---

*The Prince of Wales's favourite from 1806 to 1820, when she was supplanted by Lady Conyngham.*b*

[41]

embark upon that subject, or trust myself to say one quarter of
what I feel towards him.

*The sisters had been together mostly in London for the first
part of 1811, remaining there until July when the Duke died.
Now the elder had gone to Castle Howard and Harriet and
Granville were off on their round of family visiting – first to
the Staffords at Trentham where Monsieur (the Comte d'Artois, later Charles X of France) and his second son, the Duc de
Berri, were staying.*

Trentham
23 [August 1811]

Lady Stafford^b is, shutting ones eyes to the past, very delightful,
kind, generous, natural, se laissant aller and seeming to adore
us. 'Tis seeming all, but glissez mortels, n'appuyez pas, will
carry us through with her as well as on ice. Lord Stafford
provokes me with an importance about every trifle, sufficient to
give a man weight in all the trying circumstances of life, and he
nods and stares and screws up his mouth about the distance he
has walked in the morning, as if it was an event and a mystery to
his audience.

[Trentham]
[6 October 1811]

We do everything with extreme onction. We play upon the
piano-forte, harp, guitar, triangle, and castagnettes with all our
might, all singing at once. On Tuesday we all move to Sandon
and I cannot tell you how much I long for the repose of Tixal.

The Duc de Berri is clever, sings well, but is difficile à vivre
and tries Lady Stafford by finding fault. To-day the eggs at
breakfast were abominable. 'Ma foi, Madame, Mesdames vos
poules ne s'aquittent pas bien.' The life here is a little less easy.
We sit hours at breakfast and have a sort of conscience about
coming down in the library.

Tixal

[October 1811]

Lord Carlisle is a great deal too bad. It is like the Staffords, who would dine at four the day we were expecting the Hollands at Trentham, though we had no means of acquainting them with the hour, and they might have more reasonably expected it to be breakfast than dinner. Selfishness in these little details I cannot understand. In a great affair you may not have strength of mind to make a great sacrifice, you may not have principle enough to make a strong exertion; but in trifles light as air, ten minutes' difference in the hour, walking to the right or the left, going in an open or shut carriage, je m'y perds. Where is a mind little enough to make such matters of one moment's importance?

Mr Luttrell[b] I like better every hour. He has that don du ciel of never being de trop, and I never met with so independent a person. I attribute it partly to being used to float upon that great ocean, Brocket and Whitehall,* where a person is forced to shift for himself without any clue to guide him. I hear they wander about there all day and sleep about all the evening; no meal is at a given hour, but drops upon them as an unexpected pleasure.

Tixal

Thursday [probably 28 November 1811]

You are a great deal too kind to me. How could I not love you; think of your comfort, when I recollect that for years you were the only person who ever gave any to me. Happiness may have engrossed my time, and even altered my attentions to some of my friends, but for you I have invariably felt the same strong affection and anxious solicitude about every thing that concerns you. I do love you and Granville with my whole heart, but selfishly, because I feel that you are necessary to my happiness and that, unconnected with you both, my life would be a blank.

God bless you my dearest G. My best love to Lord Morpeth.

*Brocket Hall, in Hertfordshire, and Melbourne House, Whitehall, were Lord Melbourne's houses in country and town.

Pray tell him I won 17s & 6d last night. I owe Lord M. mints still unpaid which I thought G. had paid.

Georgiana Morpeth was once again pregnant.

Tixal

Friday evening [13 December 1811]

Pray, pray do not delay your journey to town much longer. Lady Talbot, after having had lots of children, was brought so near her confinement without being aware of its approach that they crossed Finchley Common in despair from thinking no house near into which, at a moment's warning, she could be carried.

Staffordshire is at this moment full of one subject; surmising, proving, wondering, lamenting &c &c. Lady Caroline Wrottesley, the strict, the good Lady Caroline has been discovered in an intrigue with a Captain in the Militia, brother to the innkeeper at Wolverhampton, a married man, and turned out of doors. Granville brought these tidings from Shugborough and had something to do to make Lady Harrowby and I believe that he was not delirious.

[Sandon]

[Postmark 16 December 1811]

I have at this moment a raging tooth-ache, my dearest G, and go about the house with a great bottle of tincture in my hand, whilst Newhouse [Granville's valet] is boiling pig-tailed tobacco for me. I have soaked camphor in cold water and am going to consult Hughes about the poisons. All this pain and apparatus are to go tomorrow to meet twenty six people at Lord Bradford's. I have no twitches, no throbbings, no sensations, but a sharp, downright violent pain in my teeth. At dinner I am obliged to avoid crusts and to sit as if I was leaning on my hand only, but really to conceal my cheek being all puffed out with port wine. I think of nothing else and look resigned at all the slops and washes, at this moment taking a sly sup (behind Lady Harrowby's back) out of Seaman's Tincture.

Lady Caroline Wrottesley is quite the watch word in Stafford-shire. I hear he is half distracted. He was devoted to her and supposed she was to him; she has left nine children and is forty one.

I have but a few minutes to write in the midst of this tourbillion. Weston is in some respects a very delightful place. The most comfortable house I was ever in. Lord Bradford's spirits are very overpowering and more so from not appearing natural. He must be much worse than the tooth ache, and I speak now with connoissance de cause. I have suffered very much indeed with it since I last wrote but a large cup of liquid tobacco, held in my mouth, nearly killed but cured me. I was drunk, sick, fainting, &c but the pain really destroyed. It seems to put the whole mouth on fire and the effect is like magick. Lady Talbot has done the same and we can talk of nothing else.

Mrs Sneyd is here; loud, braided, red, in white satin like an old bride. Lord Bradford is calling me with such frightful oaths that I must go for decency's sake.

[Later.] Lady C. Wrottesley is innocent and I am quite shocked at having spread so false a report. Her John has behaved like a madman. He sent to her to Brighton to desire her to come to Wrottesley till he had investigated some account of her conduct – a flirtation she had had a year and a half ago. She instantly set out and came post to him, which I think was very natural. He shut the door in her face and she was obliged to set off very ill, and you may judge in what a state for London. He now says he never suspected anything but imprudence and I hear the letter she has written him is the most beautiful thing that ever was written; she courts every investigation and only entreats she may be confronted with any person who has accused her. He has at times been out of his mind and they suspect that he was so from the violent effect some ill natured reports he heard about her had upon his mind.

Sandon

Saturday 21 [December 1811]

We dined and slept at Blithfield* yesterday. Lady Bagot is a very sensible, delightful person, more reserved than shy, and silent from habit, as I understand Lord Dartmouth [her father] never liked his children to join in general conversation. Lady Harriet was less agreeable than I have ever seen her, looking beautiful but, like some of her own family, languid, dawdling and thinking it wit to say 'How do, Dick' &c. Mrs Bagot baffles all description, in a salmon coloured gown with myrtle wreaths and rose coloured ribbands twisted about her head, rouged to the eyes, more gay, more at her ease, more impudent than anything I could have believed ever had or could exist. Lady Talbot was petrified with astonishment and indeed this new style of penitence is next to miraculous and not edifying. Charles is acting the most humiliating part and it is really impossible to pity such voluntary degradation.

Sandon

22 [December 1811]

Mrs Bagot produced the fruit of her retirement the morning we left – a yellow tunique embroidered with every colour of the rainbow, an emblem of her penitence. I hear it is supposed that C. Bagot will be quite cut out by men when he mixes more in society in town; that his conduct is looked upon as so weak and humiliating. It is really scandalous to see her manner and the rouge, the gros paquet before &c &c and too ridiculous, after all the confessions and declarations. She is much more triumphant and impudent than she ever was in all the pride of her beauty and reputation. She marched out of the dining room before Lady Talbot, talked incessantly as if she was the mistress of the house, did the honours to us all, tittered, flirted with all the men, in short, nothing but seeing would have made me believe it. It has been reculer pour mieux sauter and woe betide the next victim. It is a fearful sight to see, such effrontery in one so young and fair. Her uncommon beauty and skin deep intelligence, with experience

*Blithfield, Rugely, Staffordshire, the home of the Bagots.

[46]

that no woman before ever can have had upon such a subject, will make her next exploit no joke to the hero of it.

[Badminton]
[Between 29 December and 2 January 1811/12]
I long to see you all; we shall be in town on Sunday. Lord Apsley and a friend of his come tomorrow. The youths are about, I see and as Mr Canning once said to Granville walking with him in the streets, 'The bores are about, let us go home', I feel inclined to say now.

The Dss [of Beaufort] is really angelick, more than ever I think. Her piety, her devotion to her children, her earnest desire of doing right, seem to me stronger than ever.

You, my own G, are after Granville, every thing to me every where. God bless you dearest sister. Promise not to lay in without me. Miss [Anna] Seward talks of Lord Morpeth's marriage with the lovely Maid of the House of Cavendish.

After the death of her husband the previous year, Duchess Elizabeth did not maintain a decorous silence regarding the birth of Caroline St Jules and Augustus Clifford, her two illegitimate children fathered by the late Duke many years before their marriage.

[Badminton]
Thursday 2 [January 1812]
The Dss is really too impudent; but I think we ought (by coldness of manner) to check the sort of language she uses about Caroline and Clifford, for her own sake more than any other persons. I think if we do not she will soon avow every thing to every body.

Georgiana Morpeth's daughter was born on 11 January. The sisters were in London for the first half of the year. Harriet was pregnant and the child expected in September. Byron was now the hero of the hour. Childe Harold *had been published in the first days of March and had been received by a rapturous public. Among these was Caroline William, Harriet's volatile, capricious cousin who, passionate in all things, flung herself at the poet. For three months she conducted a turbulent love affair, pursuing him and behaving with a recklessness and abandon which by June had become not only a prodigious scandal, but a vexation to Byron himself.*

[To the Duke of Devonshire]   [Stanhope Street]
                                               10 May [1812]

My last gaiety was at Lady Essex's on Sunday, where Lady Hamilton did attitudes in a shawl of Lady Essex's, who looked inspired and will I hope shortly take to doing them herself. I was at Mrs Gordon's on Monday. I saw my Aunt Spencer, grunting and elbowing through the crowd and afterwards squatting down with a bevy of respectable women about her. Dear [Mrs] Rawdon was pushing about in a fury, her shawl upon her arm and in her countenance 'I will endure it no longer.' The daughter* very pretty, but her blooming little face quite lost in curls and nosegays. Lord Byron is still on a pedestal and Caroline William doing homage. I have made acquaintance with him. He is agreeable and I feel no wish for any further intimacy. His countenance is fine when it is in repose, but the moment it is in play, suspicious, malignant, and consequently repulsive. His manner is either remarkably gracious and conciliatory, with a tinge of affectation, or irritable and impetuous, and then I am afraid perfectly natural.

There were changes in the Government in the early summer. Lord Liverpool became Prime Minister and Granville had hoped that a Cabinet post would be offered to Canning, who as a close friend might further Granville's own prospects of promotion. In this he was disappointed but Harriet was delighted to be able to look forward to many months of settled life at Tixal where her second

---

*Elizabeth Rawdon,[b] niece of the 1st Marquess of Hastings, married Lord William Russell in 1817.

child would be born in September. True to her generous nature she had decided to have Granville's daughter by her aunt Bessborough to stay on a trial basis. Harriette Stewart (the surname had been that of Granville's mother) was a few days short of her twelfth birthday when she arrived in August.[12] To the child, Granville was known as her guardian, and when her real mother died in 1821 she seemed not to have realised the closeness of that relationship. For Harriet, as both stepmother and cousin, it must have been a bizarre experiment though one that answered with a reciprocity of happiness and affection on both sides. (Lady Bessborough's feelings one can only conjecture.) George Stewart, of the same parentage, joined the household in the next year.

Tixal

Friday [31 July 1812]

There was a report yesterday of the Prince [Regent] being anxious to renew the negotiations with Canning but I do not believe it, and even if he is, his very wishes are become too insignificant to influence a single person in or out of his Government – a Government too, perfectly satisfied with itself; they seem to me to have quite a reliance upon their own shabbiness and insufficiency and the dread of the superiority any degree of talent or character would necessarily obtain over them.

I hope my determination of having Harriette here will turn out well as I have persuaded myself it will. It is merely as a trial and the best, and indeed the only one, I could ever make, as she considers it quite a visit.

Tixal

Wednesday [5 August 1812]

I am free from pains and aches of all kinds; have secured Croft's delightful society sooner than I expected, that is, on the 24th of September and lastly, am here for good, as Mr Canning's negotiations with Ministers are entirely over and all prospect of his joining them at an end. He was willing to sacrifice a great deal, some, of course, think too much and others too little, but to act

[49]

under Lord Castlereagh he has invariably refused in spite of all their shufflings and evasions, they have never intended any thing else and at last have made this so clear that a complete rupture has been the consequence. I win two guineas but, love of gain apart, I had much rather see these ruins crumble than my friends and relations prop them up.

We hope to have the Cannings very soon indeed. Tixal is in radiant beauty all over roses, rain, sunshine and a new fire place in the hall. I really do love it beyond expression.

Tixal
[5 August 1812]

I believe the great secret of happiness is to strengthen one's mind so as to resist imaginary evils and bear real ones. The first always at our beck, and the latter but too often. For my part I hope I am growing philosophick and I have persuaded myself that I look forward to the pangs and perils of childbirth with a sort of satisfaction. The women in Staffordshire make nothing of it; a maid servant of Lady Talbot's performed it the other day in a cow loft and milked fourteen of its inhabitants in her way home. I am delighted to be at home and Tixal is to me a paradise.

There is a report of a great victory to day. [*] I wish it may be true but the account seems unconfirmed and in some respects improbable. Granville heard from Mr Canning yesterday. I cannot say how much I rejoice at his being politically free again as I have never for a moment thought the offers made to him such as to make it desirable for him to prop up the present Government without such a situation and such influence in it as would enable him to counteract the mischief they do, or to effect any good purpose himself.

[Tixal]
[9 August 1812]

The little girl arrived yesterday, Harriette appearing in very high spirits but looking out of health.

[*]The Battle of Salamanca was won on 22 July, followed by Wellington's triumphant entry into Madrid.

The Staffords seem to have turned their thoughts entirely to economy and the society of Scotch agents. The former answers as I understand they have sold Woolmers for six and thirty thousand £ and are raising all their land about here incredibly. They make Lord Gower[b*] their steward and the advertisements are all published with 'apply to Earl Gower' at the end of them.

Tixal
Friday [14 August 1812]

We have at this moment a house full. They are all going to drive and ride and I shall have my mornings entirely to myself, that is, to Harriette who gains upon me every hour. She really is a most amiable little creature and though she has nothing precose about her, her intelligence and docility make her a very delightful companion.

Caroline William's behaviour had now surpassed all reasonable proportions. On 12 August, as the result of some reproach made to her by her father-in-law, she had rushed from Melbourne House like a mad thing, supposedly to Byron, with her mother and Lady Melbourne in hot pursuit. She was eventually found at the house of a Kensington surgeon and, persuaded by Byron, returned home. As a result Lady Bessborough suffered some kind of a collapse from shock. When she recovered the Bessboroughs, taking Caroline and William Lamb with them, retreated to Ireland to avoid further scandal.

[Tixal]
[c. 15 August 1812]

I must write one line though my eyes are shut and all my faculties asleep. I suppose you have heard what an unpleasant sort of attack poor Lady Bessborough has had. The account today was better, but she must have been very ill indeed. I believe Caroline Wm keeps every thing belonging to her in a state of agitation and

---

*The Staffords' eldest son. This was the time of the clearances in Sutherland.

anxiety from the extreme and alarming oddity of her character and conduct. She has been with my aunt during her illness and I hope may profit by the uneasiness she must have felt for her.

Your account of your dear children delighted me. I read to little Harriette the part about acting. Her anxiety lest you should not bring your girls is beyond any thing I ever saw and I am obliged to preach all day patience in suspense and being prepared to bear disappointments.

Georgiana Morpeth was to come to Tixal for Harriet's confinement, bringing with her her three eldest daughters. The baby, Georgiana [Dody], was born on 23 September.

[Tixal]
[*c.* 20 August 1812]

Harriette is in an absolute fever about the Miss Howards; you really *must* bring them. She is a charming child; she does not know what naughtiness is. She is raving of fishings, rides on the donkey, walks &c with your little girls. If you can help it you must not disappoint us.

This great victory, the promising harvest &c must delight every body and I only grudge to Ministers the thinking themselves conquest and sunshine, which they certainly will do, and I fear the good they have had no hand in, will enable them to remain to do future harm.

We had a very good account of my aunt today but she must have been very ill.

Sandon
Friday [23 October 1812]

Here I am at the risk of my life surrounded with beaux. I am entirely recovered from my confinement, headache, weakness, &c and have had the ingenuity to catch a most dreadful cold & entirely to have lost my voice with hoarseness. Think how inefficient I must be here. However I listen and smile, cough and listen to Modern Europe from Pozzo and do as well as can be expected.

We go to Trentham Monday for one night. Granville has seen them – la marchesa [Lady Stafford] cropped close and as grey as an old mouse. Mr Luttrell and Mr Nugent[b] are at the piano forte going Whoo Whoo Te Whoo like the owls in Ray Wood [at Castle Howard] – Caro [George] like a nightingale.

Tixal

Thursday 29 [October 1812]

Caroline remains with me which gives me great delight, and will return to town under F. Foster's protection. By this arrangement I shall have her with me when the Irish horde [Bessboroughs] pour in upon us, to my unspeakable comfort.

We spent this morning at Sandon, measuring and weighing. I am 5 feet 6 inches and weigh 9 stone 6 pound. Caro 5 feet 3, and 8 stone 1. I have lost about two stone since I was the fattest of my kind.

Tixal

Friday [30 October 1812]

[Augustus] Clifford and the *two* Fosters are here, but it does very well and we are to send Augustus [Foster] to Sandon Sunday when this house will be quite full. Clifford is improved in looks but in conversation he is really nothing and his constant little nervous laugh makes even his silence appear less negative than that of another person. I am very kind but with the 'Spirits low that bore bestows'. He has no conversation at all and having quite left off the familiarity and childishness of manner he once had, he has nothing at all in its place. F. Foster is in tearing spirits and most excessively amusing. A. Foster rather better than he used to be.

The Beauforts arrive tomorrow. The two Cannings the next day. When all these sweep off, Sandon pours in upon me.

Tixal

3 November [1812]

Mr Canning, Mr Stratford Canning and Mr Ellis arrived

[53]

yesterday. Mr C cannot stay with us beyond Wednesday or Thursday. The new Mr [Stratford] Canning appears to be very sensible and agreeable.

Dear dearest G, I do long to see you more than I can say. I certainly love you better, or I believe it is that having roused myself from the lethargy of a totally indolent and inactive life, all my enjoyments and feelings are proportionately stronger. My times used to be spent in reveries and dread of losing my happiness – I now feel only anxious to make myself worthy of it.

[Tixal]
[Between 4 and 8 November 1812]

We sing and talk till our throats are dry. The beaux are all in high good humour. Mr Montagu is really a good and amiable creature; Mr Luttrell is more agreeable than I ever knew him; Mr Nugent very sociable and perfectly good humoured; F. Foster, the greatest love that ever was, very drole and surly and stuffing more boiled pork and boiled mutton than any person ever did before.

We hear nothing from Ireland but I conclude they will be upon us presently.

This visit took place in circumstances which to Lady Bessborough and perhaps to Granville himself (with Harriette at hand) – even in so worldly a society – must have appeared, at the least, extraordinary; but it was weathered on all sides by tolerance and good manners.

[Tixal]
[November 1812]

The Bessboroughs have been unpacked about a couple of hours. My aunt looks very stout and well but poor Caroline most terribly the contrary; she is worn to the bone, as pale as death and her eyes starting out of her head. She seems indeed in a sad way, alternately in tearing spirits and in tears. I hate her character, her feelings and herself when I am away from her, but she interests me when I am with her and to see her poor care worn face and figure is sad and dismal in spite of reason or speculation upon her extraordinary conduct. She appears to me, in short, not very far from, or rather, little short of insanity. My aunt describes it at times having been decidedly so.

[Later.] Caro has been most excessively entertaining at supper. Her spirits, while they last, seem as ungovernable as her grief. My aunt is very gay and very amiable. Poor Lord B. me pèse sur le coeur, l'esprit, l'estomac &c &c. William Lamb laughs and eats like a trooper. Rolla is grown superannuated and makes me sick – he whines, howls, coughs and what is worse, in every corner of the room.

Lilleshall
23 [December 1812]

We are here for three days, quite alone and very very comfortable. Blazing fires of Staffordshire coal, two new Reviews, early hours, wholesome dinners, a comfortable bed and Granville, adored Granville, who would make a barren desert smile. There is a tirade: I do not often let myself go and never but to you, therefore do not say it is not in good taste.

I really should like to be here all the year round with you and Lord Morpeth; it is so quiet, such thorough country and so difficult of access to the world in general. You will think I am growing quite a misanthrope but Chatsworth will make me very worldly again. How smart we must be and I have quite forgot how. It makes me laugh to think how very popular we shall be. In sapphires and diamonds and amethysts as big as eggs, doing l'impossible to be gracious and agreeable and how dearest Hart will be told by Mr this and Lady that, that we are adorable, perfect &c. I really do think, as Walker says, that we do please very much when we try *and* with the wonderful exertions I foresee we shall make, I confess I see no limit to it. It is incumbent upon us to be so very delightful, I consider it quite as a debt and duty we owe to my brother.

Tixal
30 [December 1812]

Lady Shelley*b* is not superior or clever – indeed she is not. Do observe, pray – it is all common-place and very superficial; she is not foolish and she has had an education tres soignée, I believe, in every respect, but class me below Sir John if you find, upon acquaintance, a grain of superiority in her.*

I returned this morning from amongst the Chiefs and Ladies bright at Blithfield parsonage. Lady Ponsonby is beautiful beyond all description, crushed by his affected contempt and brutality. They have, I hear, come to what is called an understanding. He is to give up Miss [Harriette] Wilson† and all that sort of thing, as Lady Stafford would say, and she is to renounce all her little manoeuvres round the ring, in the opera room &c. Lady Harriet [Bagot, her sister] is a little miracle of goodness; she is the quietest best and happiest person I ever met with, and Dick [Bagot]*b* is a good sort of man and a very good husband, the proof being in the good little pudding before mentioned.

Lady Shelley's 'bloodshot eyes' were occasioned by her having to stay awake at night until her husband came home, and since his pursuits were those of the libertine and the gambler (cards and the Turf) he was often very late. This necessitated a great deal of reading on her part so as not to fall asleep, but she displayed no false modesty in her diary, and wrote in a more elevated style of her 'eyes once so large and brilliant' beginning 'insensibly to grow dim'.[13]

Sandon
1 [January 1813]

Do not for Hart's sake, delay Chatsworth any longer.

I see you are coming round to Lady Shelley. I see her with a sort of hoisted-up look in her figure, tight sattin shoes, a fine thick plait of hair, bloodshot eyes, parched lips, fine teeth and an expression of conscious accomplishments in her face.

*Sir John and Lady Shelley will be more prominent in the Paris of 1815.
†The notorious courtesan.

Lord Aberdeen and Baron Tripp are expected here tomorrow. Lady Harrowby might parody Ariel's song: 'Where the beaux flock, there live I.' They have a natural tendency towards her habitation.

Sandon
Sunday 3 [January 1813]

Lord Abderdeen arrived this morning and is very delightful. I acknowledge he looks beautiful and there is something in the quiet enthusiasm of his manner and the total absence of frivolity in his mind and tastes as uncommon as it is captivating. He does not like me at all, which makes this praise doubly flattering to him and generous from me. His spirits appear to me very much what they used to be. He goes to Chatsworth from hence but I do not know what day. He will be the precious stone upon the dunghill and you, I am afraid, the cock who picked it up – will pick it up rather. God forbid I should mean for the dunghill any thing but C. Greville, W. Spencer.

Sandon
4 [January 1813]

Dearest Brother and Sister, I am glad to hear you are together [at Chatsworth] and well and on Sunday I trust I shall be with you. What time do you dine? That sounds like coming. What may Granville shoot? Birds, roe bucks, neighbours – you must let him have something to kill.

Dear G, how pleased you would be with Lord Harrowby – it is half past twelve and he has read aloud to us since nine. I see Lady H. is in such a fidget with it that she can hardly keep from screaming. Granville bears it like a man, but Ld Aberdeen and I hang over him enamoured.

The children set out for Chatsworth on Saturday. Susan is the fattest, flattest, broadest merriest darling. Georgiana, a little Granville in a lace cap.

After the visit to Chatsworth both sisters were in London for the first part of the year.

[Stanhope Street]
Saturday [Spring 1813]

I went to the Duchess of Devonshire yesterday and found her as I described. Her merits – great good nature and not an ounce of rancune at my total neglect of her for years. Her ridicules appear to me much more saillant than ever; she looks better, but not well enough for a white gauze bonnet with six pink roses in it and a shawl of all the colours in the rainbow.

Lord Aberdeen's wife had died and now he showed a strong predilection for Anne Cavendish, daughter of Lord George Cavendish, Harriet's uncle.

[Stanhope Street]
[28 July 1813]

I took Anne to the Opera last night [and] to Devonshire House. She is, I think, for the first time, touched beyond measure. He [Lord Aberdeen] sat by her at supper, and was most devoted to her. He has been with me this morning and said nothing. Robert [Gordon, his brother] knows all about it, approves highly of his taste, but thinks he ought not to marry whilst his mind is at all biased by his paradoxical feelings. If, when his spirits are quite revived and after his return from abroad, he persists and she relents, he thinks – and so do I – that they will act both wisely and happily in marrying. She was in her narrow breasted black gown, a creation of pinks on her large head, coq de perles hanging all over her, flippant and cutting jokes; he enchanted and approving every word. They both adore us all.

Ingestre
Friday 30 [July 1813]

I think Anne will be Lady A[berdeen] after all. My opinion is that she likes him, but Lady George combats every argument in his favour with a stubbornness and want of sense that influence Anne to repeat occasionally the frivolous objections and narrow views by which her mother is governed; but she is superior to feelings

[58]

like hers and I am convinced that if he returns constant, she will marry then. His thinking an honourable employment would advance matters was a touch above them, but they do not even pretend to understand it – 'but what has that to do with it, my dear Harriet?"

Anne was really émue whilst I argued with my Aunt and seemed afraid, but inclined, to second me. I could hardly fix my Aunt's attention – she praised my bonnet, asked after my children, but I screwed her to the sticking place and it ended with her saying, 'well, well, there was no hurry – a short acquaintance – time enough to discuss it after his return upon further intimacy.' Ainsi, gentil troubadour, si tu reviens fidèle, I think it will be, and I do think Anne the best creature in the world and that she will make him happy. The other simple good brother thinks it will be the most excellent match, has a high opinion of Miss Cavendish and cherishes us all.

[Tixal]
[? First week in August 1813]

Granville is suffering with a violent and general rheumatism. I am anxious to tell you what Mr Luttrell says: that rheumatism is *not a disease* but a symptom; that if he hears of rheumatism he says 'take care of your general health'; that there never yet was a case of its being cured by care and warmth and thinking about it; that it is the grand enemy of bile and to be met with exertion, strong exercise, regime and gentle apperients. Lady Talbot was in the room and cheered him; she has been tortured with the lumbago till she discovered it was purely bilious.

Tixal
Thursday [5 August 1813]

I have been on horseback once again but I am a tremendous coward. The roan Granville bought for me is beautiful and as gentle as a lamb, but he walks too near the ground and had a fall with the groom. I cannot bring myself to mount him, though I am held rather cheap for it. Have you any stout, safe, rough horse I can ride at C.H.; so that they neither stumble or start I care for nothing else. Lord Talbot's pony, Cabbage, almost dislocates and gives me labour-pains all down my back, but I adore him for he treads high and heeds neither man or beast.

Anne has not yet written to me. Do you know it would give me real pleasure to have them shooting here next autumn, which shows me that I have in fact a great regard and affection for her; she is so very worthy, but to see Ld Aberdeen making love to her is a sight really wondrous. The last night at D House, she was (from confidence in her success with him, I suppose) dégagé in her manner, very talkative and flippant, with a rage for making explanations about everything. He appeared perfectly satisfied, not charmed but approving. Robert talks of her with veneration and wishes it, not as a romantic but as a respectable marriage – as another choice of Hercules.

Bolton Abbey[*]
Thursday [12 August 1813]

We arrived here last night, having performed a journey of more than ninety miles. We picked up the Tavistocks on the way and brought them the last stage. Bolton is beautiful and very comfortable indeed. We are all in high good humour; the two Lords radiant, Lady T. obliging beyond measure. They are gone out shooting and Lady Tavistock, Mr Carr[†] and I are going to the Strid.

Lord Tavistock is more amiable than I ever knew him. I daresay his understanding is good, but though it vexes me to say so whilst she is sitting before me so radiant and good humoured and ready to fetch anything anybody might want, it must be an incalculable disadvantage to pass his life with so very bornée a person as she appears to be. It is nothing but a few facts and a great deal of civility that fills her head and as he seems to live but to please her, such an object can neither rouse him to exertion or allow him to wish for more improving society.

I am sorry upon Hart's account as for some unfortunate reason or other, all his friends are calculated to encourage him in an indolent dawdling sort of life. His own understanding is so very

[*]The Duke of Devonshire's property in Yorkshire.
[†]The clergyman at Bolton Abbey.

superior. I never am with him for half an hour without thinking more highly of it than I did before.

They were on the moors yesterday in broiling heat from nine till seven and my brother the only one not in the least tired. Oh G, if he was a laboring man what health he would have. One great thing is that his mind now is from various reasons occupied and amused and he has not time for fancies.

Carr, Lady T. and I went all over Strid Wood yesterday. He is a great bore but I keep him in very good order; it must be drole to hear us all. Lady T. admires even Mr Carr with enthusiasm and of course every thing he has done and intends to do. 'Now pray catch the view here.' 'I do, beautiful!' 'It was fortunate I happened to observe it.' 'Nothing could be so fortunate', with a look of the most penetrated conviction. 'The seat is good.' 'Capital.' 'A finer seat would not have suited so well.' 'Not half as well', with almost a tone of anger. This is all told in so brisk and encouraging a tone that I cannot keep pace the least, but put in languid 'oh yes, oh no, it could nots and it wills' but with small effect.

The truth is that I do not think her a great admirer of picturesque beauty; the rapture is evidently but the over-flowings of her good humour. I am sure she is the kindest, sweetest tempered thing alive, but such entire want of mind I never met with. In short, her mind and your belle-mère's are, I should imagine, exactly the same in quality and quantity and like her, she will converse and get eager at spillikins with little Russells yet unborn.

Hart sent H.R.H. three grouse yesterday. She cannot wear them, which is one comfort, unless Dow. Leeds* and her go about in the feathers.

From Bolton Abbey the Leveson Gowers went to Bridlington, near Scarborough on the north-east coast, before moving on to Castle Howard for a week at the beginning of September.

*The Dowager Duchess, once governess, and now more a lady-in-waiting to Princess Charlotte.

Bridlington Quay
Monday [23 August 1813]

Here we are at last after much indecision and endless plans and charmed with the place. We have got an excellent house, very cheap, close to the cliff, with the prettiest sea view you ever saw, the harbour covered with vessels, Flamborough Head, and excellent sands. Good beds, good dinners, everything clean and airy and neither fleas or cockchafers. Our room (the one we sit in for we have a spacious dining room), is like a large cabin of a ship – a bow window looking only at the sea.

The Wortleys and Lady Erne* are here; we walked with them yesterday evening upon the sands.

I have had today the only entertaining letter upon record from the Dss. I send it to you for le rareté du fait.

Bridlington Quay
Thursday [26 August 1813]

We sailed all yesterday morning; it was delightful, a blue sky, perfectly calm, Lady Caroline [Wortley] very agreeable, talking with great openess and interest about herself and others but not seeming to wish to have more to do with me, or my concerns, than with the bathing woman. This suits me exactly. The great tax upon female society is that necessity of being intimate and confidential beyond what is desirable when a person has as many ties and friendships already formed as I have.

We went to a play in a barn in the evening – it was very amusing; two or three excellent actors and the sailors enchanted, swinging about the beams and hanging from the top like cats. The young Duchess of Leeds was there; she has an interesting countenance, with very fine prominent teeth. But she dresses like a beggar woman without corsets and her complexion, originally I suppose fair, is weather beaten and tanned into a sort of light copper colour. Lady Caroline and she look like two people dug out of a mine, or from under a ruin; one has the greatest hopes of them after they have been well fed and clothed.

*Elder sister of the Duchess of Devonshire; Lady Caroline was her daughter.

[62]

Now for the pier. Lord Erne is here, almost an idiot – they are kind to him, give him his meals and put him out to walk.

Bridlington Quay
Saturday [28 August 1813]

Oh, dearest G, are you at that sad work again?* As for me, I believe I never shall have another. You have managed it well however in one way – at least for me. I should have been wretched if it had not been when and where I could be with you. Dearest sister, I do love you so very dearly. I do think you so adorable and such a much greater angel than any I know of besides. Granville is looking and laughing at me, for he has been hearing of it for the last half hour.

[To the Duke of Devonshire]   Castle Howard
6 September [1813]

We found upon arriving here at half past four, among the statues, G in a bedgown and dishevelled, and Lord M. 'pacing with hurried steps his room along'. The Earl had put off dinner for an hour, as four was the usual time. However this has been the only disturbance. He is in high good humour. We dine at five and he lets Granville shoot.

To make the scene present to you I will give you a sketch of us at dinner. Lord Carlisle, star-shining, lip-projecting, with a dish of his own, a sort of solid soup, by his side which he offers to a chosen few. Next to him G looking amiable and resigned, and very pretty. Lady Julia Howard† by her side with a wreath of white roses, more rouge than ever and inumerable jewels. Granville looking very good tempered between her and Lady Carlisle with a camelia japonica and a red pink in her cap, trying, like a busy bee, to extract conversation from us all by nodding and staring at us. Harry Howard is aide-de-camp at the joints of meat and never by any chance opens his lips.

---

*Georgiana Morpeth was pregnant with her ninth child.
†Lord Carlisle's unmarried sister who died in her hundredth year (1848).

The Leveson Gowers were at Tixal until the end of the year and the Morpeths joined them there in mid December. By the end of January 1814 both families were in London where Georgiana Morpeth gave birth to her ninth child in March, and their grandmother died the same month. This was the spring and summer of Peace. With Napoleon banished to Elba, it was a time of celebration. The great London houses, Carlton House, Devonshire House, Lansdowne House, held balls and receptions, masquerades and fêtes. Following so tumultuous a season the Morpeths and Leveson Gowers set out for Spa on 2 August where they stayed till the last day of the month. Together, September was spent in Paris. From there the Morpeths returned to Yorkshire, the Leveson Gowers to Tixal. By then Harriet was pregnant. At Trentham for two nights Harriet was able to discuss the newly arranged marriage of the Staffords' eldest daughter, Lady Charlotte Leveson Gower, to Henry Charles Howard, afterwards thirteenth Duke of Norfolk. 'Indeed Charlotte's radiant face', as Harriet told her sister, 'and the new born respect of the family for her, "queen that shall be", are irresistible arguments in its favour.' Another engagement of the autumn was that of Annabella Milbanke to Lord Byron.

Tixal
Wednesday [12 October 1814]

I had a long conversation with Charlotte before I left Trentham and I am perfectly happy again, for I never saw anybody so completely [in love] as she is. The man is her own affair and I find she is charmed with him. The advantages of the situation and independence to Charlotte are quite incalculable. I had also some conversation with him and found a little more sense than I had expected. He has rather a handsome face, is short and has a particularly disagreeable voice – very drawling and helpless.

Lady Stafford is made very agreeable by this marriage – in perfect good humour and very drole, fonder of us than of the aire she breathes. She said to me the last thing, 'I am glad to see Charlotte has begun him with a very easy book, she has given him a volume of Pennant.[*] He can't quite fix his attention yet, but I dare say in a few days he will like it very much.'

Lady Bessborough writes us word that Miss Milbanke's marriage is declared and all the Melbourne family full of it. How wonderful of that sensible, cautious prig of a girl to venture upon such a heap of poems, crimes and rivals.

Tixal
Saturday [22 October 1814]
After our delightful and uninterrupted quiet we are going to have a very gay and bustling week. On Thursday all Trentham come to be within reach of the Blithfield Ball. I confess I shrink from the prospect of 8 miles and back in this uncertain weather and without much inducement. Charlotte will display her little prize to the greatest advantage as he seems tres bien chaussée and to have a decided genius for dancing.

Tixal
Friday [28 October 1814]
The Ball was dull and dignified, very good company, a few long dances and a magnificent supper. Charlotte and Mr Howard made a great, but not a very lively, sensation and it was drole to see her with the most virtuous effort introducing him to everybody. He is what the author of Waverley says a natural fool is called in Scotland – an 'Innocent' if ever there was one. Lady Stafford in purple cloth and gold appliquées, was slaving for popularity.

[Stanhope Street]
[Autumn 1814]
I saw a letter of Miss Millbanke's to Lady Melbourne, a very amiable one in which she praises him [Lord Byron] with rapture and says she can never sufficiently wonder or rejoice at being the happy object of his choice, and only hopes to deserve it by her

[*]Thomas Pennant (1726–98), traveller and antiquarian. As a naturalist he wrote several classics.

constant exertions &c. Poor girl. I hope she may never be undeceived. La Vecchia [Lady Melbourne] cannot talk of it without great emotion but says Caro is very calm and reasonable.

A year ago matters had seemed set fair for a suitable marriage between Anne Cavendish and Lord Aberdeen. Now he had backed out but Lady Anne persisted in supposing that he would marry her, right up to his wedding day to another woman in 1815.

Stanhope Street
Wednesday [9 November 1814]
Granville went to the House and I sent to ask Anne to come to me; she is looking very well, her figure grown quite nice by a total reform of dress. I was obliged to be cruel only to be kind. Lady Harrowby saw Robert [Gordon] at Brussels, where he told her that his brother had written him word that all thoughts of his marriage with Anne was at an end without a chance of its ever being renewed and desired him to exert himself in contradicting any report he might hear of it. Finding her secretly just as sanguine as ever, I told her (in *mild* terms) this; she was at first very low but before she left quite revived again and I am convinced her cure will not be a difficult one.

Granville is going to see Miss O'Neill in 'Belvidera'* with the Cavendishes. Tomorrow we go to see Kean in 'Macbeth'. I hear both are transcendent.

Stanhope Street
Monday [? 14 November 1814]
Yesterday we dined at Cleveland House;† Lady Stafford very gracious and Charlotte looking happier than the case justifies. I went from dinner to Saville Row; Anne's spirits are recovering every minute and I think I have done good by a conversation with

*The leading part in Otway's blank verse tragedy *Venice Preserv'd* (1682).
†The Staffords' house close to the south-west end of St James's Street.

[66]

my aunt, in which I urged her and Lord George appearing satisfied and to have given it quite up, as the best consolation Anne can receive.

Sir Charles [Stuart][*] paid me a long visit yesterday; he is uglier than ever and very conceited, but quite as fond of us as ever and, if any thing more fidgetty about Lady Morpeth. He met you as you were going to C.H. and took it to heart that you did not acknowledge him.

Stanhope Street

[Probably 16 November 1814]

We go to see Miss O'Neill in 'Venice Preserved'. I have seen her in Juliet,[†] I thought I should have died and Granville and Lord George went the other night to Belvidera and were all but carried out. Her tones, her action are really too beautiful.

Stanhope Street

Thursday [17 November 1814]

Your dear boys are with me and are the greatest darlings that ever were. They have nothing to amuse them but my conversation, but we get on perfectly. Frederick is delightful; William is à croquer. I could not give them any dinner as they arrived at one and there was not a morsel or soul in the house. They went to Park Street and got a boiled chicken – they seem easily pleased and begged just now for some toast and water, which seems a luxury.

I died last night over 'Belvidera'. I never did see such an actress. It is a great deal too dreadful and I would not see her again in it for the world.

Stanhope Street

Thursday [17 November 1814]

I forgot to tell you that I was some time in Saville Row yesterday. Anne had received your letter and feels, I think, as she ought as to

---

[*]A professional diplomat shortly to take up his mission in Brussels.
[†]*Romeo and Juliet* had opened at Covent Garden on 6 October.

the result, but Lady George is so stubborn and obstinate that I lose all patience. She told Hart that dear Harriet meant it all very kindly but was quite mistaken as it was quite as likely as ever, since Lord A. had told Robert he would wait for a final answer which he had never received &c. She adheres to this and all my intelligence goes for nothing against this unfortunately preconceived opinion.

I have not said half enough of Miss O'Neill. The dandies and the women of the town cry their eyes out and the house is in a state of agitation almost as deep as the tragedy. I think I shall not go to see 'Isabella'[*] tomorrow; it is really pousser la tragédie trop loin.

The year had ended with the Morpeths at Tixal and 1815 opened with the Leveson Gowers on their usual country-house circuit in company with the Morpeths, but in February until July (when the correspondence is resumed) both families were in London. In May the son and heir, the 'little Governor', was born: Granville George Leveson Gower, later second Earl Granville and Foreign Secretary. The Battle of Waterloo, where the Bessboroughs' son had been badly wounded, was won on 18 June. The Hundred Days were over. The Duke of Devonshire was extricating himself from a flirtation with Margaret Mercer Elphinstone[b] ('Poor Dear' to his family), an intimate friend of Princess Charlotte. In July Granville was created Viscount Granville of Stone. As the daughter of a Duke, Harriet could have continued to call herself Lady Harriet. However she preferred Viscountess and later Countess, in line with her husband's rank.

[Stanhope Street]
Wednesday 12 [July 1815]
I went to the Cavendishes yesterday and found Anne very well and very smart, which I think a good sign, not at all en victime. I find she thinks Ld Aberdeen has married upon compulsion and attributes every appearance of good spirits she has seen in him for the last six months, to a hope at the time of freeing himself from his

---

[*]*Isabella or The Fatal Marriage*, by Thomas Southerne.

engagement to Lady Hamilton. This perfectly unfounded conviction comforts her and prevents all mortifying reflections, so I did not, of course, *interfere* with the truth.

I gave near 6£ for a very high hat which I tell you of as an instance of the weakness of human nature. It has a fount of feathers upon it and I never will buy another, which is all I can say in my own defence.

There are letters from Brussels saying Frederick Ponsonby is covered with wounds but quite in a convalescent state, only greatly prescribed. The Bessborough's are expected there almost immediately. Caroline Wm said to the surgeon, 'Pray, Sir, had not I better read to Colonel Ponsonby all day long?' He answered, 'No, but if I might venture to recommend, it would be to hold your tongue.'

> Stanhope Street
> 14 [July 1815]

Our little dinner at D House went off very well, though my brother, Mr Burrell, Granville, Monsieur de Lieven and Miss Mercer scarcely uttered. Hart was testy and did not endeavour to conceal it; Mr Burrell, fine; Granville, lazy; Monsieur de Lieven, stupid and Miss Mercer, gloomy. Mme de Lieven,[b] Mrs Burrell and I were, en revanche, so very talkative, and the former so very drole and played and sung so delightfully in the evening, that I brought Granville to confess it was very agreeable to hear us and I found Hart had been pleased in spite of his resolutions to the contrary and half repented himself of his aversion [to Mme de Lieven].

Anne was excellent and respectable, but rather schocked me with her view of herself; she says she will not marry a man who is not rich or of very high rank, that she is born for a high and exalted station, that she must not be thrown away, that she knows what she is, &c &c. This is not interesting, though satisfactory as to her feeling no humiliation.

> Stanhope Street
> Monday (? 17 July 1815]

I wish you had been here last night for I was quite proud of myself. My rooms looked so very pretty, full of light and flowers and everybody was in such good humour.

[69]

My brother was very good and gave no encouragement whatever to 'Poor Dear' who had supped with us en famille the night before owing to her good genius coming to her aid in the shape of a torrent of rain which made it impossible to turn her from the door. I am at last brought to pity her — she has so committed and exposed herself. People laugh at her so openly that she must see and hear them and the Boringdons so openly discountenance and thwart her little plans that I wonder she bears so well with them.

Then came the great news dispatched to G in Yorkshire. The Granvilles (as they were now called) and the Duke were going to Paris for a few weeks. With the Restoration a Bourbon was again on the throne in the person of Louis XVIII. The Allied Sovereigns and their armies made their entry into Paris this month.

[Stanhope Street]
18 [July 1815]

Now, dearest G, for the great events. Hart commissions me to tell you that he has quite decided to go abroad, to Paris, on Tuesday or Thursday next at latest, and what appears to me a much greater event, I think there is just a chance of our going also. Granville has a raging desire to see the Allied Armies and though he is too kind to think of it himself, I feel I ought almost to urge his going alone, if it was thought better for me to remain behind and therefore you may conclude it *brings me* to wish the expedition to be settled.

F. Ponsonby is still feeble and wounded all over and was in dread of Caro's sisterly persecutions, but she was soon prevailed upon to prefer parading about the town at all hours.

God bless you, dearest dearest G.

I am to sup with Hart upon a broiled chicken tonight and know more of our schemes.

[Stanhope Street]
19 [July 1815]

It is quite settled dearest sister. We leave town Tuesday, Hart, Clifford, Granville and I. I take Mrs Ridgeway [her dressmaker] whom I have just left roaring for joy. She 'respects my motives more than the act itself', but I had not time to hear what she supposes them to be. I mean to spend a hundred napoleons in a week, but in cheap goods, as seeds for future economy and Ridgeway and I will, betimes in the mornings, rout out Le Petit St Antoine, the Cirque d'Or &c &c. The seeing Hart's first launch into foreign parts will give me great pleasure and his delight at having us with him, doubles it. I really believe I am enchanted. Do you know, my great enjoyment is that I shall have better means of amusing you and I am contriving an establishment in my box to facilitate my writing constantly, and the hearing of Hart will be next to seeing him there. He says to me, 'seduce me back to England with you', but a week will not be enough for him.

[Stanhope Street]
20 [July 1815]

We hear very encouraging accounts of Paris. We have got a very good courier and intend writing to reserve a ship in advance to avoid the bothering of the Captains in that well-known mahogany room at Dover. As I intend to bring you over some cheap present, pray let me know what it shall be. [In the Duke of Devonshire's hand] Don't be vexed at my neglect – its universal and constitutional. When the sea parts us, I'll write every day. Are you surprised at Viscountess Granville sharing my fête? We do long to be off. God bless you, dear G, and reward you for your patience if you suffer from ennui during our excursion.

[Stanhope Street]
[21 July 1815]

I do think my new name very pretty, but it seems to me always as if I was called it for fun.

[71]

What odd terms after all Mercer and my brother are upon. He tells me he has received a letter from her saying that 'for the first time since the commencement of their long friendship, she has *reason* to *complain* of him. Why did he *conceal* from her his plan of leaving England; why make a *parade* of meeting her at Brighton, to put her and Mrs *Burrell* in a ridiculous light?' Now excepting dragging in Mrs Burrell into the phrase by the neck and shoulders, this is really a sort of coming to the point, and as times and girls go, the next move is a proposal.

The poor Dss of Beaufort is much disappointed at not being able to go with us. The Duke will not hear of it. He is one of those people who admit no reason but downright necessity for any act, with a clause, however, in his creed, concerning hunting.

[Stanhope Street]
22 [July 1815]

Nothing is to be heard but discussions of what is to be done with Buonoparte. I am now writing in the little dark banking room at Child's, trying in vain to get napoleons. I am so hurried that I am obliged to carry my letter about with me.

The Bellerophon* is not yet arrived in to Plymouth. It is reported that the Apollo, the Transfiguration,† and all that was taken from the Vatican is to be brought here. It is also reported that Blücher has claimed sixteen of the finest pictures. I do not vouch for my truth.

Calais
26 [July 1815]

We have been very prosperous. We left Dover at twelve last night and landed here at half past four. I was sorry that we arrived in a thick rain and nobody up, so that nothing marked its being France but about half a dozen clamorous sailors, the poissardes being all in their last sleeps. I regret them as part of a very curious

---

*The English ship which brought Napoleon from Rochefort to Plymouth at the start of his captivity.

†In 1816, at the instigation of the Allies, these two statues, with others, were returned to the Vatican.

[72]

scene. Hart is in high good humour and tearing spirits, bids me describe his dress – a cap with a broad gold band and some very smart grey pantaloons. I wish you could see them at breakfast – Hart with one leg making side steps for joy all the time; Clifford tittering with the garçon about the coffee and hot milk; Granville pouring over an old 'Moniteur'.

Lord Castlereagh, Secretary of State, and his wife were staying in the Embassy house in the rue du Faubourg Saint-Honoré. Sir Charles Stuart, a bachelor, was now the Ambassador; the Duke of Wellington, Commander-in-Chief of the Allied Forces, had been given, for the present, a house close to the Place de la Concorde.

Paris
3 o'clock Saturday [29 July 1815]

Here we are this moment arrived! Hart, Clifford and Granville gone to the musée and to call on Lady Castlereagh. I am left writing to you in a little back room in your lower apartment at l'hôtel de l'Empire [rue de Cernutti].

Our journey has been one of greatest enjoyment and my brother's spirits and perfect good humour have never failed him for a moment in spite of several galling little circumstances. We remained a whole day at Calais, walked on the pier and went in the evening to the play; it was amusing but not good. Loyal songs were sung and a great many old peaceable looking gentlemen and all the old women are in raptures, but the soldiers gloomy and silent to a degree not to be mistaken. I have not seen a smile upon any French soldier's face the whole way.

The journey has nevertheless been delightful – the pleasantest weather, *tolerable* health, Hart quite perfect. Today it was a very curious sight to see St Denis full of English soldiers, officers, and English women galloping in and out of Paris. My brother remains in the rooms you had at first as he does not mind noise, and is charmed with them. We have taken a most delightful suite of apartments at La Grange Battelière.

[73]

4 o'clock. La Grange Battelière

I have just trotted here between gutters and cabriolets and am established in a very immense drawing room entre cour et jardin. They are come back – my brother in a state of enchantment. The Duke of Wellington invites us to a great ball on Monday. I hear the society at Lady C[astlereagh]'s is terrible – nothing but English and extremely dull.

We have just had a very comfortable little dinner and are setting off for the play. I hear our troops behave well; they can only enter Paris with passes from their Colonels.[*]

My brother professes a determination of taking a large house here, not now but another year, and if he does but like it half as well chemin faisant as he does at his outset, I think he certainly will.

What colour will you have your silk?

Sir John and Lady Shelley had been in Paris a fortnight. According to her diary, Lady Shelley appeared never to pass a day or evening out of the Duke of Wellington's company, with whom, she wrote, she had been intimately acquainted since the previous year. She was determined to be seen everywhere with him, at the theatre, the opera, at dinners and balls and even military reviews, and the Duke, it must be said, was very assiduous in his attentions to his ambitious companion.

Although a good-humoured, fairly sensible woman, Lady Castlereagh was given to fanciful actions, as for instance at a ball during the Congress of Vienna when to the consternation of the guests she wore her husband's Garter Cross in her hair. Her husband's half-brother, Lord Stewart (also Charles and not to be confused with Sir Charles Stuart), Minister in Vienna, was inordinately vain, while his reputation for debauchery was a byword. He had a jealous eye for the post of Ambassador to France and as half-brother to the Foreign Secretary there was an uneasy, though unexpressed rivalry between himself and Sir Charles Stuart. During the latter's incumbency the Embassy house was richly furnished, not only with Pauline Borghese's

---

[*]This was the first time the British Army had entered Paris since Agincourt.

Empire furniture, bought with the house, but with his own distinguished collection.

[Paris]
Monday 31 [July 1815]

Yesterday was a very interesting and amusing day, though perhaps you may think it neither to have begun it by sitting at home with H. Pierrepoint, Punch Greville and Ld Apsley, but they had all their little possible to say. The first gave me directions to the best fleuriste and lingère in Paris; the second told me all the scandal of Paris – that Sir John and Lady Shelley run after the great Duke in a very disgusting manner but, as they run together, sans peur et sans reproche. Ld Apsley is full of the battle [of Waterloo] in which he, by all accounts, put himself forward as much as any who were obliged to do so; he is a good natured, friendly creature and has shown a great spirit where he might have got off without showing any.

I called upon Lady Castlereagh and found her in the Villa Borghese [British Embassy] forming the most compleat contrast to the locale, which is all oriental luxury, and she really is fitter for Wapping. Lord Stewart came in all over stars and tenderness. I hear there never was anything like his vanity and extravagance.

I met my brother at the Louvre; he was struck with the coup d'oeil but says he has no taste for pictures, which I was not aware of. It appeared to me to be more beautiful than ever. Blücher has taken down sixteen, but none that I remembered; no proof, however, that they may not be some of the finest. The whole length of it was filled with soldiers of every nation – some Highlanders, who attracted great attention and took it as a great compliment. One of them said, 'They look more at us than at the d – – – d pictures.'

We dined at Lord Castlereagh's; his manner is very good and calculated to please but how he gets on in French I cannot imagine. He called out to the mâitre d'hôtel, 'apresent Mounsieur servez la diner,' and asked for *cotlys* when he wanted chops, which he had better have said at once. Sir Charles Stuart is in a fever of mind which he cannot conceal, from the fear of not remaining Ambassador here, and from all I hear, he seems to be the best person, being

[75]

excessively liked by the French. He has great jealousy of Lord Stewart whom (it is said) is equally anxious to remain.

But now for the cream of the story; we went to the opera – the house was full and brilliant beyond measure and my brother in raptures (as I must say he is from morning till night). All nations, all Embassies, all English men and scarcely a *reputable* but myself. Boxes for every King and Emperor of the known world. But what do you think they shout at, applaud, pâmer de rire over, *dance* in short. They dance the Battle of Waterloo – in all its details. The Imperial Guard, wounded, form dejected groups, embrace the National Guard &c whilst a smart English officer makes most brilliant entrées. He is héros de la pièce, ends the ballet with presenting a French officer whom he had taken prisoner to his mistress who had imagined him dead. The French all kneel to kiss the hem of his garment and dance a finale of all the nations amidst bursts of applause. Metternich[b] sat by me at supper at Lady Castlereagh's and we agreed it was worth coming any distance, taking any trouble, to see this proof of national character and confirmation of what that character is now reduced to. Even the Emperor of Russia is shocked at their frivolity – jugez, he has only been out of his home (into society, that is) three times – has taken quite a new and grave line – se promène dans son jardin and only with the ugly and the old. The King of Prussia prowls about, after his own heart, without exciting much attention and the Emperor of Austria is never seen at all.

The ball at the Duke of Wellington's is a sort of test of female character – there are bets whether a French woman can stay away from a ball, but they have one and all professed a horror of going into publick, and some, la crainte des reproches. Monsieur Mesnard[*] has just been here. He says that he has advised them all to go as a proof of what the Duke of W's good conduct in Paris has effected. But few will be candid enough to believe in this motive and I wish for their sakes that those who have been most marked in their misfortunes or in their opinions, may stay away.

Frederick Ponsonby is going on well and Caroline [William] Lamb enquiring if women can come to Paris, which I trust she will not ascertain till I have left it.

[*] ADC to the Duc de Berri.

Monday evening

I have just come from a very comfortable little dinner at l'hôtel de l'Empire.* Hart has been half over Paris already and was indulging himself in all sorts of imaginations. The favorite plans at this moment are – Devonshire House to be whitened; Chiswick to have palisades, gilt like the ones at the Thuilleries, between the cedars and the new plantations; all his female friends and relations to go to the play in high bonnets. He is delighted with a gown I have got for the ball, with no waist and immense bouffées all round it.

Lady Frances Webster, with whom Byron had had a passing love affair in 1813, was in Brussels at the time of the Waterloo campaign and was said to be the régnante with the Duke of Wellington. He wrote to her on the morning of the battle suggesting she might have to move to Antwerp. Again at the close of the day when the battle had been fought and won he sent her a reassuring message of his own safety. (Lady Shelley witheringly remarked that the Duke's attachment to Lady Frances was platonic, or if any love existed, it was on the lady's side.)

'Little Mme de Périgord' was none other than the ravishing, dark-eyed Dorothea Comtesse Edmond de Talleyrand-Périgord. Possibly of illegitimate birth, she was born in 1792, the youngest daughter of the Duchesse de Courlande. In 1809 at the age of seventeen she married Prince de Talleyrand's nephew and heir, but the marriage was a failure. The duel to which Harriet refers may have been the one fought by her husband and her lover, in which her husband was wounded in the face. Subsequently Dorothea became the Duchesse de Dino by which name she is best known. She devoted her life to her uncle until his death and accompanied him to London when he was appointed Ambassador, 1830–4. In 1820 a daughter was born to her, generally thought to have been fathered by Talleyrand.

[Paris]
Tuesday 1 August [1815]

The ball was a most extraordinary one – about four hundred men

---

*The Times reported that the Duke of Devonshire had 'a suite of elegant apartments on the first floor of the right wing of the Hôtel de l'Empire, rue d'Artois'.

to forty women, for I did injustice to the French. I find they are for the first time subdued by misfortune and it is from real feeling that many of them stay away from every place of amusement. When I went into the Duke's I found in the first magnificent room about a hundred officers, but soon discovered many well known bores under these false pretences. In the doorway I met Talleyrand* waddling out; he did not speak to me so I only had the satisfaction of seeing his dirty, cunning face and long coat for a moment. After him came Fouché, a little spare, sallow, shrewd-looking man who seems to unite all parties in one common feeling – horror of his character and the policy of not betraying it. He is, I conclude, the worst and most useful man the King could have found in his whole dominion. The King of Prussia was the only royal lion; he talked to me for about ten minutes, enquired affectionately after you. Pozzo di Borgo, Metternich and Sir Charles Stuart are the people I like most to talk to here. The former tells one any thing and every thing one wishes to know from Adam till now; Metternich is more entertaining than any body and Sir Charles is like a good court guide or book of reference – he discovers what others are about and would be about, to a degree that must be very useful to him in his present situation.

The demoralisation of the French nation is become too much like the cosmogony of the world in the 'Vicar of Wakefield', one hears and talks of nothing else and I would bet ten to one that every person begins (in English, German, French, Russian or high Dutch), 'Was there ever a nation' &c &c. There never was, au reste, such innumerable parties and shades of party, and Fouché, for the last year, has paid abject court in five different quarters – to the Emperor, the King, to the Duke of Orléans, the Jacobins, and to the Duke of Wellington – to receive a retraite en Angleterre in case all the others had failed him.

Lady Shelley pursues her pursuit with the most unremitting diligence and really makes herself very ridiculous as the Duke pays her no attention and she follows and watches him quite laughably. There is no harm in her, I am sure, beyond inordinate vanity. There is, I find, a very different case – Lady Frances

*The immensely wealthy and powerful Prince de Talleyrand, with a sad reputation for immorality, was now Minister for Foreign Affairs and President of the Council.

Webster, that beautiful daughter of Lord Mountmorris, Lord Byron's 'Genevra'. The Duke is desperately in love with her and she with him and it is said to be quite une affaire arrangée. He is considerably older than he need be to be her father.

Little Madame de Périgord and her fine eyes was one of the very few French women there; she waltzed as if her husband's head had not been laid open in a duel in the morning. I suppose they cannot help dancing. Mme Juste de Noailles after a contredanse, met some body who asked her how she did: 'Aussi bien que l'on peut être après avoir dansé sur le tombeau de sa patrie', she answered, and I daresay danced another.

Tonight Granville and Punch are risking my fortune as well as their own at the Salon.

3 [August 1815]

Only think, my dearest G, of poor Granville being laid up with his first fit of the gout. It must be confessed he has chosen his time ingeniously. I went with Hart to see Mlle Mars[*] and was disappointed; she appears to me an excellent actress but not séduisante, enchanteresse &c. Eyes and gesticulations as quick as lightning, but she put me in mind of Miss Berry when she is shewing off and that does not bring the word *captivating* to my mind. My brother was much more pleased with her than I was.

[Paris]
Monday [7 August 1815]

In politicks there is nothing new. Fouché is said to look very grave. The Emperor [of Russia] whom Granville saw this morning, says the state of affairs is quite inexplicable; our military seem very much amused in tearing up and down the boulevards in the morning, filling the theatres at night, and losing their money at the Salon.

Of sights I have seen the Halle au Blé, the Marché des Légumes, the models of the Hôtel des Invalides, service performed at Notre Dame – and the Duke of Rutland in it talking in a style prophetic

[*]Famous as an actress and as a favourite with Napoleon.

of another tour, 'This is indeed a most striking and most curious sight and this is indeed a state of things in which . . .' &c, his eyes in a tame phrenzy rolling. I have seen Talma* and Mlle George act very finely in 'Oedipe' and Mlle Mars delightfully in the 'Misanthrope', but the theatres are intolerably hot. The carriages are rather worse than ever or than any thing but Lady Castlereagh.

Hart has been and bought all that Blücher has left. Nothing is agissante but Caroline Wm in a purple riding habit, tormenting every body, but I am convinced ready primed for an attack upon the Duke of Wellington and I have no doubt but that she will to a certain degree succeed as no dose of flattery is too strong for him to swallow or her to administer. Poor Wm hides in one small room whilst she assembles lovers and trades people in another; he looks worn to the bone. She arrived dying by her own account having had French apothicarys at most of the towns through which she passed and sent immediately for a doctor, but '*by mistake* they went for the Duke of Wellington'!

Hart is gone to win me a few parting napoleons.

Lord Stewart, having accompanied the Allied sovereigns to Paris, had installed himself handsomely and entertained lavishly. The Duchesse de Sagan (sister of Dorothea de Dino), whose reputation was the scandal of Europe, was now his mistress. Earlier she had shared the affections of a lover with her mother and during the Congress of Vienna Frederick Lamb,[b] Prince Metternich, the Emperor of Austria and Lord Stewart had run concurrently. The 'Baronne de Talleyrand' is unaccounted for unless Harriet confused her with Dorothea whose husband was Talleyrand's only nephew. Ney, marshal of France, was court-martialled and shot for treason in December of this year.

[Paris]
Thursday [10 August 1815]
On Monday I went with Hart to a great dinner at Lord Stewart's. The Duchesse de Sagan, who has forsaken Frederick Lamb and is

*François Joseph Talma (1763–1826). French tragic actor but educated as a dentist.

[80]

now the régente at Prince Charles' (for so Ld Stewart is universally called) court; her mother and sisters; la baronne de Talleyrand, a little thing of sixteen, natural daughter of Talley-rand and married to his nephew; Ladies Castlereagh, Shelley, Kinnaird and myself. The house is beautiful and belonged to the comte de Montesquieu. The dinner very splendid and Schwarzen-berg, Czernicheff,[*] some Princes and all the Ambassadors present at it. I sat between *Sir* Charles and Lord Clancarty and was well amused.

There was a Russian review yesterday morning, but we did not go. The three Allied Sovereigns, the Great Duke, and Lady Shelley, riding along the ranks and reviewing the whole; she makes an unprecedented fool of herself.

Paris is in the same state; the news of Ney's being taken having arrived today; little disturbances in the publick gardens and the Duke of Wellington having told somebody that in six weeks the armies will have quitted France. What will happen then, nobody even attempts to conjecture, but poor Louis must, I think, end ill after all. We go on Sunday. I have just come from dinner; Hart, Clifford and Punch Greville dined with us. Hart says he has bought all Paris. I have bought you a green silk petticoat.

Roehampton
Monday 21 [August 1815]

We went to Holland House today but did not see him. She was seated on the grass with Allen and a plate of baba, very cross and very absurd about Buonaparte, 'poor dear man' as she calls him. They are all well here; my aunt is grown thin but looks uncommonly well and is very happy about Frederick who begins to move his arm and is going on as well as possible. F. Lamb is arrived. The world is much occupied with Mr [William] Lyttel-ton's conversation with Buonaparte, but there are very different versions of it. Lady Holland represents it as having been insolent, brutal and disgraceful to the greatest degree. They all say here that he was not polished in his manners but intended, and thinks,

---

*Field-Marshal Prince Karl Philipp Schwarzenberg, Commander-in-Chief of the Austrian forces. General Alexander Ivanovich Czernischev, aide-de-camp to the Russian Emperor Alexander I.

his manner was complimentary and flattering and that he thinks Buonoparte was charmed with him.[*]

Badminton
Friday [25 August 1815]

I have but a moment to tell you we arrived here last night. I dined at Holland House and if she had been in better humour it would have been very agreeable, but she is not in a happy hour and will not suffer others to be so, without a little quiet course of pumping and teasing going on sotto voce all the time. Their politicks seem to me to be reduced to adoration of Buonoparte. Mr Sheridan was there at his best; discussing all the young women of his acquaintance with much praise and some little cuts. He says '*Silence*'[†] [Lady Jersey][b] is a pretty, purling, babbling stream, never stagnant. Lady Borino [Boringdon][b] his favorite, has hit the line between good humoured frankness and vulgarity – just touch and run.

Badminton
26 [August 1815]

Frederick Lamb is come home, some say disgusted, others relieved, at the Duchesse de Sagan's new passion for Ld Stewart. I should hope, for his sake, the latter, as I really see no charm but profligacy in her, and though one often hears it said that is one – for the honour of human nature – I hope charms but few.

From Badminton the Granvilles went to stay at Saltram in Devon (now National Trust property), the home of Lord Boringdon who became first Earl of Morley in December of this year.

Saltram
31 August [1815]

I am very much pleased with this place, but Borino is monarch of

---

[*]For the correct version see B. Askwith, *The Lytteltons*, 1975, pp. 27–30.
[†]The irony of the nickname lay in her being an inveterate talker.

all he surveys and it is almost a guilty feel comes over one when not employed exactly according to his bidding. I should say there was more of enjoyment than of beauty in what I have hitherto seen. We live in two very comfortable rooms – a small library and drawing room; keep early hours – at least breakfast was over at eleven and dinner upon the table at six, and plenty of it. The Lansdownes are here and yesterday evening was after my own heart – work, reading, talking and neither dancing, acting, romping or joking.

Saltram
1 September [1815]

The Boringdons saw the Pole who was allowed to go with Buonoparte, he seems really attached to him 'mais il ne pense jamais à lui' – a new view of his character. There are different versions of all the stories of him and his companions; some say that Madame Bertrand* is very much in love with him, others that she detests him and never calls him anything but 'l'homme'.

My own sis – I am ordered out – we are going to Mount Edgecumbe. Borino is so long murmuring and marshalling us that I have time to tell you that I had a letter from my aunt; she says she has just seen the Hollands – Lady H. overwhelmed with grief at the failure of some presents she had wanted to send to Buonoparte and Mme Bertrand; that Caroline writes that 'she detests Paris which she says is gay without interest, noisy without respite and noisy beyond bearing', that she is magnificently but uncomfortably lodged, alone or in a crowd; that every countenance bears the stamp of suppressed ill humour if a native, pique if Austrian or Russian, open insolence or vulgar wonder if English, with the only exception of Hart, who unlike all others, sees every thing couleur de rose and enjoys himself extremely.

Saltram
3 [September 1815]

Have you any recollection of Mount Edgecumbe? We went there the day before yesterday and I think I never admired any

---

*The wife of Napoleon's secretary. They accompanied Napoleon to St Helena.

[83]

thing more. The day was beautiful and the sea covered with shipping.

Lady Lansdowne is the best little person in the world. I really think she seems faultless. Her desire of gaining information in every possible way is particularly laudable in her as it is, I am sure, a more certain way of pleasing him than any other. Knowledge seems to be his deity and he is just like the account of King Solomon in the Book of Kings. We leave literally no stone unturned and all my ignorance comes to light upon the occasion.

The Cowpers will be here to dinner. I see I like Lady Jersey the best as I wish for her much more than for Lady C.[b] The former takes every thing in good part and is so frank and good humoured that thinking the other, as I do, much the most agreeable, does not turn the scale in her favour. The thoughts of the Earls sit heavy on my soul at moments when my spirits are not high, but I know I shall like it when they all come and Messrs Luttrell and Nugent will be a great addition. The only real black spots on the horizon are Secrétaire,[*] the system of joking and the muscles of my mouth unable to look gay and affable, with the deep remorse of that inability. I feel shy and an idiot always in that society.

We have just been at the most mitigated church service, as Mr Ward would say; so curtailed and shortened. I was in agonies least Borino should, if the sermon exceeded his wishes, hold up a watch or drop a curtain.

Saltram
6 [September 1815]

We went down or up the Tamar to see Cothel[†] (I only know that it sounds so) – an old house of Lord Mount Edgecumbe's. It is a beautiful expedition but a fatiguing one; you may judge – six miles of carriage road, at foot's pace, up and down perpendicular hills; fourteen of water, rowing against the tide; a long walk to see the place, sailing back and driving home in the dark; groping up the hills every now and then for safety. I will describe ourselves to you walking up the steep hill at Cothele, pour vous orienter

[*]A card game.
[†]Cotehele is now a property of the National Trust.

compleatly amongst us. 1st, Lady B[oringdon], an old green shawl swinging over her shoulders, the corners all wrong, her hair about her ears, a cap just sticking on to the back of her head and her hat in her hand – shouting out for the housekeeper to be in readiness for us. No wonder that a maid who first appeared to us, told her she must not *per-sume* to come in. Next – Lord Lansdowne, very fat and out of breath, in a black chip hat, very much enfoncé over his head. Lady Cowper, swinging after them, her nose very red, a high hat tied on with a veil under her chin, flounces draggling, sashes untying, shawls floating. Myself, ditto. Lady Lansdowne, towed up by Miss Smith in a little crushed muslin poke, a sweet smile and an immense protruberance,* Lord Cowper striding after us, every now and then stopping, taking a position with his hand shading his eyes to look at the view en maître.

We lead the life of tourists, have delicious weather, little repose and no time. Lady Cowper is more animated than I ever knew her; she talks more and is not quite so much ' " 'Tis seeming all " ' as usual, though she occasionally looks bored and resigned and gives us sly cuts.

I am writing for dear life. Ld Lansdowne and I are going to perform a journey on foot, Lady Boringdon in a whisky, Lady Cowper and the Lords on horseback – she has no habit and is a coward on any horse but her own.

Saltram
Thursday [7 September 1815]

My brother arrived yesterday without a single note of preparation at the very moment we sat down to dinner; you may judge how we shouted and rejoiced. He looks even better than when I left him at Paris. Tanned into quite a dark man with a great colour in his cheeks.

Friday morning [8 September 1815]

He is very amiable and I think so essentially improved by his *travels* – so much more considerate and facile à vivre. I have been walking with him, as we have, with great difficulty, obtained

*Lady Lansdowne was expecting a child in January (who became the fourth Marquess).

[85]

from Borino one day of rest and free will. It is burning sun, delightful to bask and saunter under, but quite unfit for exertion.

Saltram

12 [September 1815]

We had a great ball last night in the great rooms, which upon lesser occasions we are not allowed to frequent. Some very pretty girls and smart men – two quadrilles, la Coquette, walzes, contredanse anglaises. Lady Boringdon danced as gaily and as well as ever, flumped down upon knees and nose in the middle of a chasse and minded it no more than I did looking at it. Granville and Lady Cowper persevering round and round and Hart enjoying it with all his might.

Tomorrow we go to see Miss O'Neill act 'Belvidera' at Plymouth. Think of Mr Luttrell's look who has never seen her. We are to go blubbering to a Plymouth ball afterwards, which is not the best part of it. I am now ordered out to Plymouth to call on Miss O'Neill and to settle a farce.

Saltram

Wednesday [13 September 1815]

We are all resting upon our oars in the hottest day I ever felt to enable us to go through Miss O'Neill and a Plymouth ball. Lady Borino and Lady Cowper called upon her yesterday; they say she looks exactly the same off stage as on, has very good manners, only a little too theatrical, motioning them to sit down with her pocket handkerchief in a arranged shape, and looks too earnest for the occasions that occur in the course of a visit in the Plymouth hotel.

Saltram

14 [September 1815]

Miss O'Neill acted some parts of 'Belvidera' beautifully, but I think her a little spoilt, I suppose by success. She occasionally over acts and especially in the mad scene – after her hysterical laugh she makes a noise in her throat between suffocation and sickness that is really horrible, most disgusting. She is also grown very fat, which in a part where she is to throw herself about, is a very serious disadvantage. We had a tolerable Jaffier, but a Pierre* whose beau ideal is Barrymore and but a bad imitation of him. The theatre is very good and was very full.

We went to a dull ball and returned to mutton broth at about one as Hart had threatened to leave Saltram if he had not some. We are now expecting a visit from Miss O'Neill and Sir Diggory Forrest, the Mayor, under whose protection she is here.

Saltram
Saturday [16 September 1815]

We are at this moment setting out; Hart in his barouche which we were to have gone in with him if it had been fine, but it is pouring.

We had a visit from Miss O'Neill, who is odious. She snubbed us all, which to begin, is not prepossessing, strutted about and throws out sentences in a low tragedy tone, looks short, thick and vulgar, carefully avoids and coldly receives any conversation bearing the least upon her art and when Lady B. mentioned Mr Ward as having acted Jaffier tolerably at the Plymouth Theatre, said 'Mr WHO? I was really not aware of his name!' with the most dignified touchiness. She is pretty but her figure in blue sattin is quite ugly taken in the lump – the details of it, when brought into play on the stage, is what is beautiful.

Tixal
23 [September 1815]

I am so happy I do not know what to do with myself. We arrived here at eight and found Susan bolt upright in her little bed with her little round night cap on; a fat boy whom I took at first for Georgy, fast asleep, and Georgy herself, whom not all my endeavours could keep awake for a moment; Harriette fatter and happier than ever. We came all the way 105 miles today, so you must allow for a short sleepy letter.

I am sorry to see in a latter from Paris the following account. 'Lady Caroline Lamb is madder than ever – she has broken two busts in the Duke of Wellington's house because she pretended

*Jaffier and Pierre are the leading male characters in *Venice Preserv'd*. Barrymore played secondary tragic parts at Drury Lane.

they did not do him justice and he has been seriously warned of her, as it is said she will not leave Paris till she has stabbed herself or him.' I had heard nothing of this new pursuit had you?

Tixal
Thursday 28 [September 1815]

I have been a long ride this morning and should be quite à mon aise if my poney had not a great mind to run away. He set off with me once – I tugged and hollowed for Granville. He would not come but bade me hold my tongue and tug on, which succeeded. He ran away once with Harriette but he has no vice and one is quitte pour la peur.

Probably because of her husband's impotency Caro George now fancied herself in love with Henry Brougham.[b] No chronicle of London society in the first half of the nineteenth century would be complete without reference to the Lievens. He was Russian Ambassador in London, 1812–34. His wife, Dorothea, had a passion for high politics and intrigue. Brilliant, shrewd, and observant, she was never an easy companion.

Tixal
Wednesday 4 [October 1815]

I think her [Caro George] spirits are better than I have for a long time known them and I should say it was a new, though not yet a strong interest, that makes them so. I should think Mr B[rougham]'s faults and merits must equally tend to make him a very dangerous person.

I hope Mme de Lieven will not be very offensive to my monde. I dread tiffs.

Tixal
Friday [6 October 1815]

Mme de Lieven has a fluxion – as her temper is not of the sweetest and as she thinks a good deal of herself, you may conclude that she does not appear to advantage. She will not have a breath of air and frets over her pain and necessary *wraps* from morning to night. My women are very good humoured and bear with her I think almost better than I do.

[Tixal]
Sunday [8 October 1815]

Mme de Lieven has not shown herself to advantage. Her cleverness is her only charm and alas, it does but little towards making her attractive. It is every thing that makes a person amiable which is wanting in her – gentleness, sweetness, cheerfulness, kindness, abnégation de soi. There is a great deal of decorum and propriety and I cannot believe in any very ardent feelings under it. Mounsieur de Lieven looks black occasionally but prend sur lui and behaves very well.

I do not think Caro at all in love with Mr B. now, but I think he will take unlimited power over her mind if she sees much more of him. He flatters her understanding and excites her compassion – two strong measures for acquiring influence – and I know he has that peculiar sort of ugliness (like truffle with white teeth), which charms.

Ingestre
[10 October 1815]

Each hour my spirits and friendship decay – I cannot describe how maussade she [Mme de Lieven] is and the decorum and reality so ill concealed, schock me.

On Saturday we shall all be at Chatsworth – Mrs Lamb is there already. Mr Brougham is, I believe, coming to Chatsworth and a few mitigated dandies. Tell the girls I will give them some beautiful patterns.

Lord Gower was carrying on a flirtation with Mme de Lieven which Harriet described as 'very great but babyish, not passion, and there is a great contrast in her very cross dry way and his perpetual titter'.

Chatsworth
Saturday 21 [October 1815]

Today two coaches full have gone to Castleton, but yet I am seizing a moment, equipped in Mrs Lamb's riding habit, trembling with fright, whilst Granville is ordering the horses. In a body coach are Mounsieur and Mme de Lieven, Lord Gower and poor Caro – but she preferred even this to the risk of getting a pain in her face, – Lady Cowper, Elizabeth Somerset, the Albanians[*] and Sneyd in another. Poor Mounsieur de Lieven is wretched and more jealous than any thing I saw; she is a mixture of the strangest impudence and most artful contrivance. They go on Thursday to Sandon where, I conclude, they have menagéed themselves another meeting. Lord Gower goes Monday and Mr Brougham comes on that day. Lord Cowper pines for the latter, as, to do him justice, he is not unworthy of a clever person. Mr Luttrell being the most brilliant person here, he leads him off from morning to night and watches every opening of his mouth.

[Chatsworth]
Wednesday [25 October 1815]

Mrs Lamb is drinking broth at my elbow to see that I write no harm. Mr B[rougham] is arrived and shy, dark and clever as he is, he puts me quite at my ease from appearing so fearful of us all, that one's courage gives one a feel of superiority that his *renown* would rather check. I feel as if I should admire him most extremely but he is like the sensitive plant and shrinks from the advances universally made him. The Dss [of Devonshire] plies him incessantly and tags after him with well informed questions about Edinburgh, Paris &c &c. Mrs Lamb is very right and amiable but not the least in love to my mind; she mentions, 'not at present and that we neither of us know, what may happen. I could be . . .'

They amuse us both here by their violent abuse of his looks, yet we are all after him from morning to night. I think the Dss and Lord Cowper are the most assiduous. The Lievens go tomorrow and I am much touched with regard to her. I pity her so profoundly for her education and a thousand things. It is a bad concern but with thousands of excuses – and very unhappy.

[*]Luttrell and Nugent.

[90]

Tixal

Friday [1 December 1815]

I have been in my room all day with a complaint, dining upon tough partridge and reading Mr Scott's 'Tour in France'. He is editor of the Champion and has advertised another.

I am sitting now opposite the Dean [of Lichfield] – the Silent Dean – with black eyebrows and a cup of cocoa; Nugent thundering out Figaro to Harriette's accompaniment and Granville listening attentively on the other side of her. You have no idea what a comfort she is becoming to me – she is not shy but she is not in the least forward. In the evening she stays from half past eight till eleven. She saves me the intolerable bore of sitting boxed up amongst the singers and plays delightfully.

Nugent is really quavering like a lark.

[Tixal]

Sunday 3 [December 1815]

Granville and Mr Nugent are buried in a game of chess and I have left Scott and an arm chair quite in the fire to write to you. I cannot say enough of Scott's Tour – it is living in Paris all over again with every thought cleverly expressed, every feeling defined and no stomach ache. Passe for a soupçon of vulgarity and it is one of the cleverest, certainly of the most entertaining, books I ever read.

Read Mr Brougham's speech upon the trial – it is very like a man who prefers a platonic attachment. I get frightened about him – every body talks of him with a hitch and a 'clever he certainly is – no body can question his abilities – one tells me that he is famous for taking the hue of every person whom he wishes in a way to controul'; another that, 'qu'il y a longtemps qu'il a étè honnête homme', is all that can be said and none of these political enemies.

[Tixal]

6 [December 1815]

I have had a long letter from Caroline today – it made me miserable – she is so low, appears unhappy, she doubts Mr B, says she must go abroad, that she is quite unable to remain with George. Dearest G, ever since I have known it seems to me as if something was pulling at my heart strings whenever I think of her. There is no sacrifice I would not make to see her even a degree happier; but think of her imprudence.

[Tixal]
23 December [1815]

I think it must be very melancholy – the moment of leaving Lord C[arlisle], but I am extremely impatient for you to be in town with Mrs Lamb. Have you observed how her letters dérouter one? And every fresh one I take an entire new view of the subject. It is a terrible responsibility to write or advise at all at such a moment. I trust you will not blame any thing I have said. With great risks, I confess I think it is her *only* prospect of happiness and perhaps virtue. I do not think she could now, with a shade of either, remain in the Melbourne family. Her feelings toward them are all so embittered. I cannot say how anxious I feel about her. My only doubt rests upon the misery to her if he should ever repent or even regret.

Sandon
1 [January 1816]

Many happy returns of the new year. Somebody told me today of a caricature – a figure reposing, with little figures representing colds and rheumatism twitching at and pinching him, written underneath – 'The compliments of the season'.

How are you dearest sis? I do not know how I shall have patience to stay at Badminton when I know you are in London. God bless you my own dear G.

[Sandon]
[First days of January 1816]

Dear love, I do not care how late in January you stay so that you are in town by the last week in February.

Thank you, my own dearest sis, for all your kind expressions. I am indeed as happy as I can hold together.

[92]

Tixal
6 [January 1816]

Granville tells me he means to go to town the 30th of January. I am so stout and well that I fear it will entail upon me a great deal of business. I weigh 10 stone 14 pound! and look like a dairy maid – rouge excepted. Granville, though well upon the whole, has little *ails* hanging about him.

The subject of the following letter, the boisterous and high-spirited (if a shade vulgar) Duchess Georgiana, had shocked society by marrying the sixth Duke of Bedford as his second wife, having been as near as may be engaged to his brother the fifth Duke, who had died. This had been engineered by her scheming mother, the Duchess of Gordon, who had two other Duchess daughters.

Ingestre
Thursday [11 January 1816]

The only thing that has amused me here have been some of Lady Talbot's accounts of Woburn. The Dss, so big with child that she can hardly walk, is grown in person very like the other sisters; her face and neck as red and her look as coarse. This, with much added want of decency and refinement, must, I think, quite destroy her charm. She invites people to feel the Duke's sides with this appropriate speech, 'Why, Johnny, you are as fat as your sheep', and screamed out to the Duke of Manchester's eldest daughter [her niece] who came down with a gown very low in the back, 'My dear, when do you mean to favour us with a sight of your *bottom*.' I am ashamed to have written it. Johnny still simpers and looks pleased with all this.

Lady Holland was all attention to Lady Talbot who with all her abuse and prudery, will, I foresee, undergo the pumping ordeals after dinner at Holland House next year as well as the best or the worst of us.

[93]

Lilleshall
15 [January 1816]

I never was so well in my life and I think I owe it chiefly to air and temperance. To the former I wish you could by degrees bring yourself. I do not take much exercise but whenever I feel *withered* or fusty, I open the window, put on a hat and shawl and walk quick up and down the room about a dozen times and it cannot be indifferent the sort of feel of *purified*, *clarified* sensation with which I shut myself up again. I do it between dressing and breakfast – it avoids the trouble and plague of going out for a minute at that time and airs me. About diet; I drink either madeira or sherry in the middle of the day with bread. At dinner I eat meat in both courses, sometimes when I am very hungry twice helped to each, with vegetables.

I must now tell you a story – Lady H. Bagot has had the most dreadful unaccountable pains in her face – she is entirely cured, – but when she had them she was strongly advised to write to 'Mr Perry, Surgeon, Liverpool'. He is one of the cleverest men that ever was but has turned his thoughts principally to *odd pains*. Lady Harriet begged me to write this to you – whether it is not worth while for you to write to him a full statement of your case from its very beginning. I know one of his remedies is having the coldest water poured upon the cheek from a very great height.

Badminton
Thursday [18 January 1816]

I have for a long time been a little uneasy about Granville's health; he has had more or less ever since his illness in town, headaches, full feels, in his head and a very full, heated look in his complexion. I arrived here, half reason, half fancy, in a very great state of anxiety. We persuaded him to see Taylor this morning. I found that my fears had been much more than occasion required, but he immediately bled him 14 ounces, till he fainted dead away. He is going to take Seidlitz waters four times a week for a month and calomel about once in three weeks. He has urged him so strongly to get up every morning at 9 o'clock and never omit 4 miles *walking* exercise every day. He is tonight (by his own confession) better than he has been for a long time. He has a relieved feel, a weight taken from his head.

[94]

I have had a letter from Mrs Lamb with every thing in it but a final resolution and I have written one to her attempting to represent no one objection but the question whether she can in conscience, resolve to blast all his [Brougham's] future prospects, or dare to think any thing could make up to him, or to the world, for the rendering useless such abilities as his. Granville saw it so strongly in the same light as myself that I ventured to urge it as much as possible.

Sir Charles Stuart, nearing forty years old, had made a bid for the hand of Lady Elizabeth Yorke, the Hardwickes' third daughter – still unmarried at thirty and with no pretensions to beauty. The marriage, contrived by the Berry sisters, close friends of the Hardwickes, was one of convenience. Sir Charles was well known for his more than indecorous behaviour, particularly in the lower life of Paris, but he had money and position (though not yet created a peer) and the Hardwickes needed a husband for their neglected daughter.

Stanhope Street
Friday evening [2 February 1816]
Mrs Lamb was here this morning with a dozen people in the room; she looks worn out but is now behaving with great calmness and what she always has – a strong wish to do right. Clifford is perfect – so right minded and high principled, but it is, I fear too late for her to take the only virtuous line. He, however, urges it without ceasing and if any body can have influence, he will.

Saturday [3 February 1816]
Miss Berry is going in the course of next week to 'comfort Papa and Mama Hardwicke' – but who will comfort Sir Charles? I hear he behaves shamefully, goes about saying she is laide à faire peur and has no thoughts of parting with a French actress whom he keeps. Adieu best and dearest own G.

Stanhope Street
Monday [5 February 1816]

I have been sorry to hear Mr Brougham's speech very much
abused; * it seems to have been thought coarse and with very
little to recommend it. I understand his friends are much annoyed. I do not think the peace between him and Lady H[ol-
land] will be lasting, in which case it had been better not made;
if he gives himself out as upon friendly terms with them he
should not act exactly as he would have done if he had contrived
to be as independent of them in society as politicks. Lady
Holland has taken up a line of civility and sweetness. To Mrs
Lamb I find she has been really licking the dust under her feet –
to get at the chestnuts – but it is not only when she has an object.
She ran to open the door for Berry, which little event has not
missed its mark, for she repeats it every 5 minutes. She had I
hear quite an assembly in Savile Row† last night. Granville went
there and to Mme de Lieven's, who has soirées and suppers
every Sunday.

There is a little novel going on – Miss Mercer affichérs
desperate love for Flahault,^{b‡} which he acts a most assiduous
return to, but is really épris with Lady Cowper.

Your children all drank tea here last night. Blanche and Suzy
came to desert. Blanche is too great a darling; she is shy in general
but I suppose it is some likeness in voice or manner, she forgets
with me that I am not you, calls me 'Mama' and is full of jokes
and animations.

[Stanhope Street]
7 [February 1816]

It is said to be true that Lord and Lady Byron are going to be
parted; she has written to him to say that unless he consents to a
legal separation she intends bringing it into a Court of Justice.
They say his profligacy and ill usage of her have been dreadful.

---

*On 4 February, the first day of the Parliamentary session, Brougham had delivered
an onslaught on Government policy.
†The Hollands' town house.
‡Reputedly the illegitimate son of Talleyrand; also reputedly he had fathered a son
(Comte de Morny) on Queen Hortense of Holland in 1811.

[Stanhope Street]
[8 February 1816]

I have been visiting but have gleaned little news. I found Lord Gower with Mme de Lieven which embarrassed me, but not them. The Byrons are certainly separated. Lady Ossulton told me a horrid report of its being in consequence of an improper correspondence having been discovered between him and Mrs Leigh. It must be impossible.

[Stanhope Street]
[? 11 February 1816]

Granville went to see Miss O'Neill in 'Measure for Measure' last night, Monsieur de Flahault and Benjamin Constant were there; it is a bad play for foreigners to see, and he says they seemed terribly wearied. Benjamin has brought over a novel [*Adolphe*] which he is going to read to a select few in C[avendish] Square* next week, and I mean to be present and I have begged C[aro] W. Lamb may – to cry and make a sensation for us. I hear that Miss Mercer is desperately in love and that Charles de Flahault acts it quite like somebody in a play; the most extravagant speeches before every body which Margaret swallows.

[Stanhope Street]
[14 or 15 February 1816]

Mme de Lieven, whom you enquired about, is become famous for civility and empressements to every body; her manner much softened and as far as the most propriety in all one sees and [on] the most amiable terms with her husband and greatest égard for him – so great a change has taken place – but I suspect that her little affair with Ld Gower goes on à la sourdine. He looks more discreet than ever; his eyes are quite closed and his mouth like a dot. To *me* she is much less éxigeante; she calls here every three or four days, is very agreeable and always in radiant good humour and we dined there on Sunday. It was, I suppose, a dinner quite unrivalled in the records of dullness. The Arch Dukes [of Austria]

---

*The Bessboroughs' town house.

[97]

who scarcely utter, though the eldest looks intelligent, and it is said that they are just as bored as they look; Lord Liverpool, Ld Castlereagh, Ld Bathurst, nearly as silent.

I went from thence to Savile Row which always looks as if there was to be revolution the next morning; Ld Kinnaird, whispering, gesticulating and prophecying; Flahault who is discreet upon politicks, dévoués aux dames. The Duchess of Bedford affiché-ing her labour pains and assuring them all that Johnny would never get her safe home.

[Stanhope Street]
19 [February 1816]

I was all Saturday listening to Benjamin Constant; his novel is very clever, very well written and very *true*. It is, in my opinion a glowing, deeply felt description of what the misery must be of having inspired Mme de Staël with a violent passion and the difficulty of getting rid of her. The heroine dies, but the fatal notion I had formed, steeled my heart and Benjamin must think I have a cor di tigre, especially as I sat next to my Aunt, who was a sort of fountain. Mounsieur de Flahault came in for the end. I have seen very little of him; I think him spoilt and less like an Englishman than I had imagined. He is very gracious but with a look of protection that is rather irritating.

I went yesterday evening to Mme de Lieven's. Mary and Agnes Berry in velvet gowns, ruffs and hats and feathers like very old Queens of Scotland. Lady Downshire in blue Turkish attire. I sat with Lieven – the man Lieven. I never was so comfortably bored and I can conceive the connoisseurs thinking it a sort of little Paradise.

The sisters were together in London. There are no letters until July.

[Stanhope Street]
24 [July 1816]

I enclose you a letter I received yesterday from Lady Byron, in consequence of which I have ordered the carriage to call on

Mrs Leigh; I think Lady B's wishes upon the subject quite conclusive.

[Stanhope Street]
Thursday [25 July 1816]

I went yesterday morning to Mrs Leigh and found her radiant, in high spirits and uncommon good looks and constantly alluding with very meaning smiles to all the past.

Evening.

I must now faute de mieux, talk of my own health. I find that the rhubarb and ginger are the philosopher's stone to me and I have felt better these two days than I had for a long time past. Hart has withdrawn to Chiswick from whence he has sent us a fatal galantine of peaches, for I cannot resist them.

Mrs Villiers gave me a long account of what has passed between the wife [Lady Byron] and the sister [Augusta Leigh] since the accouchement of the latter.* Mrs Villiers persuaded the former to bring the whole thing to a crisis and I saw the letter giving the account of what had passed – it is wonderfull beyond all measure, but accounts for what has seemed more so – the calmness and intrepidity of the guilty person explained by a total perversion, or rather destruction, of principle. She does not imagine any criminality to be attached to her conduct. She has simplified her creed of morality to this – you can do no wrong if you do no pain. According to this it is a perfect salve to her conscience to have behaved strictly and conscientously during the whole time that the wife's happiness and honour were concerned and except the single expression in one letter – 'For pity's sake what can I do?', there is not one betraying the slightest remorse, or even regret. She is not aware that Mrs Villiers knows a word of what has passed but simply tells her that in a transaction she has had with Lady — [Byron] she has been very kind and amiable.

Is all this being a devil or not?

*Birth of Medora, 1814.

[Stanhope Street]
Wednesday 31 [July 1816]

We dined in Savile Row yesterday. H. Pierrepoint grand and
evidently *thinking* himself a pearl thrown amongst swine. I have
been nowhere. Mrs Pole's I hear was dreadful – a circle round the
room with the Regent bodkin between Lady Cholmondeley and
Fanny* for four hours. The latter swallows the bore for the
honour's sake. C[aro] W. Lamb came in and made a diversion,
swinging with her two arms round her mother's neck and hiding
her face upon her shoulder. This is pretty at thirty in the authoress
of 'Glenarvon'.† I have no patience.

[Stanhope Street]
Saturday [3 August 1816]

I am so transported at this being my last day in town. I saw Miss
Rawdon at Berry's – not very agreeable, too foreign in snuff
coloured silk and talking like the Tower of Babel every language
under the sun but her own. Fanny ran in amongst us and was very
infantine and playful with Berry who was fiercer about us all than
ever. I have been walking to Savile Row and back and am quite
knocked up. There is nothing about but Lord Petersham in a gig.

[Leamington]
[12 or 13 August 1816]

I received your letter about Mr B[rougham] yesterday. I cannot
quite agree with you as to his conduct; I confess I think he has
been very hardly used and has in consequence of encouragement
and even promises, been led not to profess, but to make actually,
the greatest sacrifices. I believe what he says because I think it like
her to have done it. You know when I exclaimed to her upon the
Dss [of Devonshire] having (on hers and Mr B's first acquaintance) proposed his bringing her over to England, she told me it
was herself and that she could not imagine (when I reproached

---

*The sisters' name for Lady Bessborough.
†A *roman à clef* published anonymously, containing a caricature portrait of Byron,
of Harriet herself, of Lady Holland and others.

her for it) what made her do it. One must be fair to him, in considering the case.

I am quite stout again today. Yesterday I think I had a narrow escape of producing a seven month's child,* but being perfectly still and taking great care has quite set me up again.

[Leamington]
Tuesday [20 August 1816]

The Arch[bishop of York]† always seemed to me full of petitesse. I think it is the undiscriminating favour and familiarity of our Royal couple that makes one hold their attentions cheap. They have aversions, but as unwise as their likings, and though Princess Charlotte (by far the best of them) sometimes seems to have better taste and more discernment, she is capable, for example, of an engouement for Thérèse, Princess Esterhazy, whom I assure you, is the most signal goose going and totally without attraction of any kind, though I hear she has the complaisance to say that she wishes there was a book written of all I say. Judge what I think of her when cette forte dose only mortifies me.

[Tixal]
Saturday [7 September 1816]

We have been enjoying the whole of this beautiful day climbing and driving, walking and eating boiled chicken with a boisterous degree of health. My suffocation is gone and I believe the child too for I feel as light as a feather.

Lady Bath, I am convinced, eats herself into half her complaints. I too have committed excesses but of the most primitive kind: rice, cauliflower, French beans and potatoes. Hughes has put me on dry meat and cayenne pepper, carbonate of pot-ash with lemon juice three times a day.

---

*Harriet was expecting a child at the end of September.
†Vernon Harcourt.

[101]

[23 September 1816]

I am very well, my legs plague me as they are like fine large columns and I can hardly get my stockings on, but my sickness is gone and yesterday I walked to church and back.

Did I tell you that Granville and Ld Gower went from hence for a night to Beaudesert.* They returned quite ill of ennui – a fine house, without window shutters, large rooms, without one book or chair in its place, no conversation at all, excepting a little clap trap and a great deal of bad taste from Lord Anglesea. Lady Anglesea perfectly nulle and never opening her lips; the girls melancholy and never uttering any thing but sighs; some of the heavy, pompous brothers, who never opened their lips but to say occasionally to each other, 'Give us some snuff, there's a d – – – d good fellow', and Mrs Charles Paget, grown a very ugly old woman, silent, hemming and only occasionally saying of the children, 'This is the greatest beauty in all England', a watch word in the family, for it was repeated by some one of them each time they appeared. Granville heard Lord Anglesea say it three times.

[From Harriette Stewart]   [Tixal]

[2 October 1816]

Dear Lady Georgiana,

I am so glad to be desired to write to you to tell you Lady Granville was brought to bed this morning of a fine boy; they are both doing very well, but I know Ld Granville is going to add to my letter some details which will satisfy you better. Susan is delighted with her brother, who really is excessively pretty, and Georgy is much surprised to hear he can neither walk nor talk. Will you please, dear Lady Georgiana, give my best love to the Miss Howards. I am,

Your affecte and obliged

HARRIETTE STEWART.

[In Granville's hand] I have not many details to add, dearest Ldy G, but Harriet has specially instructed me to tell you that the boy is beautiful, that it was very *tough* work. She is tonight wonderfully well and in delightful spirits.

*The Angleseys' house near Lichfield.

[From Harriette Stewart]   [Tixal]
                                            [7 October 1816]
I am writing from the best authority, sitting by Lady Granville's
bed. The boy's personal beauty beggars all description she bids
me assure you. That it is a thorough Leveson; his name is to be
William.

[From Harriet] God bless my own beloved Sis, thousands and
thousands of times.

                                                         [Tixal]
                             Wednesday 16 [October 1816]
It is a winter's day again, my dear G. You may well ask the
question you do about Mrs Villiers' letter. Guilty; you know I
saw all the account in a letter from Lady Byron of her [Augusta
Leigh's] confession and penitence, but this is that she has
behaved whilst with Lady B. in an amiable and satisfactory
manner. I do think an offence of such magnitude beyond the
sort of language Mrs Villiers uses and I shall be provoked if she
parades her about next year after all she has said to me on the
subject.*
    Ever yours, carissima.

                                                         [Tixal]
                                Monday 21 [October 1816]
I think Lady Byron's conduct quite perfect. I think it must partly
come from a feeling I can well understand – the effect a *confession*
has upon me. It is a proof of sincerity and greatness of mind, the
two things perhaps most to be loved in the world. It seems to me
that they, accompanied with feelings and penitance, could make
one forget and forgive almost any thing. In Lady B's first letter she
writes coldly of *her* [Augusta Leigh], and comments on the want
of the two last qualities and it is therefore I conclude, the having
found them in her during this last time they have spent together,
that must explain what Mrs Villiers says in her letter. But I have

*For a clearer account of the intrigues and counter-intrigues on Mrs Villiers's part,
see M. Elwin, *Lord Byron's Family*, 1975.

no sympathy with Mrs G[eorge] V[illiers] and hope she does not mean to parade about with Mrs L — [Leigh] every where. Sympathy and pity has power to make one feel and it is not only, I think, mercy or justice that act in one but a feeling of humility, 'Here I stand with 1000 offences at my beck but keeping them all to myself as a judge or a saint, with this creature confessing one fault, with all those virtues to which have been promised "though thy sins be scarlet yet shall they be as white as wool".' Do you agree with me? I know if I had been a father confessor, I should often have been inclined to kneel to my penitent. Goodnight dear dearest.

[Tixal]
Thursday 24 [October 1816]

The Bessboroughs arrived about an hour ago; she is looking uncommonly well and in high spirits. I hear he has brought all his unfinished sketches to make drawings from them and as till Sunday we shall be a partie carrée I rejoice at his having something by way of resource.

Lady Talbot is come to Ingestre raving of the delights of Paris – the amusements, the cookery, the shops, the ease, the climate. She says Mounsieur* was all civility and telling whilst he lived he could never repay them for their kindness to him when he was in England. Sir C Stuart and his Mama make themselves detested; they go about with their John Bull faces and heads completely turned, cutting all the English and sneering at all the French, whilst poor Lady Elizabeth makes all the little jokes and affabilities she can think of with but modest success.

High heads are gone by – a tress very low and a little wreath of flowers round it but no pinnacles or battlements or Chinese dragging up the hair. The gowns are all made in this shape [sketch], en coeur ou en vierge at top and bottom with behind [sketch] – that sort of projection.

*The Comte d'Artois, younger brother of Louis XVIII, succeeded as King Charles X in 1824.

[Tixal]
27 [October 1816]

I have no news for you from Lady Bessborough. I never knew her so agreeable and we have weathered our three days solitude most perfectly. I do not dine or go downstairs but receive my monde upstairs. Borino, you know, says no house ought to be without an invalid, the advantages to society in general being great. I am as thin as a whipping post; pea green, black and blue, but strong.

Mrs Peterson[*] came to see me last night. She says the Brocket ménage is going on terribly; that they are alone there, Caroline more irritable and peevish than ever and going into such furies with her servants that the history of the page was very near being acted over again with a footman one day last week;[†] that Wm is become very nearly as violent and that the scenes going on there are really dreadful. She thinks Caroline's mind has now decidedly much to do with it; that she wanders about the house tormenting the servants, swallowing all the physick she can get at and will not cross the walk before the house or take exercise of any kind.

Lady Bessborough has had a letter from the Dss dated the 11th; Mr Brougham still at Florence but she says Caro [George] and him do not meet *often*! Were you aware of this? Good night my own G. Go on telling me about all your cramps and stitches.

[Tixal]
Monday 4 [November 1816]

I heard today (or rather I have seen with my own eyes) that Mr Brougham is settled at Florence and 'we behave as well as possible; they see but little of each other, are as prudent as possible – nobody suspects anything.'

I have also seen a letter from Lady Melbourne saying that Caroline [George] has written to her saying that all is entirely over and that she hopes never in any way to offend any of them again. Is not this strange?

[*]Sally, Lady Bessborough's servant.
[†]Earlier in the year, in a fit of hysterical temper, Caroline had injured one of her pages.

[To Georgiana Morpeth and the Duke of Devonshire]

Tixal

Sunday 17 [November 1816]

Dearest relations,

It is very tantalizing to be so near you both. I see dearest G, enormous in silk stripe* spying at the drawings.

Lord Talbot came to see us today and filled me with horror with details of his discontent, poverty, ruin &c &c &c: as to us we are singing our sweet dying notes and shall soon beg at your hospitable doors. Fanny is very French in her toilette and more infantine in her manner than I have seen her for some time; she walks out and meets fearful objects and falls down and hurts her presence &c &c and laughs and starts and looks unutterable things.

Trentham

Friday 20 [December 1816]

We arrived here an hour before dinner. Lady Stafford (that tower of strength in form) is all in friar's grey, looking old and stormy. I have had little conversation with her; she praises your tribe of children with more appearance of sincerity than I have seen in her upon any other subject.

Lord Cawdor and I flirt violently, but he is sorry I cannot play 'volle cogliere una rosa'. He has been praising Lord Morpeth in a way that made me love him. He thinks him the first of men.

Saturday

The Staffords, poor people, have been obliged to retrench many of their comforts, cards and suppers are abolished. Lady Stafford and Elizabeth walk off to bed at eleven and Ld Stafford looks big at me till I follow them. Elizabeth looks beautiful[14] but really stark naked. Lady Stafford talks of nothing but your girls and her hopes that Ld Gower and Ld Francis[b] will marry a couple of them!! She has a new phrase – she talks of 'liking people, that is liking them with a sort of disgust'.

*She was expecting a child in December.

[106]

Monday [13 January 1817]

I went yesterday morning to Edensor Church, it is very comfortable and Mr Smith preached an excellent sermon. He has persuaded Hart to have a stove in the chapel, which will be a great point gained as the distance to the church would make it often from weather or hours, impracticable to many people here.

Yesterday evening we had no whist and the evening passed rapidly – a great deal of reading, talking and some musick. The whole difference of being at some of his places to me is Hart's no longer having habits of doing nothing and the library here facilitates everything to the busy and idle. The dinners are very good, the rooms excessively well lit, no appearance of retrenchment and much more consistant appearance in every thing than at the time when there was extravagance and profusion with much that was manqué.

I am delighted with Harriette's début; she pleases everybody and to me is perfection, – guided by a thread, never in the way and as quiet as a mouse, – my beau idéal of one's girl tacked to one. They might make themselves disagreeable to one.

Tixal
Thursday 16 [January 1817]

One day more, my dearest Sister, and I think our leaving Chatsworth would have been impracticable. We came here today through a driving snow in which those lovely creatures, Newhouse and Lucas [valet and maid] were mislaid for some hours. Do you remember a line in Lord Byron's poem of Darkness,* 'and of their [mutual] hideousness they died.' This might have come to pass I think.

The Granville and Morpeths spent the late winter months and early spring in London. In May the Granvilles took both their daughters and Harriette to Paris for two months.

*Written in 1816.

Dover

Friday evening, ½ past 8. [9 May 1817]

We are all in spirits in spite of the prospect of being shipped off tomorrow at four. The Captain says we shall have a rough passage and he hopes to be in Calais at eight. The weather here today is like winter, cold and raw. I cannot understand how I have contrived to get rid of my cold, for this inn seems made to give one. The room smokes, none of the doors shut and the wind blows in every where.

Saturday.

It is four, a very fine morning, we are all very well and just going to embark.

Paris

Wednesday [14 May 1817]

Here we are, dearest G, lodged in the most delightful manner. The prettiest salons for ourselves and the children, with a large garden, in an Hotel at the end of the Boulevards nearest the Tuilleries, as quiet as Chiswick and only making me feel a wish never to stir beyond it into the rattle, stink and tourbillion of Paris.

Poor Mme de Staël is in the most terrible state; paralytic, dropsical and dying, she sees people and talks of it, which must be very painful.

Paris

Saturday [17 May 1817]

Sir C. Stuart is all graciousness; he was here yesterday and very entertaining, le moins marié que possible, affiché-ing the worst company and lowest connections, but I understand, has des égards for Lady E[lizabeth] with which she is perfectly satisfied. He lent us his box at the Opera. It was the 'Carnaval de Venise'* – very gay and pretty. Bigottini acts better than she dances. I do not

*Composed by André Campar (1660–1744), creator of the opéras-ballets, but choreographed by Milon. Emilie Bigottini (1784–1858) was a French ballerina.

think her very handsome; her petticoats are about five inches long, consequently when she makes a pirouette she is stark naked.

[Paris]
[? 23 May 1817]
Lady Elizabeth Stuart is very popular and Sir Charles as unpopular, his low amours are the scandal of Paris. Certainly no one could guess he was married.

Mme de Staël continues in, I fear, a dying state but she gives dinners and is as agissante as ever.

Saturday
Lady E. Stuart called here today. I think her manners very pleasing and with a little rouge she looks sensible and pleasing.

[Paris]
[29 May 1817]
[Lady Cowper] writes us word that Ldy M[elbourne] was angry at Mrs — [George Lamb] refusing to go to the opera, knowing it was to stay at home to see le fameux [Brougham]. Tell me when you write how they go on. Where will she be when I die of joy driving into London the beginning of September?[*]

[Paris]
Friday [30 May 1817]
I think French women are grown uglier. They wear little Mrs Bunting-looking[†] turbans and small round gauze-looking hats and feathers. The élégantes in little round heads with flowers upon their noses.

Saturday
Mme de Coigny[b] called upon me. She says Lord Gower is dying for la Princesse Pauline [Borghese]. The D. of Wellington comes here today and we are going to meet him at Sir Charles Stuart's.

[*]After Paris they were to spend two months travelling in Switzerland and Italy.
[†]Mrs Bunting had been housekeeper at Devonshire House.

Sunday

It was a dull little English rout – one or two hideous French women and one or two stupid loyal subjects to Louis 18. Ce Roi has been painted in all ways at the Louvre – but the chef d'oeuvre is a full length of him en habit de voyage at the moment of his quitting the Thuilleries at the return of Buonoparte; he looks like Puss in Boots. The subject is said to have been chosen by himself, but the factious say it is a malice of his ministers.

I am *half* ashamed of not liking Paris better, it would give me no pain never to see it again. I am lazy about society and even about amusement and in every other respect it is in my opinion deplorably inferior to England. The idea of a reunion at Chatsworth or Tixal is too much for my understanding.

Talk to me of Hart and Mrs Lamb. The former will leave no girl but Miss Berry unmarried in England, for the moment when he decides upon throwing his handkerchief. I hear of him: Monsieur mon frère. Do not think them forgetful of Lady Morpèze.

Paris
Tuesday [3 June 1817]

Yesterday was a very busy day. In the morning I sat for a whole hour in the magazin de St Antoine bargaining for silks. I went to Court and was very graciously received. The King looks ridiculous in an arm-chair and the Duchesse de Berri[*] nearly as much so in another. She is very ugly, not much bigger than your Harriet, very big with child and ungracious in manner.

Wednesday

We went to see 'Bagatelle' after I had written; the day was delicious and it is a pretty little quinqette-looking château dans le genre du petit Trianon. A garden all full of little surprises, bridges, rocks, turrets, cottages, souterrains and pinnacles every minute. There is a beautiful Marie-Louise octagon salon and little fringed or-moulu bed-rooms.

We dined at Mme de Staël's; she was too ill to see us. Mme de Gréfuhle and Mme Girardin did nothing but compliment each

[*]The Duchesse de Berri was the daughter-in-law of the Comte d'Artois (the future Charles X) and was widowed in 1820.

other and die of laughing over their own little jokes and demi-mots so that I felt fièrement embarrassée de ma personne. The men were partly occupied in a discussion whether a large wreath of natural bluets on Mme de Broglie's* head became her or not, and partly with criticisms upon plays and pamphlets I had neither seen or read, the whole carried on in a scream.

Paris
Saturday [7 June 1817]

I have been at two great dinners since I wrote, at Lady Mansfield's and Sir Charles Stuart's. The Duke of Wellington is here with one American branch, Mrs Hervey, but he has neither love or hatred to display, his wife being at Cambray and his loves dispersed over the earth, so that il se laisse admirer as a great hero with very simple, unaffected manners. Lady E Stuart is very agreeable and aimable and by dint of rouge and an auburn wig, looks not only pretty but nothing worse. Sir C. praises her to me with enthusiasm and as she does not seem to mind his theatrical career, I am sure I do not know who should.

I shall see 'Nina', the famous ballet in which Bigottini acts to Paisiello's musick; it is beautiful and very affecting.[15] The French are all in fits and, when in the middle of her délire she dances a little entrée, they die.

Sunday

I have been at Church and am now come to rest in my pretty garden till four, when I set out for a great dinner, seven miles from Paris. Imagine me in a chip hat with white and red feathers and a tulle gown, flounced and ruffed, looking draggled and weary, making smiles and civilities to a number of little black starred and ordered French men.

10 o'clock.

Now see me, dragged and weary, stripped of my finery in a white bedgown, just returned from St Cloud. The drive there and back was very pleasant. I went with Sir C. and Lady Elizabeth. They are both very agreeable and though there is no sentimentality between them, they seem the best friends possible and I believe

*Mme de Staël's daughter.

[111]

half his bad behaviour is put on and that he is mauvais sujet par air more than anything else.

I must tell you what amuses me. I have his great Grace several times and with the weakness I have about great people, treated him de haut de ma grandeur. I suppose he was pleased at the rareté du fait. He called me to sit by him and was quite à mes pieds. The fact is that I really believe the Duke finds so few women that do not kneel to him that he must feel a sort of respect for any who do not make up to him and Granville, who has rather suffered at seeing us sit through two dinners dos à dos will be rather pleased to hear of my successes, obtained d'après ma façon, for an ugly good sort of woman to be attended by a man, into whose good graces beauties force themselves by dint of bassesses. Pray forgive my *virtuous* exaltation.

[Paris]
[13 June 1817]

Thank Mrs Lamb from me for writing and Caroline William. The Duke of Wellington talked a great deal of the latter. I see she amuses him to the greatest degree, especially *her accidents*, which is the charitable term he gives to all her sorties.

Saturday [14 June]

We were surprised by Lord Gower walking in to the room this morning. He looks very well and very gay and seems glad to return to England. He did not mention the Princesse Borghese and I had not the face to do it. He says the Duchess [of Devonshire], Cardinal Consalvi and Souza are all digging à qui mieux mieux; that they rout up great curiosities and that the Duchess is adored as she protects the artists, employs and pays them magnificently.

Lady Jersey is at Lyons and arrives Monday in Paris. She stays at all the towns, dines with the Préfets and enjoys the tumults. I think I begin to hear her.

[Paris]
Wednesday [18 June 1817]

Lady Jersey has been with me some time yesterday; she is very cordial, kind and amiable, looks very handsome though she is tanned almost purple, is more agissante than ever and has already done more and seen more than any other given person does in a month. She is a noble, innocent, unsuspecting creature and I love her quite. Is it like Mrs Candour to add that she bores and fatigues me; it is true and to you only. But she gives life to society and every thing is more sprack and we all are the better for her presence – it says 'up and doing', she looks so reviving with her black hair and coral beads.

[Paris]
Friday [20 June 1817]

We all ship off for Epinay, and for the Duchesse de Raguse on Tuesday. It is immoral, but I think these sort of things do so much better when there are a few lovers in the case; I mean there must be a great deal of pairing off together. Now as things go, poor dear Lord Jersey will probably have to lead me about and sit by my side two whole hot days running, and how he will be able to bear it I do not know.

I have been dining with Sir Charles [and went to the theatre]. He stays almost all the time behind the scenes and winks and nods are going on all the time between him and the actresses. Lady E. is not more romantic than is to be wished, so that I do not think any body has a right to object to any thing but the genre of his infidelities, which is, I think, deplorable.

Saturday evening.

Lord Jersey goes to England on Wednesday and she stays here six weeks. They seem just as well together as ever – 'Sarah put on your shawl.' 'Thank ye, Villiers.' Don't you hear her? She goes on calling Lord Morley, Boringdon,* and it entertains me to see the half-affronted, half-simpering consciousness with which he endures this misprision. Lady Hunloke at the play looking very handsome – she is just as childish and handsome as ever; 'Now I say I don't like the French; now I can't help it – I always say what I think, Lady Harriet, now they are not well-bred, now I am sure you will laugh at me, but I can't help it.' I think Hart is as well without her, weighing women and wives.

*Lord Boringdon was created first Earl of Morley in 1815. His first wife, from whom he was divorced, was Lady Jersey's sister.

Wednesday 25 [June 1817]

Yesterday was the day of our dinner at Mme de Raguse's. The 15 miles drive there was very broiling but once arrived it was delicious as there is great deal of shade, rooms kept as cool as cellars and in the evening from seven till ten we walked, sat out of doors and came back to Paris in open carriages by moonlight. Lord Jersey is so gay, so like a bird who sees his cage open, that we got on famously together. You would laugh to see us; 'Come Lady Granville', and off we go together as playful and happy as possible. Sir Charles was wretched, voué to the little fat Duchess [de Raguse] and Lady Elizabeth after him to prompt the due civilities, which he performs like a pug dog just going to snap. Lord and Lady Morley, 'Economy's my plan' never being lost sight of for a moment, toiled there in a heavy chaise and pair, but he is not happy when he cannot be master of ceremonies. Silence looked very handsome though she is thin and burnt to chocolate colour.

On 3 July the Granvilles (Harriet with a toothache) set out on a pleasant tour of Italy and Switzerland. At Geneva she was very bilious which she ascribed to her fright in winding down the Jura close to the precipices. 'Do you see me', she asked her sister, 'riding on a mule up to Montanvert, like the sides of a house I daresay.' It was an 'unspeakable relief' to ship off the children to Neuchâtel for a month and there to rejoin them later. Their journey took them to the lakes of Maggiore, Como (where Cadennabia was a special attraction) and Lugano. They did their sightseeing in Milan, and enjoyed Berne, Zurich, the falls of Schaffhausen, and Basle. They were back in Paris towards the end of August.

Paris
25 [August 1817]

Here we are, my dearest G, children and all. All was well as possible in very delightful rooms at the top of the Hôtel de Paris; the Hollands in those we had at the bottom. I have just been with her enthroned in the corner of a green and gold room looking very well, a little discomposed with the mistress of the inn, who will not let her tame cook even look into the kitchen. Lord Holland,[b] an angel, has been with us since but was sent for [by] her just as he had got quite comfortable, owning himself delighted to warm himself over a fire on the coldest, draughtiest day I ever felt, the rain pouring without ceasing. Lady Jersey is here, worn to the bone. She begins the day with a dancing master at nine o'clock and never rests till night.

Paris

Wednesday [27 August 1817]

Lady Holland dined the other day with the Stuarts and was very much pleased with Lady Elizabeth, but there was a very great man there [Wellington] who chose not to acknowledge her or Ld H.[*] This has caused much discussion; the great man says they would not bow to him and the welkin rings with the different versions of the story.

Lady William[†] is very pretty, very pleasing. Lord William looks very quiet and pleased but a little small between his accomplished bride and exigeante mother-in-law who talks all the time as if Lady William was dead. 'From the time I lost my poor Bessy.' It is clear Ld Wm will not love Mrs Rawdon.

Calais

10 o'clock [18 September 1817]

I cannot feel very much depressed at any thing the day I am returning to England, yet our affairs this morning do not wear a very favourable aspect. Granville is a little gouty. The wind is not favourable. Our captain seems very lazy and smells so intolerably of brandy that I am afraid it must be his only pursuit.

I return with a very safe conscience as I do not smuggle over a single thing; my goods are all to be sent for me and a little box of china and one of eau de Portugal which I take with me, I shall pay

[*]Owing to a misunderstanding occasioned by a letter written by Lord Holland.
[†]Lord William Russell had married the gifted Elizabeth Rawdon that spring.

the duty for. Your silk is no longer a green silk; I saw one afterwards so much prettier and more uncommon that I determined upon it – it is a deep lilack and coffee coloured *stripe shot* thing, but does not look at all glaring. You must let me know which you will have as it is just the same to me. I must also give you another *useful* piece of advice; always buy enough stuff to make a little body to the petticoat. It will only take half a yard more, without sleeves, it looks as well of a morning with a white body over it and is an evening gown at any time by tacking a pair of short white sleeves into it.

[Tixal]
[24 September 1817]

I have been reading, that is hearing, 'L – – – R – – – k' [*Lalla Rookh*] (I cannot fill it up) Moore's poem and I think some of it quite beautiful. There is so much *radiance* and tenderness. Lord Byron has so much thought and passion that it makes every thing flat in comparison, but it is also a repose to escape from crime and read of birds of paradise and innocent loves.

[? Lilleshall]
[? 3 or 4 October 1817]

Think of the odious Lord Douglas who has succeeded Lord Gower as Pauline's [Borghese] lover. My head is a little better but I have very disagreeable feels in it. I feel after I have walked up the stairs, or when I first get off my chair, a full tingling feel, chiefly in the back of my head, as a watch if it was alive would feel when it was being wound up. Dwell a little on these topics I beg.

Tixal
Sunday [5 October 1817]

Ld Gower is here as quiet as a mouse. I think him rather out of sorts. The family have, I believe, quite given up going in body to C.H., but she [Lady Stafford] muttered some thing about trying to get over there by herself for a day. She gave no cuts and only mentions you when she talks of her sons marrying and then she always brings in 'the Morpeth girls'.[*]

[Tixal]
Wednesday [8 October 1817]
I have been hearing some details of the Dandy race which I think curious enough to repeat: they wear dressing gowns with landscapes on them – houses, castles, bridges, as you may have seen upon bed curtains at an inn. They have also reading boots, which they wear only of a morning for one hour which they devote to study, made of yellow leather.

[Tixal]
[25 October 1817]
I send you the enclosed[†] – Granville and I have read it over many times without being the least able to understand the purport of it. As you are more in *her* confidence than I am, you may perhaps have some key to it. The only thing we can guess is that she is gravida [pregnant] – if not what means her alternative, the risk, the reasons, the approaching necessary éclat. What is it, dearest G? Il connait son monde. I always feel touched when I get one of his long open energetic letters and wish immoral things.

[Trentham]
[November 1817]
We are all very much interested for poor Princess Charlotte. I fear it is bad. Lord Gower writes word that there is a difference of opinion; they are uncertain whether she has twins and whether she will have strength to go through the labour.

[*]Lord Gower did indeed marry one of 'the Morpeth girls', Harriet, well known as Harriet Duchess of Sutherland, Mistress of the Robes to Queen Victoria. Earlier, Harriet Granville had written of the Staffords' other son, Lord Francis Leveson Gower: 'Francis must marry some of us. He is quite a perfect love, so handsome, tractable & unfrivolous.'
[†]Evidently a letter from Brougham concerning Caro George.

Sandon
[6 November 1817]

We found the Staffords here yesterday; you are in very great favour with her, she says Lord Carlisle doats upon you and is always talking of the delight and comfort you are to him. We get on very well by dint of whist, piqué and chess.

I quite agree with you about B[rougham]. I have half a mind to fire away at him, but do I dare?

We are all very anxious to hear of Princess Charlotte. I hope it is a boy this time.* Lady Stafford drove with me to Tixal this morning to see the children. They were four adorable loves but she was cold and spiteful; said Suzy put her in mind of an old French woman and only praised the baby because she sees I don't take to him. Lord Stafford is as happy, as gay as he can stick together, in a titter from morning till night and half in love with us all. He is shut up till he don't know whats what.

[Trentham]
[8 November 1817]

I feel quite unable to write upon any subject but one. We are all heart sick at this terrible event. Poor Princess Charlotte.

I have seen a letter from Lord Melville to Lord Harrowby – some thing in the position of the child was wrong, I believe, but from some of the symptoms it is supposed inflamation within must have taken place. She became restless and agitated; they gave her brandy, she then said, 'if you leave me alone I shall be well', turned about two or three times and died.

Tixal
16 [November 1817]

I have been hearing a great many melancholy details of poor Princess Charlotte's death. She bore her whole labour with a patience and courage that were quite heroic. It is true that she never shrunk or complained but only held out her hand to him [Prince Leopold] and pressed it when the suffering was great. It is

*The baby, a boy, was born dead. Princess Charlotte died on 5 November.

said that there was no one cause sufficient to account for her death, but that her whole *machine* and constitution was in so bad a state that she could not possibly have lived long.

At this moment I am listening to a most violent argument upon the subject of the probable wish of the Prince Regent to bring forward the subject of a divorce. If he does, and I suppose he will move heaven and earth to do it, it will to be sure be the most tremendous piece of work that ever was made in the country.

Tixal
Saturday 22 [November 1817]

I cannot describe to you the sort of oppression and depression of spirits that the idea of Lady Stafford's visit tomorrow gives me. It is not only that I do not like it, but I am always afraid of not coming off with a clear conscience, of being false, or so non-enduring that she will not be able to resist knocking me down. This will be less the case, as I expect the finding my brother here will put her into such good humour and activity that I shall have nothing to do but to bear her smiles.

[Hart] is thin but looking uncommonly well – sunburnt, which becomes him, very delightful, so kind, so amiable, and so much with his wits about him – which is, after all, the reward and effect of trotting all over Europe.

Tixal
25 [November 1817]

You have no idea how amiable Hart is. He contributes to make the Stafford visit go off much better than I could have expected. The men are shooting in a snow storm and we are all reading and writing. It has only just struck one and I feel as if five hours more morning would be severe; my only consolation is that dullness is their element and agreeable people who did not suit them, would be more perplexing than a gloomy silence – all intent upon our books.

The Morpeths were at Tixal for the larger part of December. Early January they all spent at Chatsworth before the migration of both families to London, where they remained, seeing one another constantly, until the end of July.

Chatsworth
Tuesday [11 August 1818]

We arrived here before dinner and found Hart in uproarious spirits and looking well. I was in despair at first at finding the Leinsters and Tavistocks with a host of Derbyshire squires, but their harmless, goodhumoured faces have quite disarmed me. The young Duchess* is very like Lady T. with, I should think, more sense and less beauty, but she is a fine good humoured healthy thing, capital as to flesh and blood and looks happier than any body I ever saw. He is very pleasing and handsome and seems as happy as she does.

Wednesday.

We were up between seven and eight and had a capital breakfast; the Duke and Duchess sitting next each other aux petits soins with the sugar, bread and butter &c. At ½ past two I am going to drive with the Duchess and Lady T. I have taken Hart's advice – not to be the least sensible but very merry and good humoured. I have taken the joking line with a very good grace; we light fires where fires should not be, blow them and die with laughing when they blaze. They were all shy of me at first but begin to think I have some fun.

The Duke of Leinster has great captivation of look and manner, though he is very Irish and begins many of his sentences with 'ye'll be begging me'. Lord Tavistock is grown fat and looks as if he was perpetually purring with comfortable delight. I think a cleverer wife might have made more of him, but I am sure none could have made him so perfectly happy.

I enjoyed myself very much yesterday evening. The couples played together at one end of the room and Granville, Hart and I looked over books at the other – a beautiful edition of Camoens given him by Mounsieur de Souza, bound here in brown and gold with D and the coronet inlaid in diamonds. It is like a book in a fairy tale.

---

*The Duchess of Leinster was ten years younger than her sister.

Bolton Abbey
Monday [17 August 1818]

Today we all got up at six. The men are gone to the moors. The weather is delicious and I walked yesterday to the Strid with Granville and Hart. Chemin faisant, Hart called out to us, 'Get out of the way. I am afraid the dog is mad', and, en effet, the sweet little creature began howling horribly and foaming at the mouth. He darted round us in this state, we expecting a bite every moment. I underwent all the pleasures of imagination – dipping in the sea, bits of our flesh cut out, painful death. At last he shot off in a straight line to the house and we followed, I expecting to find Lord Russell bit, and shaking so I could hardly get along. He had, however, retired to my brother's room, upon whom we have with great difficulty prevailed to let us forego the pleasure of his society. I believe it may only have been an acces de fièvre, but still he is to be shut up whilst we are here.

F. Lamb is not yet arrived to d — us all, but we expect him every hour.

Bolton Abbey
Tuesday [18 August 1818]

F. Lamb arrived last night; he is in very good humour but rather too clever for the state to which fatigue and people who require no exertion of intellect have brought us, and his shrewd observations, backed with oaths, make us nod and stare like Lady Carlisle.

[Bolton Abbey]
Wednesday [19 August 1818]

Ld George [Cavendish] comes tomorrow. My boy is as happy as can be. So is Hart, when he does not overeat himself. We live luxuriously upon hashed venison and moor fowl.

Frederic Lamb would be bored if it were not for food and sleep, which share his affections. Our evenings are short, sweet and sleepy as we dine at eight and go to roost at ten.

[Bolton Abbey]
Friday [21 August 1818]

Hart bids me tell you that he would write if he could do anything but pull a trigger, but that he shoots, eats, and remains – when he does neither – in a state of torpor; and this is la verité toute nue.

I admire F. Lamb perhaps more than I like him. I think him uncommonly clever and agreeable but he sees life in the most degrading light and he simplifies the thing by thinking all men rogues and all women —. He looks old and *world-beaten*, but still handsome. He seems to enjoy being here, and sport, food and sleep fill up all his time and at any spare moment he reads the 'Heart of Midlothian'* of which he says, 'Why, if you wish for my opinion, I think it's the d – – – dest bad novel I ever read in my life.'

God bless you dearest G. Castle Howard is my terre promise.

[Bolton Abbey]
Monday [24 August 1818]

We dined at six yesterday and had a long evening and a very pleasant. F. Lamb is certainly uncommonly clever and agreeable. I think him very like Lady Cowper [his sister]; they are both remarkable for good temper and ill nature and the question is whether one should not prefer a blow or a little praise. It is one sweeping condemnation of man, woman and child and if there is one exception to the word 'fools' it is qualified by 'D – – – d disagreeable.' As a member of society, however, he is very pleasant; living abroad and seeing a great variety of people, with the necessity of exertion, have given him a sort of rude polish which his brothers want; he is less like an animal, does not roll about and snore as they do. At meals the real Lamb breaks out, but at other times he is civil, gentlemanlike and gentle.

He likes Hart though I daresay he does not spare him any more than his fellows. He says 'He is an odd chap and tells one what another would conceal, but all those Cavendishes have a d – – – d deal of sense at the bottom.' What we have at the top I conclude he reserves for less partial ears than Granville's.

*Sir Walter Scott's novel had been published that year.

I have been so comfortable and happy here that I should be sorry to go to any point of the earth but C.H. – as it is I count the minutes.

The bull, G, the bull – I read it ten times over with a sort of shuddering horror. They have been tossing to right and left and even the cows, those disgraces to their sex, have taken to it. Promise not to take me out of the Ray Wood, not over the grass to that melancholy building [the Mausoleum], not round the lake, not into any *gills*. I confine myself here to the kitchen garden and the length of the house backwards and forwards.

After ten days at Castle Howard the Granvilles were back in Staffordshire.

[Trentham]

13 September 1818]

Here we are, dearest G. The Lievens, Neumann and Fagel and alas, 'ma chère, je m'ennuie' has already escaped the Countess [Lieven]. It has been very severe at dinner; we pumped in French with gêne and solemnity and I eat in despair.

Elizabeth [Leveson] looks pale and grave; Ld Gower like one of the statues he is soon to see in la belle Italie. The Staffords are galled at his departure, fearing that Pauline [Borghese] will come home for their blessing.

Trentham

Monday [14 September 1818]

The wind is blowing hurricanes and it looks black and dismal; Mme de Lieven, however, rides the storm, which is a very great relief to me as she knows I cannot canter after her and I am spared by this means driving and am left entirely to myself.

Elizabeth tells me that she thinks Ld Gower more driven from home by them [the Staffords] than attracted to Italy by Pauline; that they are as cold as ice to him, snub him every word he says and that he says he is treated at thirty two as if he was ten. They tell Elizabeth that it is necessary that he may not be spoilt. How people are punished even in this world, for their faults. They are wretched at Lord Gower's departure and yet I hear he says that they have made him determine to live with them as little as possible; that he had rather die than be condemned to live at Trentham. She told Mme de Lieven that he was a fool, 'un être absolument abruti', and only longing to be Marquis of Stafford. What a rogue she is.

Trentham
Thursday [17 September 1818]

Lord Stafford is, as he usually is after two or three days junket, in a perpetual titter and perfectly happy. We played at whist last night. Elizabeth says that alone with her he sometimes says how pleasant it is when people are here, but never before Lady S. Now I will tell you a great secret. Grandpapa [Lord Carlisle] and Lord Stafford fell out here and the consequence is that the latter declared he would never go to C.H. again. I cannot make out from Lady Stafford's account which she thought to blame, though she did say Grandpapa was very sneering and provoking, but she seemed to think Lord Stafford also had worked himself up into a blind rage.

Tixal
Friday [18 September 1818]

You will be surprised to hear that the Earls fell out about politicks. For three days Lord C had talked violent opposition language till Lord Stafford was worked to the fatal pitch. Lord Carlisle then crowned it by saying Sir F. Burdett was very popular in the House of Commons. Lord Stafford denied it flat. Lord C. said, 'Well, I may be mistaken as I never was in it.' 'No, you had not that advantage', retorted my beau-frère, and got up and walked about the house by himself the rest of the evening.

Lady Stafford asked me today what made Monsieur de Lieven so grave. I told her the Comtesse had told me it was uneasiness about his health. 'Oh', she said, 'I suppose he lives in constant fear of her poisoning him. You see what horrid things come into my head.' Then after a pause, in a mutter, 'they always do'. She asked me the other day out right if I thought it was likely that any of 'these men going to Rome would poison the Princesse Borghese.'

I am convinced she is going to take to it; she will try it upon the French fowls or something of that sort and then administer small doses to her acquaintances.

[Tixal]
Sunday [? 4 October 1818]

Between my children and my company I have scarcely a moment for writing. We are very agreeable, but I am grown languid and stupid and as Mr Wilmot is not with child, I put the whole responsibility of general conversation upon him.[*]

You know how I worked at making Harriette talk loud? We are all now in a dead silence, some reading and some writing and she is conscientiously holding forth in a moral discourse with Sandon about all the virtues in a voice that might be heard at Litchfield. I cough when I am ready to die and he whispers all his responses in vain. He must think the devil is in her – it is now about the language of the heart and I shall really expire.

They all rode to Beaudesert today. Ld Anglesea was very grand and looked, they say, like the great Bengal tyger, shaggy and fierce. The Beauties were all about.

The Granvilles had given up their London house in Stanhope Street and had taken 16 Bruton Street. This would not be ready for them for a few months and meanwhile they had nowhere of their own to go to when they moved to London at the end of the year.

Tixal
Wednesday [21 October 1818]

I want you to undertake a most delicate mission for us. We shall be on the pavé for about a month or six weeks upon first arriving in town and I dread a dirty noisy hotel for myself and the chicks. If

<hr>

[*]Harriet was expecting her fifth child in May of the next year.

[125]

Hart could let us be in D House it would be a benediction to us, but as we had rather be in the gutter than there against his inclination, we want you to sound him about it – as a favor he might do us, not as a request of ours.

Tixal
Sunday [25 October 1818]

I am only vexed at the idea that it vexes you to think we are vexed, which I beg you will unthink as soon as possible. We shall manage our matters perfectly; a thousand thanks for your kindness.

Sandon
30 [October 1818]

Mr Luttrell we expect every day; he has been living at Ampthill[*] and Brighton. Lady Holland seems to be a greater despot there than any where – she has forbid shooting and cards and Ld H. and Rogers are found at chess, hiding in distant rooms and when they are found she says, 'Lose, Mr Rogers', and Mr Rogers loses.

Tixal
Wednesday [25 November 1818]

One hundred thanks for Park Street – it is only for Granville and myself. We shall want as little as possible of attendance and all I wish for is a little bed in one of the children's bed room.

Tixal
Thursday [26 November 1818]

I long passionately for another girl and rejoice at being with child. I mean to have her with me as I now have Granville, whenever and wherever I please. All my hopes are fixed upon a girl who may be the plague of my life. I long for the grunt, pat my gros ventre and jump for joy.

[*]The Hollands' country house in Bedfordshire.

Our cook goes to town and several servants so we shall want nothing but a chair woman who is in the house. We are both penetré with your kindness.

Park Street
Friday [4 December 1818]

We arrived here at 4 o'clock yesterday and found every thing as comfortable as possible and this morning it looks quite gay with a bright sun upon the large windows. Thank you both again, dear Ld and Ldy Morpeth. I cannot say how strange it appears to me to see it and not you.

[Park Street]
Monday [7 December 1818]

I went to our house and am happy to find that we can come to it in January though it will be in a very unfinished state. I then went to Mrs Lamb who has been unwell and is staying in town; she looks very ill and is very low. B[rougham] was with her looking like something just dug up. I met the Lambs and C[harles] Greville at dinner at C[avendish] Square yesterday; it was rather a mournful ceremony – les convives were all triste, the room looked funereal and Rover howled and whined without intermission. A dinner the day before at Mr Canning's was somewhat more lugubre; she was ill and he was silent and the people all thin, grave looking men whom I had never met before with the exception of Lord H[enry] Howard, a fat bon vivant – an accumulation of many years sturtle and venison.

Park Street
Friday [11 December 1818]

Have you heard from Hart lately? Pray let me know when you do. I hear he is living entirely with Lady Hunloke. It is very silly of her. Abercrombie says she must be his mistress, and how much more the rest of the world must think so. I do not.

Trentham
Wednesday [16 December 1818]

I ascend from one of those cruel confidential tête-à-têtes that freeze ones middle aged blood. We have gone through all the lovers, past and to come; asked civilly after the Morpeths – praised George, by the bye, up to the skies, and in a way that makes me think Grandpapa has been extolling him con amore. Dear G, he is an angel.

Tixal
Saturday [? 26 December 1818]

We set out in a fortnight. The children for Chiswick. I shall find you in Park Street. I certainly do look forward to being in London with very great pleasure.

Sandon
Wednesday [30 December 1818]

The Staffords went this morning – she turned stormy yesterday evening, locked in a high black gown and black crape turban like the prints of Erasmus as Mr Sneyd observed, and finished by losing a mint at whist, I expected her every moment to detonate like the bulls.

The following months were spent by both families in London. Besides the move to Bruton Street, where Harriette Stewart was launched into society in July, the Granvilles left Tixal and rented Wherstead in Suffolk. Frederick, the Granvilles' last child, was born on 3 May.

[Wherstead]
[? June 1819]

Granville is quite afraid of my talking of Wherstead. He says I shall raise every body's expectation and you will all be disappointed. I will therefore only say that seen in the month of June, all hay and roses it is very very pretty and more enjoyable than I can say. I long to shew it you – if you could but come down for ten days in July. I am happy to tell you it is the most open, high, healthy, airy, dry (consequently probably digestive) feeling place I was ever in.

Bruton Street
Monday [19 July 1819]

What delicious weather and how I envy you living out of doors, unlike your worn sister hanging calico and planning floors,* and seeing her lank pale face reflected in endless mirrors which Mr Orchard has the goodness to put up all over the house, pour rien, in the style of Mme Dessart who has just sent me a bill of 42£ for a dress which upon an exaggerated calculation taking finery into account, is worth 20£.

I dined at the Dss of Beaufort's Saturday with the Cannings and some wits, but malgré cela, we were as dull as we were innocent. Mr Ward looks at Mr Ellis with a mixture of interest and amusement, a sort of 'How is it I do' in his little intelligent phiz and the other flourishes and squeaks most obligingly, to enlighten him. I went from them to Lady C. Greville's.*b* The Duke was there, but I must say nothing could be more 'genteel and respectable' (as Orchard tells me my ball will be, forgive the ruling subject) than their conduct, and the little Dss [of Wellington] literally, and old Charles Greville figurativey snuffed up the air in approbation.

Yesterday I did nothing but walk with Granville in Kensington Gardens – where I saw most of the little affairs, with no difference but sun and shade upon them. The Miss Fitzclarences† all but astride upon the wall with all the young practitioners Sandon, Greville, Villiers*b* at their feet; wretched girls pacing after their chaperones and the dandies on horseback, gazing at us; I don't know why, but follies are more glaring by daylight, and I felt like a clergyman or Miss Trimmer – and held tight to Granville and the unsentimental Punch, as if it was catching. Dear G, since my early youth I have not poured forth such a tide of ill nature mais c'est toi qui l'a voulu – and light a fire even in these dog days to purify us all.

*For a ball to bring out Harriette Stewart.
†Illegitimate daughters of the Duke of Clarence, later William IV.

I went to see Mrs Lamb yesterday and thought her in pretty good spirits – what I think is that she feels very strongly the repose of certainty, and that her whole history with Brougham had all the torment of an attachment without the love, which however it may excite and preserve from dullness is my beau ideal of misery.

I think d° of the 1st canto of Don Juan. There is a description of love by moonlight that beggars all praise.

Orchard is turning my house literally inside out. God bless you dearest, my love to Ld Morpeth and perfect George.

I have a bower on my landing place which will be a very convenient retreat for ladies and gentlemen who wish for a little private conversation.

Bruton Street
Thursday [22 July 1819]

Though the laudanum made me wretched all yesterday it enabled me to enjoy my ball which really was as pretty and successful in every department as possible. My front room was as light as day, and the back room very pretty all pink muslin – flowers – and candles which prevented its getting too hot. My bed room was converted into a very good assembly room, with places for fifty people to sit down in, and my little dressing room with lights, flowers and the old blue divans all round it, into a very recherché boudoir. The two large rooms below were filled with little round supper tables, and all the flirtations went down together, to back their sentiment with soupe and entreés. They danced with such spirit till near six o'clock that Colinet said he was dead and could play no more, which did not grieve my tooth and me. You must forgive me if I puff as much as the Morning Post. I was very lucky in having out of 340 near a hundred excuses, which reduced me to a right size and they were almost all chaperones and married women, and the girls came in tribes with some one elderly.

I think parts of Don Juan more beautiful than almost any thing he has ever written – some with a great deal of bad taste.

I must tell you that I have given up a second ball – all the young men are going – and I find if I send home the decorations now it will cost me little – but mints if I keep them, and as I feel you have no decided wish for me to do it, I have no regrets upon the occasion.

We are all going, as is our duty, to Prince Leopold tonight. Harriette is not asked and I do not promise myself much pleasure.

Middleton [Park][*]
Friday [27 August 1819]

I arrived here and found Hart, having already taken a long drive with Lady Jersey – and waiting with his new temper for an 8 o'clock dinner. I cannot tell you how I feel already the bodily advantages to getting from town into the country, the perfect quiet, the freshness of the air and the possibility of repose without remorse, all more or less impossible in London. The luxurious comfort and beauty of this house much surpasses my expectations. There is not one inch of it that one may not either admire or enjoy. Lord Jersey has one (Miss Berry would say) 'very pretty thing in his character', his fondness for and manner to his beautiful little boys. She is looking enormously well, but suffers from fidget and the hot weather – being very large indeed. Hart is not happy here – and he owns it tires his new temper amazingly. He does not like dining at eight, and a life which is only conversation.

Our evening was very short, we walked till the men came out, we talked till the supper came and went to bed soon after eleven. The only thing galls me, a number of wasps, in on under over everything.

Badminton
Wednesday [1 September 1819]

How do dearest Sis? The post brought me a letter from Mrs Lamb. She appears to be grown extremely fond of Lady Byron, admires her beyond measure – and says the child[†] is uncommonly clever with stormy passions and a look like him. She is tall of her age, and Lady B looking at her said with a melancholy smile, 'she will not be dumpy'.

[*]The Jerseys' country seat in Oxfordshire.
[†]Ada Augusta Byron, born in 1815.

[131]

[To the Duke of Devonshire]   [Badminton]
                                                  [3 September 1819]
I cannot let you forget me, and therefore, with but little to say, I
must write. I thought you low at Middleton under the tree, my
dearest brother, and feared you might mistake my silence for
coldness. Believe me, it is not indifferent to me to see you so, but
you know I dare not venture upon subjects which might seem like
a wish to extort the confidence which, very likely most wisely,
you have decided not to bestow. Only be persuaded that
affection, interest, sympathy, indulgence, all wait your bidding as
far as I am concerned. How far in a world like this it is happiness
or duty to exchange them for concealments, conversations where
the thoughts are not, is not even a question in my mind, but may
be conviction in others. The purport of all this is to let you know
that I am attached to you, interested in you, anxious about you
under a mask of indifference, worn under the belief that it is your
wish it should be so.

                                                        Ampthill
                                  Monday [13 September 1819]
Here I am after a very pleasant journey. We slept at Oxford last
night. Granville shewed Harriette the lions this morning – and yet
we are here. Granville shooting and I having taken a tolerably
long walk with Mr Luttrell.
   We met dear Lord Holland ogling the rabbits (I believe the
courtship goes no further) at the first gate. Granville joined him
and Mr Luttrell took me round the garden. His mind is troubled,
but I cannot tell why. It may be that they have changed the dining
room, it may be that Lady H. is going to have some Chinese roses
which grow into the window cut down – it may be that he hears
too much of Georgina's* illness, as the first thing he said was
'Mary [Fox]^b is ill, very ill at this moment. A blister on her
side, and a Burgundy Petite Plaister on her chest but her name is
not even mentioned. However to make up for it we have plenty of
Gina.' Then in a suppressed tone, and squeezing his hands tight
together, 'nothing else is talked of'. Mr Rogers has taken to his

*Georgina Fox, the Hollands' elder daughter; she died in November of this year.
Mary was the younger.

room and says he is ill. Mr Luttrell led me to suppose only by his manner that he supposes it is to avoid seeing me,[16] but I cannot believe in such a practical piece of satire – or so great an event from so slight a cause.

As I came to my room, I met, what I took for a housemaid – Lady William [Russell] in a coarse sort of gingham – snuff coloured three cornered shawl, a close white bonnet, and her hair all pinned up under it – very pale and very big. The house looks so comfortable, my room is delightful. I thought Lord Holland looking uncommonly well, Mr Luttrell says he does not think he has been very stout.

Ampthill
Tuesday [14 September 1819]

It was very pleasant yesterday evening. Mr Luttrell was entertaining, Ld Holland delightful and Lady Wm, Allen, Granville and I in high spirits. The dumb were Lady Holland – whom I really think very much annoyed about her little girl – but Mr Luttrell is right about the shameful difference about the two – Harriette who is very shy here, and Ld Wm, and Lord Tavistock and Lady Tavistock, save when she agreed with enthusiasm in all our different opinions. Lord Morpeth will be glad to hear that Ld Holland thumped the table yesterday, and said he had not felt so well for ages – and he looks blooming and radiant. The Hyena [Samuel Rogers] has issued from his den after a regime of spinage and water. Jugez de la mine. We dine in a long room upstairs which is very comfortable.

Ampthill
Wednesday [15 September 1819]

These are the dog days – it is almost too hot to sew. After a most dangerous dinner I shipwrecked upon some bacon from Winterslaw. Lord Holland is too adorable. He is in high spirits and very well. I wish you had seen him at breakfast almost quarrelling with 'Leveson' [Granville] for fighting the wasps – and all at once, jumping up from his seat, running with pocket handkerchief over his head and face to guard him from the sun, exclaiming 'Odds

[133]

Bobs, why did they not tell me.' This was to see some fish put into the little pond before the house. Mr Luttrell adores him but the weather lowers in another quarter – he is respectful and discreet but 'looks in my face, and his heart is nigh to break'. I think the principal key to it may be a speech of his own this morning, that 'there is no accounting for Lady Holland's attention to Mr Rogers', who does not receive them in public at present as he lives entirely in his own rooms, but I suspect it is a variety of little sick dishes and posset, carried up to dite room, that anger the man of the town. Lady Wm is very agreeable and looks beautiful.

We had a great dispute yesterday about age. Lord Holland sighs for from 16 to 26. Mr Luttrell from 26 to 35. I ventured alone to stand up for the next 20. Lady Holland gave fling at all the years. Mr Allen 'only knows that as men grow older they grow worse'. Ld Holland then said he should like to have his favourite 10, 4 times over. Mr Luttrell was very contented to remain as he is only there is 'no casting anchor'.

Ld Holland has just crept into my room to beg me to send Harriette to 'poor dear little Mary'. What a love he is – all the perfections of every different character, all the right to think himself one of the first of men, and without one thought of any thing but being and making others happy.

[Wherstead]
Friday [24 September 1819]
We have such appetites that there is likely to be a famine in the country. I do not think the difference of climate would do so much to you all who are used to C.H. but the difference from Tixal where my children had damp little pleasure grounds to disport themselves in – and this high open airy situation, is quite incalculable.

[Wherstead]
[Monday 27 September 1819]
The house is a low square white house with a green viranda to the south before the viranda grass, with two baskets of rose trees, not

very brilliant now, and some large trees with benches under them. [Sketch] The side I shew you is that and between the view of the church and water there is a broad gravel walk under the windows and another round a lawn.

George Stewart went away this morning; he is a very good and amiable boy and almost as fond of me as his sister is.

[Wherstead]
Saturday [2 October 1819]

I cannot comfort you about the rising Fitz Clarences. I hear one of about fourteen is a perfect Venus. Mr Montagu arrived yesterday. He is in high spirits and brought some Cowes and London news. The Regent sits at the helm of his yatch with crowds sailing about to look at him. Ld Anglesea follows in another, to go messages, order dinner, fetch visitors &c. Sir Arthur Paget next in a large open boat with one mast, to which he ties Lady Augusta* in strong weather in case of accidents.

[Sandon]
[1 November 1819]

I write because I did not write yesterday; for I am so tired and stupefied that I have no other reason. We went this morning (I must say against my earnest entreaties) to Tixal. I knew how it would be – but G – Lady Harrowby overruled me. I prefer Wherstead but I spent seven of the happiest halfs of my life there and I was so terribly overcome, that I could not command myself and so ashamed for the men seemed to think me crazy – it has had the effect of reducing me to a perfect bûche – and I am come to my room to confess unto thee, who will understand me better than they do.

I am going to add a little by way of countenance to look busy without being obliged to talk. Granville is going to the Lunatic Asylum tomorrow to remind himself of his old pursuits – though not like me to weep over them.

*Lady Augusta had been Lord Morley's first wife.

At the close of January *1820* George III died and the fifty-seven-year-old Prince Regent succeeded as George IV. There are no letters between the sisters chronicling this event; presumably they were in London and there was no need to write, but by the summer Georgiana Morpeth was in Yorkshire and there was plenty to report. The country was in a turmoil for the new King was seeking to exclude his wife, Caroline of Brunswick, from church Liturgy, and on the grounds of her misconduct abroad wished for a divorce so that he could marry again and beget an heir. For a Queen regnant to be found guilty of adultery the sentence was death. Pressed by the King, the Government introduced in the House of Lords a Bill of Pains and Penalties which was read for the second time on *17 August*. Though there was damnatory evidence in plenty it was unlikely that there would be sufficient proof to carry the Bill through the House of Commons. The Queen had arrived in England to defend herself, and Brougham acting for her as Attorney-General (while fairly assured of her guilt) gave his support in the hope of overthrowing the Tory Government and bringing in the Whigs.

[To the Duke of Devonshire]   [Bruton Street]
                                               [30 July 1820]

I have been nowhere but to Burlington House.* You need not be jealous, for though it is magnificent and in very good taste, it is not to be compared with Devonshire House. Its fault is the great darkness, notwithstanding seventy-two candles in the large room, but vu the colour, or something or other, it looked very sombre. Aunt George was perfectly happy, an added or moulu border to the Polonaise, another roll to the turban and another erect black feather. As an assembly its merit was space, and its fault inumerable old maids running about and several families from the provinces, curates, land-surveyor-looking people with wives hanging on their arms.[17]

I am so hipped about the 17th and very much afraid of the mob.

---

*Lord George Cavendish had bought Burlington House in 1815 but owing to alterations, including the new great staircase, he did not move in for several years.

[Bruton Street]
16 [August 1820]
Lady Bessborough, heaving with laughter, bids me tell you that
no two people are in the same mind except as to the extreme peril
we are all in, but if there is une ideé dominante it is that the Queen
will be carried through in triumph. There is an unhappy aunt of
Sir John Shelley, come to England and settled in Berkeley Square.
They have put it about that she is a witness and a weary life she
will have of it.

[Bruton Street]
[17 August 1820]
After I had written yesterday Mr Greathead called, a wise old
man and a Whig. He doubted the Guards, blamed Ministers,
dreaded consequences, hipped me to death. If the Guards are
steady, nothing can be safer. There has been a sad petitesse. They
have forbidden her going in at the royal entrance to the House of
Lords. Urged by me, Lords Granville and Morley and Hart mean
to get up when she enters. Honi soit qui mal y pense. I breakfasted
this morning at a quarter before eight with Granville and Mr
Wilmot and saw them off, armed with hard biscuits, and have this
moment seen William Hissey, who went with the carriage and
says that nothing can be more peaceable than the mob. Darlings
they are. I am considerably happier.

[Bruton Street]
18 [August 1820]
If I had not fancied a large hot buttered roll at breakfast I should
be happy. London is as quiet as a mouse and the mob cut their
jokes even upon the Queen. There have been gay doings at the
cottage at Windsor.* His Majesty, Lady Conyngham,† Princesse
Esterhazy, and Lord Francis. This latter I hear makes a great fool
of himself and is always showing off his favour with the King,

*Converted by Nash and enlarged to a Gothic cottage ornée, Royal Lodge in
Windsor Great Park was the King's country house.
†The King's new favourite; Lord Francis was her second son.

displaying watches, snuff boxes, and rings which he receives from him. The King is in outrageous spirits, discussing as we do.

[Bruton Street]
22 [August 1820]

The witness [Teodoro Majocchi] examined today is a man who travelled all over Greece and Italy with her as courier, a very shrewd, intelligent man, perfectly undaunted, and giving his strong evidence without embarrassment or hesitation. Granville says that when he was brought in the Queen stood up, threw her head back, and put both her arms akimbo, and looked at him for some time with a countenance which those who saw it said was quite terrific. She then exclaimed 'Ah, Theodore',* and trundled out of the House.

The interpreter is the man that delights them all. His name is Spinetto; he is an Italian teacher at one of the Universities, as quick as lightning, all gesticulation, and so eager he often answers instead of the witness. Between them they act all the evidence, and at times they say this is so irresistibly comic that the noble Lords forget all decorum and are in a roar of laughter.

[Bruton Street]
Thursday [24 August 1820]

To give you an idea of the difficulty of forming opinions from what one hears. I sat at dinner between Lord Holland and Lord John Russell. The former told me that the evidence of the new witness had been most favourable for the Queen's interest, Lord John that it had made decidedly against her. The dinner was pleasant, Lady Holland radiant, Lord H. gayer and happier even than usual. After dinner there was a great deal of talk.

Lady Jersey really looks the colour of a guinea and her face all drawn into strong lines and fifteen years older. She takes on sadly about the Queen and cries real tears all the time she is talking. Her Majesty is not so low, they say that when she withdraws to the room prepared for her she talks incessantly and bursts out into

*By some she was thought to have exclaimed 'Traditore'

such loud and intemperate fits of laughter that the people with her are in an agony lest she should be heard in the House.

[Bruton Street]
[25 August 1820]

The morning's work has been an examination of the captain of the polacca, and the beginning of the evidence of the cook, an assassin-looking man, whom they say they could not look at without shuddering. Their noble minds are much occupied with a magnificent luncheon Lord Gwydir gives every day in his room adjoining the House, and much of their discourse is of salmon pies and cucumber sandwiches. They all seem worn.

[Bruton Street]
Sunday [27 August 1820]

The House broke up yesterday at one and we drove in the curricle to Chiswick. There we had a very agreeable little dinner. George and Mrs Lamb and Mr Ellis and Ld Clare. She looks thin and bilious but in good spirits. She was very kind to me till I in the innocence of my heart began talking of the Queen and then I found her so irritable, and once almost crying, that if I had not recollected all at once that B[rougham] was so nearly concerned in it all I should have been totally at a loss to account for it.

Monday 28

Granville has just gone to the House and where do you think I am going – to sit at Cleveland House with the Duchesses of Kent and Gloucester, Princesses Augusta and Sophia. And this all because I cannot say no when confronted with the person who asks me. I mind going out less than I did at first because I am easy in my mind and because of a morning I scarcely see any body so that it is not talk all day, which is my aversion. Somebody said with truth yesterday that the proof of our safety is in the dullness that is come over us all. Je m'ennuie, elle s'ennuie, ils s'ennuient. In short nous nous ennuyons. Life is fear in some shape or other and despair of ever being easy should make one so. A mad dog went pleasuring up and down St James's Street the other day; a hornet

[139]

flew into my window yesterday; Granville went in a boat from the House of Lords to Child's and was nearly upset by a man unable to guide his sailing vessel. A large rat came just behind Lady Harrowby's ear as we were wrangling about the Queen last night. God bless you dearest.

[Bruton Street]
[29 August 1820]

I have been doing my duty reading the debate. I suppose it would not be easy to find an act of that sort so devoid of pleasure. The Lords seem to me to flounder deeper and deeper. You will see that Copley attacked Brougham whom he affects to despise as not being what they call a close lawyer. Brougham flew into a passion, was flippant and insolent, and uttered the most unjustifiable falsehoods as to the conduct of the government.

I have almost forgot to talk of my royal morning. I spent two hours at Cleveland House with the Duchess of Gloucester, an amiable and good soul. The Duchess of Clarence, ugly with a good tournure and manner; the Duchess of Kent, very pleasing indeed raving of her baby.* 'C'est mon bonheur, mes délices, mon existence. C'est l'image du feu roi.' Think of the baby. They say it is le roi George in petticoats, so fat it can scarcely waddle. Augusta, good-humoured and jolly, stuffing filets de sole and veal cutlets, and Sophia very clever and agreeable. I had to go with each of them the whole course. 'How many children has Lady Georgiana Morpeth?' 'Eleven, ma'am.' 'God bless my soul, you don't say so, it seems but yesterday' &c. They all seem to dote on Lady Stafford, and I have no doubt think her the most exemplary of women.

[Bruton Street]
Wednesday [30 August 1820]

I have not been able to make out a word of yesterday. I went early yesterday evening to Lady Cowper's and found Lady Holland, the only really undisputed *monarchy* in Europe, sitting in a

*The future Queen Victoria.

corner, throne a footstool, courtiers and dames d'honneurs all dans les règles. Lady Jersey quite insane, a tear in either eye.

Brougham told Granville during yesterday's debate, that he did not care a farthing which way it was decided.

[Bruton Street]
Saturday [2 September 1820]
The Lords are all tired and suffocated, some ill. Lords Wellesley and Hardwicke among the number. Lord Portsmouth takes to the late but desirable task of strengthening his mind. Granville anxious to ascertain the nature of his studies looked over his shoulder and saw he was deep in the list of fairs in the Red Book.*

The Staffords, the Archbishop [Harcourt, of York] and Lord Morley dined here. Upon Granville talking in a moderate strain and saying he had doubts as to the result, Lord Stafford flew into a positive fury – such language was very well for the immoral school but did not do for the moral one, and even Cobbett was deserting the Queen – that she would soon have no champion but Granville – he sat in the House of Lords to judge, and judge he would. The Arch is much calmer. He will not vote without a clause against divorce. They are all agreed as to the Attorney General† that he had done incalculable mischief, that Brougham is the Queen's Attorney General, but he is the Queen's man. Lady Stafford is in very good humour. I think chiefly because all her children are away from her.

[Bruton Street]
[3 September 1820]
I have been looking over Granville, who has been writing to Mr Canning and there I spy, progress slow, result uncertain, not sufficient evidence to carry the bill through the House of Commons. The Bishops will insist on the divorce clause being left out. This would reconcile the saints in the other House, but the majority would be for her, not on the ground of her popularity, but of his unpopularity. The answer to 'Is she bad?' is, 'He is as

*Probably the *Annual Register*, for which the 'Red Book' was a popular name.
†Sir Robert Gifford.

bad' in the mouths of the country gentlemen. The Crown lawyers have conducted the business infamously, letting Brougham &c, go on without interruption when they were irregular and insolent in their proceedings, stopping and interfering with them when there was no occasion for it.

The Archbishop is happier than the happy. Lady Stafford drives him about in her barouche to air him after the House. He continues not to squabble with the Marquess, as he says he always rows ashore when he sees the storm gathering. A prudent plan in all cases, and I recommend the same course to Granville.

[Bruton Street]
Monday night [4 September 1820]

Hart came to see me on my return from a dowager drive by myself up and down Constitution Hill in a chariot. He was charmed with his Chiswick, says Lady Jersey was very amiable when she forgot (as she frequently did) her despair about the Queen. Granville rode in the Park with the dite Countess and Mr Tierney. They met the Marylebone dames returning from their address [to the Queen] covered with feathers and white cockades escorted by the mob. Silence made the welkin ring with her admiration of them: it was refreshing and delightful to see such feelings in the country. Yes, Tierney said, one feels for the first time proud of being an Englishman! She took it good humourdly, only laughed and said nobody but herself thought properly on the subject. Tierney told Granville afterwards that he was more and more convinced that the Queen is quite mad. I hear it said that todays evidence has been more against her than any other day. Lord Holland says he is so tired of the subject that he shall go and live in Cotton Gardens with the witnesses.*

[Bruton Street]
[6 September 1820]

Lord Morley says nothing will induce him to vote for the bill if it comes to a division now, and I see both he and Granville are

*The Italian witnesses were kept together in a house in Cotton Gardens, now built over by the House of Lords.

anxious to have the thing knocked up in the Upper House. They think that without the divorce clause the proceeding is nonsense, with it quite unallowable. Ministers hold a different language. 'What is to be proved if this is not? What would you have more, no two witnesses contradicting each other? The Queen, the disgrace of her sex. How can anyone pretend to morality, decency,' &c. The fallacy of all this is that what we want is not belief, but proof; witnesses, but credible ones – ten Englishmen instead of a hundred Italians. The real grievance is its having become, as everything does so much in England, a violent party question.

On 9 September the House of Lords adjourned until 3 October and the Granvilles hurried to Wherstead.

[Wherstead]
Sunday [? 17 September 1820]

Do you remember my complaining so of premature old age – a swelled feel and fatigue after exercise. Well all this the blue pill aided by the bitters and salt are removing daily. I do not feel the least tired after walking. I am growing quite slender. Let me give you a journal of my day. I get up at eight drink a draught, omitting or adding the salt to Columba root at my own discretion. I walk and potter about in the poultry yard till ten when I return as I used at Spa with a raging appetite which I subdue with tea, a spoonful of powdered ginger in it, a dry toast. I talk, read the papers and write till 12 when I sally forth again and work with the children in their garden till two during which time I quaff my other bottle. At three I drink a nauseous slop, arrow root without sugar and a spoonful of brandy in it with another plate full of dry toast. I then read, write my letters, teach Georgy till near five when I generally go out again to the top of the chemin privé, to the church, or dawdle about near the house till dinner. At dinner I eat roast beef or roast mutton with cayenne pepper and a hunck of bread. At ten I allow myself a cup of tea with ginger in it and at ½ past eleven I go to bed. The blue pill I take every other night. I have today a feel of strength and elasticity that I had almost forgot. For heavens sake do not let Ld Morpeth see this performance.

[Wherstead]
Tuesday [26 September 1820]
Agar Ellis arrived to dinner yesterday. He adds very much to the aisance of society but less to its harmony. He is rude, fastiduous and overbearing, which is the more wonderful as he has a good temper and kind heart, but he is cruelly spoilt and the result is that he sets people most irreparably against him.[18] I am sorry to say Granville pronounced him to be 'quite odious' when we went to bed last night.

[Bruton Street]
Saturday [7 October 1820]
Do you know the agony of bustle of a London morning sometimes – in my bed gown – Mr Wilmot having dropt like a bomb into our early breakfast, on his knees for news till eleven, when young Scanner (60 at least) arrived and kept me till twelve. Mrs Wyatt tapping at the door with caps and bodies, Mrs Villiers waiting below with all G[eorge] Villiers letters from Russia to read them – and now see me, ere yet my destined day half done – still in my bed gown, with the carriage harnessing for Chiswick.

I dined at Cleveland House. Lord Stafford like the noble Leonatus, outré, bursting with rage, for there is nothing else for it. The Archbishop sat on the other side of me, he looks upon the thing as over and says 'it is better that the bill should be thrown out with the moral conviction, in the higher orders that she is guilty, than with the moral conviction in the lower orders that she is innocent', very sensible, Lady Morpeth, and my own view of the case. Ministers are in a nice kettle to be sure. Mr Wilmot is furious, we suspect him of an early preparation to rat.

Monday [9 October 1820]

I think I observe a change of language de part et d'autre.
Ministerial people less violent and Lady Jersey & Co. bearing
their honours meekly. It is said that there is much squabbling and
difference of opinion in the Cabinet.

Chiswick was very agreeable with only one fault (I don't see
why or how) of the evenings being rather long and décousu. Hart
and the vedova [Lady Hunloke] appear to me the two happiest
people I know. Mrs Lamb tells me that it amounts when the
society is smaller to shouting and romping from morning to
night. She looks very handsome but older and the lines of her face
stronger. She is good, amiable and at times sensible, childish,
vulgar, and at times silly. Her two girls are pretty selon moi, ugly
selon Mrs Lamb; very foreign and distinguished looking, long
flowing hair and waists d°; broken English and the second clever.
It is like a farce, little Sir Henry Hunloke is a thorough John Bull
and sickens at his sisters. Their sash, shape, flounces, all in the last
perfection, a sort of human tripod.

I returned to town yesterday after walking a great deal with
dear Hart who was as kind and amiable as possible. He is
improving Chiswick most amazingly, opening and airing it and a
delightful walk is made round the paddock, open and dry, with a
view of Kew Palace – and a few kangaroos (who if affronted rip
up a body as soon as look at him), elks, emus and other pretty
sportive death dealers playing about near it.

[Bruton Street]
Tuesday [10 October 1820]

I have lost ten minutes in consulting myself whether I should
write, or walk twenty times round Berkeley Square. I gave up
my duty for my pleasure, and if you were to see the colour of
the air, a sort of thick grey almost tangible fog, you would not
be too much flattered. Mrs Lamb is quite right in admiring me.
There is a visible increase of tone. I look lighter, clearer and
gayer.

I dined in Cavendish Square; Nugent very uneasy at seeing me
eat a couple of wings of a large fowl, with rice, pour tout potage,

thoughtless young man, not reflecting, that veal, and dindon aux truffles, left me no alternative.

Now I must go my rounds in the square. I really had rather do many other so disagreeable thing. If I see anybody before five I will add a line. If not Addio, carissima.

Granville is just come. The day, they say, has gone against her – enough at least to give hopes and spirits to min isters – and to make it likely the whole thing will go on much longer.

[Bruton Street]
Friday [13 October 1820]

We dined at the Duke of Wellington's. I never saw anything so beautiful as the contributions of the known world to him. Services of china, the Dresden was beautiful with views of Spain. Plateaus, table linen that would make beautiful gowns.

I never saw anything – rather felt anything – like the improvements already at Chiswick. I never took a wholesome walk there before.

Camden Place
Monday [October 1820]

Hart looks much better than I ever saw him and his spirits outrageous. I suppose it is discretion but he never takes the least head of her [Lady Hunloke] when we are there. It is an odd contrast to what it is when we are not. The familiarity and intimacy being then unbounded. He calls her *beauty* and *large*, and hollows after, and orders her about, as he does his dogs. She looks old I think though very handsome of an evening.

[Bruton Street]
Monday [30 October 1820]

Lady Stafford walks a footstep and there is no turning of a street or square safe from an encounter with her. She is in a prodigious stew about politicks, it will be such very hard work to turn upon her pivot once again.

I have had an answer from Hart beginning 'The devil take you', but very good humoured. It really is too severe a junket into the country to dinner on a November night.

[Bruton Street]
Friday [3 November 1820]
Great oratorical guns are to be fired today. Ministers expect (poor loves) a majority of 50, but you shall have politicks later in my envelope. I can frame no thought about Hart and every supposition has an undesirable objection to it. Why do they meet, why do they part, why live together, why live asunder, why marry why not marry?

[Bruton Street]
Saturday morning 10 o'clock [4 November 1820]
The Queen has never read the newspapers and is now just aware from being told it by someone, that she is abused as having made herself the tool of the radicals. She is in despair, has shut herself up and says she will see nobody. Brougham has urged her very much to go down to the House with her speech but she will not and says 'it will be poison to me to do it.' She seems to me to be growing quite cracked as fast as possible and àpropos of crackedness Lady Jersey wears a miniature of her as a clasp, about the size of a sixpence.

Carlton House is called Nero's Hotel and somebody said of the Queen that no body could now deny her being pure innosense and with these witticisms I bid you buona sera.

Sunday
There never was such a day, the wind howling and torrents of rain. I forgot to tell you that Mrs Lamb told me since Lady H[unloke]'s appearance Hart's familiarity knows no bounds. That he goes up to her before them all, pats her on the cheek &c. It is certainly marvellous take what view of it you may. Agar Ellis, is I find, very much abused for toadying Hart. I took his part warmly as it seemed to me so absurd an idea, but on questioning

Mrs Lamb she rather staggers me. First she told me that when first he came to Chiswick he (Agar) told her what made it difficult to talk to Hart, was that to a man of his rank, no body could begin first, but must wait to be spoken to. Dearest G, can you conceive so small and vulgar an idea? Then she says, that with his hatred of musick when Hart performs his well known voluntaries on the piano forte, Agar sits by him saying all the time 'Dear Duke how beautiful that is. Pray play that again', &c &c. This is strong presumptive evidence and as I will not give him up I am glad I have not to meet a cross examination upon it.

[Bruton Street]
Saturday [8 November 1820]
Mr Ellis is abused very much for the court he is supposed to pay to Hart. I think he likes him, though perhaps not to the degree that one should suppose by his assiduous attentions to him. I think he finds his house, dinners, carriage &c extremely conven- ient and that it is his habit, to follow up a new acquaintance, with a sort of dévouement founded more upon circumstances than feeling. It is in his nature (I am afraid I think it is a small one) to follow, to imitate, to be more of a shadow than a substance.

[Bruton Street]
Friday [10 November 1820]
They divided dearest Sis, a majority of nine for the bill, upon which Lord Liverpool withdrew the bill. Tonight we shall all stick lights in our windows and there will be an end pour le moment.

[Bruton Street]
Monday [13 November 1820]
On Saturday we drove to Chiswick where we found Hart who will write to you about Hardwick for the beginning of Decem- ber. If it can be atchieved what happiness it will be.

Agar and Mrs Lamb are worn out. The lawn beautifully variegated with an indian bull, his spouse, and goats of all colours and dimensions. I own I think it a mercy that one of the kangaroos has just died in labour, vu that they hug one to death.

We dined at Holland House, it was a very delightful one. Lady H. was very good humoured and agreeable. Lord Holland as merry as a grig though begging in vain for one glass of Johannisberg. Lord Lauderdale, Brougham next him whose nose, either from fatigue or triumph, twitches twenty times more than ever. He told us he had received an anonymous letter, beginning 'You two-faced and rascally Whig'; I felt quite distressed and did not know how to look.

Wherstead

Wednesday [15 November 1820]
We arrived here at six yesterday and though I am confined to my room with a very bad cold, what happiness it is! They are all as well as possible. Granville an elancé little man instead of a perfectly round ball as I expected. Dame Georgy is as shrewd as she can stick together; Harriette contented and radiant. The rooms are so airy, the view from my balcony so pretty and (for all my reasons are not sublime) what a comfort it is to have time for a doze and not be obliged to put ones hair into eighteen papillottes.

The Jerseys come here Monday. I believe she does not want any thing but one or two patient listeners.

[Wherstead]
Thursday [16 November 1820]
After walking alone through the foggy streets for six weeks you cannot know what it is to me to walk about here in weather like spring with the darling children. This place has certainly a power over my health that is quite magical – inasmuch as it acts upon it immediately. It is not that I felt ill in London, but heavy, languid and old, and here I grow young again. In spite of our spring weather yesterday we had some snow but very little, only just enough to destroy illusion.

Saturday [18 November 1820]

There is no chance of our failing with regard to Hardwick if Hart is steady to our plan.

The day is thick sea fog but my children make it very bright. Granville is shooting in the thick of it. I long for gloomy Hardwick more than I can say.

Woburn [Abbey]
Monday [18 December 1820]

We arrived in good time to dress for dinner. I went into the large blue and gold saloon and met at the door Johnny [Duke of Bedford] pulling a face, 'The Duchess is very sorry, she is ill and cannot appear.' I pulled another, the wrong way I fear and went to Lady William [Russell] in a corner. She is looking very well again, very pretty, curls dangling on both sides – not to mention a gown of velvet and ermine – such as hang on Hardwick walls. When I could breathe I saw the Duke of York. Lady Worcester éblouissante in diamonds. Theresa [Villiers] in a fancy dress; Tavy [Lady Tavistock] beggaring all description like a litter toller on fire at both ends. In the evening the men went to whist and billiards and we talked. Lady William is delightful. The Duchess is, or is not with child, that is the question. I hear she looks wretchedly, is grown very thin and very low. I think what I think Lady Morpeth but says nothing.

Lady Jersey comes today. Punch is seriously uneasy thinking her really about to go crazy. She walks with measured step and slow, proclaims it to be in the highest degree wrong and unfeeling to think or talk of any thing but the Queen – has worked poor Tavy up into a state of harmless phrenzy, she who never opened her mouth but to say 'Capital'.

Woburn
Tuesday [19 December 1820]

The Duchess has not yet appeared. She has seen toutes ces dames, but not me. You know I am not touchy therefore I take the goods the gods provide and swallow the affront with a grateful heart.

It is very comfortable here, neither more nor less. Lady William is the only one who really likes me therefore the preference I feel for her conversation I am able to indulge sans peur at sans reproche. Lady Jersey sits netting and raving and really it sometimes comes across my mind that she will go out of hers. Her countenance has become so stern and political that it affects her beauty. She occasionally stands up and gesticulates with so unfeminine a vehemence and tone that it makes me long to administer a calmant. Yesterday she seized Lord William by both sides of his coat – I believe what is called 'collaring a man' – exclaiming 'And why should we have Germans to reign over us.'

Addio dearest loved sister. I think we shall go Sunday. Tout est bien pourvu que cela dure but nothing can prevent me whooping and hallooing all the way to town.

Woburn
Wednesday [20 December 1820]

We are new dealt every day at dinner and yesterday I sat between Lords Thanet and Worcester. The former is very agreeable and we are becoming rather particular. Monsieur de Flahault was the only new personage. His singing is quite enchanting and made yesterday evening much more agreeable than either of the former ones. The Duchess appeared; she was to me quite what I wish her to be – uncommonly cold and uncommonly civil. She looks very ill, very much out of spirits and it is the first time I ever saw her quite unable to make a fight. Lady William I like better every time I see her. Theresa wears a thing like a gold cream cheese on her head.

[Woburn]
Wednesday night [20 December 1820]

The Duchess, though they all say she is much better, has shut herself up the whole day and none but the chosen have had a sight of her. Poor Punch is gone to bed – in a way – he lost 160£ tonight to the Duke of York, besides a hundred to him at Middleton. 'Now Sir, I have done, I shall play no more. I have lost my last shilling to you.' 'No, no, dear Punch, mistaken by God.' 'I don't know what you mean, Sir, you have won my last shilling', and flounced out of the room. Lady Jersey mentioned you once with kindness but she is too absorbed to think or care about any thing or any body. Do you know she will soon be avoided like a contagious disorder and even the Whigs slink away from her light headed politicks.

I was delighted to receive your letter from Hardwick. I see you bustle amongst our ancestors and envy all the dead and the living who see you.

[Woburn]
[21 December 1820]

I am not very much charmed here. Granville wishes to be well dans ce château. I declare I do not know why I am not more. I think very few people are more agreeable than Lady William. The Duchess I do not see. Many of the men I like. Lord Thanet, Punch, Lord William extremely. I have a delightful room and find the day too short for all I have to do in it. These people I have named are all kinder to me, one [more] than another.

Well, my dear G, now let me sum up. Why do I count the day that I am to go. Why do I feel that I shall not be able to refrain from screaming for joy when I drive off. It really is no affront to Woburn. I do justice to its comfort, ease splendour and society. It is simply a strong unconquerable wish to go.

Woburn
Friday [22 December 1820]

I am just returned from a long tête-à-tête walk with Lord Thanet. The ardour of my love is only lessened by the dreadful chill I experienced as we did not go above 100 yards an hour. My reason for my tête-à-tête was this. Dear Lady Jersey has had a violent scene with me but it has ended most enthusiastically and affectionately though it was, as you will hear, a little lady maidish and boarding schoolish. Lady William has been kind enough to take a great fancy to me and I seeing Lady Jersey (I thought) in queenism and fearing to enter upon the subject, and wishing above all not to sit with any of ces Messieurs, accepted, with grateful pleasure and with little Lady Worcester at nos trousses, we have generally escaped from politics to musick and to look at the billiards &c, &c. What was my dismay yesterday evening when Silence came up to me and before half a dozen people burst into tears. I led her off in an agony, she sobbing out 'Its all you, its all you.' She then began 'I thought you would have been my friend at Woburn, and you talk more to Lady William than to me', &c. I then quite honestly explained how her political phrenzy (yes, dear Lady Morpeth, I hazarded the word) has unwittingly made me shun her.

She was then all amiability and sits triumphantly, me, her rescued prize in her hand. Lady William very drole about it.

[Bruton Street]
Monday night [25 December 1820]
Our journey to town was bleak though joy kept me warm. We called in our way on Lady Bessborough. We went to dinner at Holland House, Lord Holland in a black velvet cap tied under his chin with a muslin handkerchief looked a great quiz and a great love. My Lady complains very much of her palpitations and bile but was in good spirits and good humour. Late in the evening Brougham, his hair and beard grown, looking exactly like an ourang outang. Mr Canning's resignation[*] has made little sensation, I suppose from its having been so much calculated upon.

I have been dining at Mme de Lieven. It would have been tremendously dull if Mme de Lieven's gaiety and cleverness had not overlaid all the weight of her convives.

The Granvilles were back at Wherstead early in the new year, entertaining the Duke of Wellington and other friends.

[Wherstead]
[*c.* 7 January 1821]
I quite love the Duke of Wellington. He is neither an agreeable man nor in my eyes a héros de roman, but he is the most

---

[*]Canning resigned as president of the Board of Control owing to his former close friendship with the Queen.

unpretending, perfectly natural and amiable person I ever met with. The shooting and the dinners have been as good as possible. The Duke and Mme de Lieven played at whist, so we had no want of occupation.

[Bruton Street]
Monday night [22 January 1821]

Hart is in a most amiable humour. You will sympathize with me as to a new acquisition he has made – a sweet little pet called an ichneumon, the size of a large rat, with a nose like a weasel's, so tame that it springs up into ones face, gets into ones plate at dinner, and when one drinks tea runs rapidly up ones back, over ones shoulder and puts its dite nose into ones cup. Its peculiarity is I believe, a delight in sucking human blood.

Granville dines with Charles Ellis and I consequently perform alone upon a roast chicken and mean to devour Kenilworth* with it. There are different opinions. Charles Greville told me last night that he did not stir out or go to bed till five in the morning the day he began it.

[Bruton Street]
Tuesday [6 February 1821]

I was at Mme de Lieven's on Sunday evening. Lady Morley and myself sat on a couch, she saying, 'now we have nothing to do but to look as fascinating as possible, and we shall be surrounded with all that is most exquisite.' The reverse of the medal was less intellectual but more beautiful, a pendant groupe. The rest of the room was darkness made visible – swarms of small back diplomates. The Bathursts in cherry coloured velvet, Lady Castlereagh looking as if she was going to stand prostrate covered with diamonds and gold, Lady Davy who is everywhere, Lady Fielding who ought to be no where. Hart joined us and we all went to tea at D House and the same party junket on Friday to Chiswick, we had the happiness to be introduced to the ichneumon. You will never stand it dear Lady Morpeth. I believe

*Sir Walter Scott's *Kenilworth* had been published in January.

it is harmless but as rapid as lightning here there and every where over and into every thing.

[Bruton Street]
[February 1821]

I heard the other day that the King is more in love with your friend Lady C[onyngham] than ever, and that he sits kissing her hand with a look of the most devoted submission. I suppose she persuaded him to go to the play.* It is very wise and answered perfectly. You would have felt for him as I did. He looked as white as a sheet, but did it uncommonly well. First of all, not like a fine lady behind the curtain of a cage grillé, but with the Duke of York on one side and the Duke of Clarence on the other; Lord Cholmondeley, with a handkerchief to his eyes, sobbing con amore, other lords behind. Bloomfield, Sir Thomas Lawrence, and Lord Mount Charles yelling for joy like a young bull dog, in the orchestra. Lady Holland opposite, tapping her longest, most Indian fan with energy on the outside of the box. The house was crowded in every part, and believe me, Lady Morpeth, the applause was stunning and thrilling. Hats and handkerchiefs in the air, and shouts almost the whole time. Twice a voice called out 'Queen', and once, 'Where's your wife, Georgie?' But the hissing, 'Shame, shame', 'Turn him out', instantly stopped this. In short, John Bull was pleased and shewed it. It proves the King's folly in shutting himself up. He goes to Covent Garden tonight. I saw him trundle down stairs, and I never saw any thing look so happy.

[Bruton Street]
[February 1821]

Lady Morley came here for a moment on her way from Covent Garden,† where the applause was as great as at Drury Lane.

*Lady Bessborough's box was fitted up for the King at Drury Lane that night. The performance included *The Antiquary* and *Harlequin & Friar Bacon*, as well as the opera *Artaxerxes*.
†The performance that night was *Twelfth Night* (arranged as an opera) and again *Harlequin & Friar Bacon*, in which Grimaldi, the clown, excelled.

White silk flags waving from the gallery, with 'Long live George the Fourth' in gold letters upon them. She says His Majesty, though it was evidently painful to him on account of his stays, lay back on his chair in fits of laughing at Grimaldi's jokes, York roared again, Clarence was dull and did not twig them. Good night dearest; my eyes draw straws, and having given you this sketch of Royalty, I go to bye-bye.

The sisters were in London for the rest of the season. Harriet was said to have had a miscarriage in July from which she took a long time to recover.

[? Wherstead]
Sunday [2 September 1821]
[George Vernon] just arrived from Ireland where he says the people are absolutely mad with joy and loyalty.[*] Lady C. appears but little, but that little is high. She was in a box opposite to him at the play and not content with making her ses demonstrations all the time, he wrote to her in pencil, and sent it round by Ld Mount Charles. Mr Luttrell who detests the Irish is quite beyond his patience on the subject. 'Royalty has generally some restraint, some schackle upon it – but here is a new case – a thing unheard of – a King broke loose. There will be no catching him again.'

[Wherstead]
Friday [14 September 1821]
I am better a great deal dearest G, have been out all the morning, malgré the blue pill and Bartlett who has been here says there is a decided amendment in what has been so long in a wrong state. He says I have a pulse like a clock and my tongue is less white and my skin less yellow. I have felt well enough to enjoy the finest weather and a récolte of French beans, with the children to the greatest degree.

[*]The King's visit to Dublin took place in August.

I cannot endure the thoughts of Monday fortnight – I am *so* happy here. You see the misfortune is that there is scarcely a thing in the scale of London, to weigh against all I enjoy here. Breakfast by candle light in a fog, no interest to make society piquante, no time for air and exercise after the House is up – away from the chicks.

Nos messieurs are very agreeable. I see nothing of them in the morning, at dinner they are very gay and conversable, and in the evening after tea and an hours discussion they play at whist. F. Byng's*b* conversation is all in the style of 'a word to the wise, let him heed who hears' &c &c, how it is better to buy tea at the India House in chests, silks to be had at a shop in the Regent's Circus as good as French ones for eight or six shillings a yard. French silks stain English ones do not.

Bless you my dearest sister. I am going up the chemin privé to prepare myself for a large under done bif stake which I have had inserted into the bill of fare for my private eating.

[Wherstead]
[23 September 1821]

Your letters are so sprack and full of news that mine must hide their diminished heads. Let us boast of our children, as we are always humble and say we don't know. I think my girls are certainly Minervas, and perhaps Venuses, but with a perfect resignation to being told every day, when I produce them, that they are peu de chose. Could you see me seated in a new chaise longue at my beautiful window, my darling children with their Papa on the grass.

You will see the Duke of Wellington's plans. They say the King proposed to him to show him the field of Waterloo: very right of him, I think. He will end by being, as Lady Morley would say, a very sweet young man.

[Bruton Street]
Tuesday [October 1821]

I have just read your letter from Chatsworth. What magnificent doings. Pray my dearest G do not ever regret not having been to me – it never entered into my head. I know all your difficulties and indeed every bodies who travels with a family – and I have never for a moment been a case.

I saw yesterday Miss Berry – still furious with you Lady Morpeth, and as this virgin grows in years I am sorry to say she grows in fury. Ah Ha Ah Ha – she means however to see you somewhere but upon all subjects her violence, her bitterness, her clamor, is just double what it was.[19] She is however true, honorable, upright and I think in many ways to be much pitied – her health seems very bad. After her came Ld and Lady Holland and staid with me above an hour – he was adorable, as merry as a grig – laughing spouting and mimicking, she grudged us our happiness (forgive me dear Ld Morpeth) and would cram him with stale bread and ask me distressing questions.

You have but one *real* fault Lady Morpeth and that is sealing the corner of your letter upon the seal of the enclosures so that, upon the first touch, both seals together with paper, precious words &c &c are torn up by the roots. Turn your inner seal under your outward direction. Din Wherstead into Hart's memory.

News of Lady Bessborough's death in Florence on 14 November reached the Granvilles while they were staying with the Harrowbys at Sandon Hall. Harriet was deeply shocked and Granville, who though very happily married for the past eleven years had once been Lady Bessborough's lover and adored by her, was quite overcome. It was a fortnight before Harriette was told of the death of Lady Bessborough, but even then not of their true relationship.

Sandon
Friday [17 November 1821]

The stunning intelligence of poor Lady B's death, has been my dearest sister, to both Granville and myself, very terrible. You will feel all we do better than I can express it. He is very calm and has with the most heartfelt grief, a command over himself, which for his sake I strive to imitate. It is a hundred thoughts that rush upon me, and seem to give added tenderness to my remembrance of her. She sacrificed herself to others – her nature was a most unselfish one. She had a life and strength of constitution about her that double the blow to those who loved her.[20] It is fortunate for us that we are here – where we can be alone as we please. I shall remain in my room, till my mourning is made up. Adieu my beloved G my head and heart are aching.

Sandon
Saturday [18 November 1821]

You will not, my dearest sister, receive more than a line from me today – as I still feel very nervous and good for nothing – and have been writing to Wm Lamb from whom I had received a few lines today – written and missent upon the first accounts received of her illness, so that I know nothing of Caroline since. I am glad that Granville has been obliged to pass the day at Stafford where he had necessary business to transact. He rode there and back which must have done him good. He means to make the effort of dining below today. I have obtained Lady H[arrowby]'s leave to pass another day alone in my room. I feel shattered and shall be better able to exert myself for the delay. I walked this morning. Lord Gower joined me – his kindness and feeling have endeared him to me. Agar has shown a singular want of both – but I wish not to feel or make you very severe upon it. He has a great deal of skin deep warmth, and is a spoilt child – and a want of *reach* of mind and heart may make him incapable of entering into the shades of feeling on such an occasion as this. But you will not think me unjust when I tell you that yesterday evening, when he knew me unhappy and with many painful necessary letters to write – he sent me up the following note. (As I have neither the wish or power to shew him what I think of it, and that it still leaves him an amusing companion and pleasant friend for the gay moments of ones life – do not ever lead him to think what I think of him, in these respects.) 'Dear Lady G. Please to write a line to Gregoire to tell her I shall dine and sleep at Chatsworth on Thursday. Pray suggest that the bed sheets be not damp. I am so sorry you are not coming down.'

Adieu my dearest sister – you feel, comprehend all – and are to me a second self. Granville is very low, but he has great habitual command over himself – his angelic kindness to me makes me love him if possible more than ever.

[Sandon]
[19 November 1821]

I am just returned from Church, have since been walking and feel well and able to exert myself.

Lord Gower and Mr Ellis are going to Trentham this morning. As I do not feel able to talk much about other subjects I will have done today. Granville is very low but able to make the effort of mixing to a degree in society. I intend dining below and have got over seeing them all, which is a nervous moment.

Country-house visiting took the Granvilles to Trentham at the beginning of December. Mr and Mrs Canning had brought their daughter, Harriet,[b] hoping to marry her off to Lord Gower (or Govero as he was called in the family). This would have been a great marriage to Lord Stafford's eldest son and heir.

[Trentham]
Wednesday [5 December 1821]

We arrived here just in time for dinner today and are in number twenty. This is certainly very large for the state Granville's mind is in which is one that unites to a power of exertion great depression of spirits.

The Cannings are here, the daughter does not as far as one days observation goes, make any impression. She is now singing very loud and very false, which makes me quiver and quake for her. The parents whisper and seem agitated in their minds. I own I think people never came so determinately upon a crime of prize taking and the failure will I fear be very much felt.

Mr Ellis is in high spirits at the thoughts of his going to you and at having me en attendant.

[Trentham]
Thursday [December 1821]

Govero does not even take enough notice – it is really distressing
for nothing ever was half so obvious as the intention on the part
of *her* family. We go on au reste very swimmingly. I sometimes
feel as if it was a want of feeling in me to have recovered so
quickly the power of being as if nothing had happened.

Mr Ellis is now sitting opposite me with a very sickening
mixture of weak warm brandy and water. Piquet, écarté, are
thriving in all parts of the room. Miss Canning and Heneage are
singing and nobody attending to them.

[Trentham]
[December 1821]

Agar sets out tomorrow. I think the Cannings look very black and
blank. The fact is that Govero is barely civil to them, and takes no
more notice of the girl than if she was not there.

Harriette was much affected but she is happily quite ignorant
of what would have given the severest pang[*] – and for a length of
time they have met but little. Can you conceive Mr Ellis saying to
Lord Clanwilliam 'What is the matter with le beau Granville?
how grumpy he is – he has not spoken for the last twenty
minutes.'

*Harriet suddenly awoke to the fact that Agar Ellis was likely to
propose to the Morpeths' seventeen-year-old daughter at Castle
Howard – 'to make a leg to her' in Granville's words, a scheme
not even remotely desirable.*

[Trentham]
[December 1821]

I cannot help feeling convinced that Agar is gone to try his chance
with Georgiana. He has never said one word to me of it, but his
going, the irritation and nervousness of his mind, his admiration

[*]The knowledge that Lady Bessborough was her mother.

of her and above all his telling me constantly that he means to marry somebody I am very fond of, carry perfect conviction to my mind which is now wholly engrossed and agitated on the subject. *I cannot wish it* – yet I am aware that parents would be mad to oppose it as this terrible world goes. If the girl herself is taken in by him all I urge and implore, is that you will recollect health, fretfulness, selfishness as opposed to all that makes a match of a man – and agreeableness in society. If she falls in love with him we must hope the best, but if she does not for God's sake do not let any consideration lead you to persuade her to it. My anxiety to hear from you will be without bounds. Let me hear from you daily.

[Trentham]
[December 1821]

I think you clearly should put to her merely a doubt, a speculation, whether he is a man she could really love. She is *so* young, *so* ignorant, so aimante, and recollect he is her first lover. I cannot think she will accept; if she was twenty seven, on her last legs, but at seventeen! and so attractive. Granville is actually not for it. He thinks the evil to the degree he has it in his blood, not to mention that he thinks him selfish, petulant and not calculated to make a woman happy. He told the Governor [Govero] that if he was refused 'he should go instantly and propose to another very nice girl, Georgiana Somerset.' This is not touching or romantic.[21]

Georgiana Howard became engaged to Agar Ellis and Harriet was obliged to backpedal. The Granvilles now moved on to Heythorpe, the Beauforts' house in Gloucestershire.

Heythorpe
Friday [21 December 1821]

I must devote my last days here to the Duchess. She has finished my conversion. She thinks Agar was at the time he first came amongst us perfection, that the adoration, almost worship of his tutors, friends &c proved it. That he has been spoilt but wanted nothing but his present prospects to bring him back to his original brightness. She thinks you and Georgiana may make him what will render her fate the happiest in the world. Forgive me beloved sister for having thought nothing good enough for her. I am quite happy now. The mistake of my friends with regard to me, is the not finding out that I am a fool, a very great regular fool. 'Never mind, it is only Lady Granville' ought to be their only feeling after listening to me. Tell Georgiana that I shall look upon her and Agar as my two eldest children – and love and scold them accordingly. I swell like the frog in the fable when I think of the enlarged scale of Auntitude which I have entered upon.

[Wherstead]
[*c.* 8 January 1822]

One line only my dearest for I am devoted to la Comtesse [Lieven] who can only stay till Thursday. They arrived here yesterday. We get on very well with our tongues and her music. Mme de Lieven could be more in love with Agar than almost any of the youths she sees. Lord Clanwilliam told me that he had seen him in town – embelli and smartened with happiness. Do not you and Georgiana take my sayings au pied de la lettre. I hear that you are to be in town in a fortnight and that they are to be married in a fortnight.

Mme de Lieven is in great beauty and the highest spirits. Mr Montagu talks without ceasing which as we are now is invaluable. Today we expect F. Lamb, tomorrow Wellington and Francis Leveson. Adieu dearest. The men have a heavenly day for their first chasse – and Granville's gout is gone.

[Wherstead]
[*c.* 9 January 1822]

The Duke and the Lievens stay till Sunday. The Duke is as merry as a grig. We were occupied all yesterday evening with conjuring tricks and patiences of every kind. Francis Leveson looks very large, upright, and handsome. He speaks but little, and I think the fault is que cela ne coule pas de source.

[163]

Lord Worcester, the Beauforts' eldest son, had got into marital as well as financial difficulties, and his uncle Granville, and aunt, spent a further few days in Gloucestershire with the Beauforts.

Heythorpe
Tuesday [probably end of January 1822]

I am very glad to be here as I think it is a real duty to show every sort of affection and respect. The weather is very cold but wholesome and bracing, and when I have done my letters I am going to take a long quick walk. Relaxation is my bane, Lady Morpeth. All my habits and tastes lean that way and in consequence I am going to wage war upon them all. I dread a languid yellow old age, hot, perfumed, and dawdling, and I prefer our Julia's course, active, smart, burnished and braced.

Heythorpe
Saturday [2 February 1822]

The Duke, Mr Napier, and Plantagenet Somerset are breakfasting with us in over alls. Their under alls make Heythorpe terribly dull, so borné a set of minds I never met with. All the élans are kept for the hedges and ditches. I love the Duchess better than ever and her angelic mind lights up even such an alentours as this.

Wherstead
Sunday [February 1822]

I can only write a line to tell you Agar arrived last night. He looks better, is much gayer, much more agreeable than I have ever seen him. Every body is edified at seeing for once matrimony have such happiness attend the prospect of it. He goes about with a hop step and a jump. We are better friends than ever and he has not a shade of sourness or any rancour for the past. Indeed he is too radiant, too really happy to see any thing on its dark side. He *does* deserve Georgiana with all her perfections and her charms. I am so happy about it all that it gives me nearly the same elasticity as him.

Govero is here, a sedate darling, and Mr Ellis and I have been agreeing that were it possible it would be the happiest thing for him to marry Caroline in the whole wide world. *

Frederic Lamb is certainly a most uncommonly clever and agreeable person but there is about him a degree of kindness and coarseness that goes against my taste. He is always going too near the wind upon subjects of morality and taste and his manners are occasionally too laisser aller ish.

[Wherstead]
[February 1822]

I thought the *Ellis's* did not intend to have a house in town this year. I wish I did not. No, dearest Lady Morpeth, I shall be very happy trundling through the fog to Park Street.

Bless you dearest, best love to Lord M and Agar – and Hart if he is with you. We are not touchy but we think it like grandmama Carlisle 'comical enough' that he has never seen Wherstead.

[Wherstead]
Wednesday [February 1822]

Wherstead is winding up with frightful rapidity and I do not know what I should do if I did not see Park Street at the end of it.

What an adorable woman she [Lady Morley] is – never did any one person unite so much – pretend to so little, so bright, all the comfort of solidity, and all the ease of légèrté. I esteem her, love her, admire her, but it is impossible to praise her as she deserves. She quite adores you and yours.

The Granvilles were invited to the Pavilion at Brighton by the King. The Ellises were married on 7 March at Chiswick.

* Instead of Caroline he married her sister Harriet Howard the next year.

[165]

[The Pavilion] Brighton
Sunday [10 March 1822]

This is infinitely better than I expected. The society very agreeable and we are all in the highest good humour with one another. The King complains of his health and is rather low[22] but I never saw him so slim and active. He scuds in to dinner with Lieven on one arm and the Marchioness on the other. In the evening beautiful musick. His band playing all Rossini.

I breakfasted in my room this morning; at twelve we go to church which I hear lasts till half past two. The day is horrible. I should despair of being able to look at the sea. I must say I see no designs afloat for either of the sparks who are supposed to be objects, and no little projects of any sort or kind. De part et d'autre the gentlemen and ladies all seem to me to behave as well as possible.[23]

I long to talk for I cannot write all my *thinks*. Hart means to write if he comes home in time but for fear he should not here is the state of the case: the King doats on you and is dying to have you here next Saturday. He thought the day of the marriage undecided so did not ask you before. You will of course hear more of this.

Until the summer the sisters were in London. Like Lady Stafford, Harriet was also inclined to worry at Harriette's being still unmarried. As Granville's natural daughter, and without a dowry, her position was an equivocal one.

Trentham
Monday [c. September 1822]

It is quite drole to see Lady Stafford so degagée and I have just left her in the beautiful room with Pahlen, Mr Montagu, Mr Sneyd – all roaring with laughter at her jokes. She lets out il diavolo occasionally but he is upon the whole more kept back on this occasion than I ever knew him before. When we came out from dinner today she began praising Harriette very much and told me she felt a very great interest in her. That she must give me some good advice: 'None of these men will marry her, you had better not keep her amongst them. Can't you send her to Lady Gertrude Sloane[*] where there are hundreds of men with five thousand a year – or to Brighton with the Duchess of Leeds.' She went on to tell me of a Colonel I don't know what, and always the refrain 'its of no use keeping her amongst these *pipple.*'

I cannot say how difficult I found it to keep my countenance, but I saw in all the gloomy lines of her countenance, that as she was in earnest I could not dare to be in jest.

News was scarce for the rest of the year except for marriages and deaths, flirtations ('making a leg'), conquests and disappointments. The year 1823 began with the Duke of Wellington spending a few days at Wherstead in the middle of January, and Georgiana Morpeth giving birth to a daughter in London at the end of the same month, and of course Harriet was with her for the event. They were not apart until the end of August.

[Bruton Street]
Wednesday [20 August 1823]

I went last night to the Haymarket to hear Liston sing 'and when I hunts and asks for mercy, It does no good, but wice wersa.'[†]

Today is Lord Dudley's dinner. The Cannings &c &c. He has long been pregnant with it and the delivery will I have no doubt be proportionately painful to him. Lord Ashley[b] is out of town. I will tell him of Miss Howard [Blanche][‡] when I see him. I expect he means to marry her, he is so extremely fond of you all.

Lord Cornwallis's death vacates the Buckhounds. There was a rumour of its being intended to give the place to Lord Morley, which Granville tells me is a false one. He met Lady Holland driving who said 'Well, is your friend Lord Morley to appear drest in green, blowing a horn.' The picture is a pleasing one like

---

[*]Lord Morpeth's sister.
[†]'And when I kneel and ax for mercy/It does no good – but wice worsay', a burlesque song from *Sure Mortal Man* was sung by John Liston in the operatic comedy *Sweethearts and Wives* by James Kenney.
[‡]Blanche Howard was thirteen years old.

the men who come forward to sing 'Hark! Hark!' in the melodramas. Adieu dearest of Ladies

> Your devoted servant.

[Bruton Street]
Friday morning [22 August 1823]

Lord Dudley's dinner was magnificent. The house to begin is magnificent though not in the best taste.* Plantations of hot house plants, a staircase, the walls being entirely built of looking glass so that as you walk up you see a dozen repetitions of yourself walking up with you – before and on each side. Large rooms, brilliantly lit, with too many pictures, too many looking glasses, too many painted blinds on them, but altogether more striking than any I ever was in excepting D[evonshire] L[?ansdowne] and C[?arlton] houses. The mangeaille, excellent and profuse, an army of servants in and out of livery. Nothing could look less at home than the little Lord himself in the midst of all this wonderful [illegible] sort of establishment, absent at the head of the table, polite to his domestics. His spirit rose as the hour of our departure arrived and for the last ½ hour he was very animated and entertaining.

[Bruton Street]
Thursday [28 August 1823]

We dined yesterday at Gloucester Lodge.† Lord Ashley means, I announce to you, to live with you 'like your son'. It is the way of all flesh, my dear. I wish Blanche joy.

We walked by moonlight. I with Mr C[anning]‡ and as five girls and Mrs C. had only Lord Ashley left to esquire them, the other sparks being gone to a soirée, they must I think have had a regular civil war amongst the bushes for him. The Ashley girls and Mrs and Miss C. are inseparable and their gaiety and good

---

*Lord Dudley's house was in Arlington Street.

†The Cannings' house, named after the Duchess of Gloucester who had lived there previously, stood on the exact site of the present Gloucester Road Underground station.

‡Canning had been appointed Foreign Secretary in September 1822.

humour cheer us up amazingly. To night we all junket to a public box at the Lyceum.[*]

[Bruton Street]
Friday morning [29 August 1823]

We went to the Lyceum last night, Mrs and Miss C, Lord Ashley and Mr Planta. It was very tedious and dull and consequently yawns and headaches on all parts. Lord A. does not make up the least to H[arriet] C. and prefers talking to Harriette Stewart, but it is our daughters he will throw his handkerchief to. I never saw any body so little inclined to matrimony as he is at present.

I hear Lady C[onyngham] told La Donna [Lady Morley] that the King 'has taken such a fancy to Lady Granville', and he has proved it is not verbiage for he sent a paper to Mr C. with the names of those he wished to have the Buckhounds, and Granville amongst them. I think this makes a prospect of something ere long more likely – but all this – dearest G – is senza dubito – most private and confidential – and burn it in the fire, that so nearly burnt me, in the days of my youth.

I have not a word more to throw at a dog – much less at my ever dear honored sister Morpeth.

Granville has just been in to my room – vide what follows in consequence – The King's list of names – sent to Ld Liverpool – of course not Mr Canning – with his (Granville's) entreaty that you will not let this fact transpire.

[Bruton Street]
Monday night [1 September 1823]

I am just come from the Haymarket.[†] I am afraid poor H C[anning] is a little wounded but any thing so unconscious or guiltless of being the cause as the other party concerned, I never saw. Luckily for her he sets off the day after tomorrow. I only hope she will not feed up this fantaisie during his absence. It will only prepare mortification and disappointment for her.

[*]To see *Too Curious by Half*.
[†]A farce that night at the Haymarket Theatre was *A Fish out of Water*, by Joseph Lunn.

Do you know what makes me enraptured at leaving London early tomorrow morning, it was the sight of Mary Berry! in a side box in a parisienne negligée with a clamorous touchy expression in her long forgotten face.

Real summer is come and Wherstead will be a paradise. I have had a most gracious note from the régnante [Lady Conyngham] begging me to go to the play with them some day this week.

[Wherstead]
[5 October 1823]

I know no news – I love you dearly – excepting that Lord Blessington is come to England saying to every body he meets: 'Do you know D'Orset? He is an excellent man. I have left him at Lyons to take care of Lady Blessington;* when she is old enough he is to marry our daughter.' So much for 'Husbands made easy'.

Wherstead
Sunday [October 1823]

You would be annoyed with such swarms of wasps and hornets – that I seldom am without one of these last and dozens of the first in my room. At Church this morning it really was too agitating to be obliged to sit still. I will write a line from Bruton Street tomorrow. I will be kind to the Maiden† of other days – but I never could much see where the duty we all think we owe her originates.

Rumours of an appointment for Lord Granville had persisted for the last few months, and now Canning, as Foreign Secretary, was to send him as Ambassador to The Hague. This would be only a temporary posting, with the Paris Embassy as the final destination.

[Bruton Street]
[11 October 1823]

I saw your dear boy yesterday evening. I only saw him for ten minutes and those so grudged by Mylady [Holland] who wanted

*The Blessingtons and Count d'Orsay constituted a *ménage à trois*, the latter being Lady Blessington's lover.
†Miss Berry.

to pump herself. He looks well and is more improved and beautified than any body I ever saw. Lord Holland is uncommonly well and Mylady runs about and prepared and ran about with water for me to wash my hands. 'She thinks she can walk round the Square if the Duke of Norfolk's porter will just bring out a chair for her for a few minutes.' It will be funny to see her sitting in state upon the trottoir.

Now my beloved Lady Morpeth and dearest Lord M, listen but first let me tell you that I write in the face of Mr C[anning]'s injunction *not* to mention for a few days, even to you, what I am big with and must therefore entreat your discretion till I release you from it. Lord Clancarty sent his démission on the 6th and Granville will be appointed to the Hague as soon as some matters of etiquette are got over. I listen to nothing but the real advantage of this – in every way – and to me a spring passed in the performance of a very quiet duty instead of London dissipation, four miles from the open sea, and with the hope you may perhaps, after all the accouchements, come to join us there, has its charms, and to those considerations which indeed turn only upon the degree of absence from you which must necessarily be at times, I shut my eyes and thoughts. Of the time of our going or anything else I have no account to give for I know nothing beyond the fact.

Your adorable son is just gone. I could not resist telling him. I know he is to be trusted.

During the next two months the Granvilles were on the move with country house visits to the Bathursts at Cirencester, the Wilmots at Calton, the Littletons at Teddesley, the Baths at Longleat, and a fortnight at Saltram with the Morleys.

Bruton Street
Sunday [? 12 October 1823]

As we set out at six tomorrow and near ninety miles to go to Cirencester, I prepare my despatch today.

Lady Holland has sent for me, but I cannot go to her. My

[171]

thoughts are all dutch. I really think I shall be very happy there – if you will come (Granville, George and I are certain you will) – about the middle of July, two months of sea bathing before Castle Howard. In October we shall follow the Court to Brussels.

Saltram
Friday [17 October 1823]

We arrived here last night. This morning I have been walking with Lady Morley to the river which was waving, and saw the sea and inhaled it with delight. The place looks excessively pretty and the weather is delicious. They are now all mounting their horses and no body has even hinted at a side saddle, or wheeled vehicle for me. Tout est bien pourvu que cela dure. We dine today at half past five as all but Lady Morley and myself are going to the play at Plymouth to see Miss Brunton, whom they all rave about. The library is a delightful room. I am quite of a heap with the improvements. Lady Morley is an amazing love in her usual rapturous gaiety and running about for mere joy.

They are all gone – frisking away upon kicking poneys and heavy war horses. I am (do I live to tell it) alone in the house and I have persuaded Lady Morley to go to the play – and now like a sensible woman I am going to stroll about upon my ten toes.

Saturday

Cela ne dure pas. How peculiar it is; I tell them honestly I hate junketting and mark what follows. At half past one Lady Morley is so obliging as to take me out in her whisky to some far distant precipice. The happy Earl [Morley] flings his reins upon the neck of his volonté and does and goes où bon lui semble. The weather is quite delicious, my health robust and my spirits very low. Dear G, I mean to have a low little carriage to drive you down to the sea every day, but on a straight dutch road, broad and unvolatile as the natives. I do not believe there is a single hill in Holland.

I open my letter to tell you that I am enchanted. I have giggled round the new rail road, sans peur et sans reproche. I never did see any thing so beautiful.

Tuesday [21 October 1823]

We are not yet at liberty to talk of our plans but all our minor ones must yield to the necessity Mr C[anning] says there is for our being off before the meeting of Parliament. We shall in consequence go from hence to town but our stay here will be prolonged till the end of next week as it is a great object to Granville to see as much as he can of Mr Canning who is most unfortunately so unwell, that he is now getting up for the first time since he has been here and will probably be unequal to society and *talk* for some days longer. All that we shall be able to perform is one week in Staffordshire where Granville will be able to transact his Shropshire business from Teddesley.

It is very pleasant and comfortable here and on physic days I am allowed to bide at home. I cannot believe in my avenir. The hurry of it adds to a feeling of its being a dream.

Thursday [23 October 1823]

Mr Canning is better but still very weak and almost entirely keeping his room. I think it was so very good natured of him to go to the Plymouth play last night. He had not appeared all day – had not been equal to dining with us – but as he did not wish quite to break Borino's heart he went – only staid an hour. He was very much applauded for his pains.

[October 1823]

Charles Ellis has, like me, knelt for a morning and obtained it. The Earl is gone in his buggy to Plymouth. All the rest to Mount Edgcumbe. Having seen it I could better spare this junket than any other.

I have been walking down to the full tide, turning my thoughts and tossing them as the haymakers do their hay, but I cannot define the different degrees of different feelings I have about the future. I would give all I possess to talk to you for one half hour, there are so many little things which it is easier to say than to write. I am sure Granville likes it which is more than half the battle, and I think I shall when I am once there.

Mr C. is quite well again. The girl is marvellously unpopular amongst the sparks. Mrs Canning has been very amiable and facile à vivre. We have neighbours every day, chiefly 'Knavish and militious characters' as Lady Morley calls them. In the evening she heads a round game – you should have heard Mr C. and her bawling 'my sow pigged' at one another. The sober minded and elderly, C. Ellis, Mrs C. and I, écart. Granville reads his book, Lord Morley sleeps.

Saltram
[October 1823]

When our plans are more regularly dated, we shall be able to see more daylight perhaps. But time is swallowed up and today we dine at five to go to the ball. I really have hardly time to blow my nose, for the evening is all active service, every woman expected to do her duty.

I sometimes think of going up England in a chay.

Saltram
Thursday [? 30 October 1823]

I have liked even the boating to the breakwater and the Plymouth ball, yet no words can describe the delight of the day I am now in complete possession of, impassable, impossible rain *set in* from the early dawn, no question of junketting.

Yesterday we went to the ball. The two Hts* danced till past one. We of the middle ages played écarté. We were twice on the point of being over turned, once into the Lary on our way home, lamps out, blind horse, drunken post boy. Howard obliged to get out and lead the horses, but here we are safe and sound, nothing impending but the St Germans. Mr Canning has a bad cold owing to the quantities of Plymouth he was obliged to perform yesterday.

---

*Harriet Canning and Harriette Stewart.

[Bruton Street]

10 [December 1823]

We are bidden to the Pavilion from the 24th December to the 2nd of January. If you will just run over in your mind my boys' holidays, the children who will have about three days of us, and those the high days, of Dukes &c and new gowns &c &c, all to be ordered *now* when I have hardly a moment to spare. Were the object a more interesting one you may sum it up to what amount of désagrément you please.

Wherstead

Friday [19 December 1823]

The joy of being here again with all my children. Suzy is une femme charmante, Dody a great warm hearted shrewd clumsy girl. The boys are very nice satisfactory little men. They are quite wild with joy at the prospect of the Hague.

I am so pleased Mrs Arbuthnot[b] is coming on Sunday. As I hear she plays at whist all night with the two Dukes – and scolds violently – I have a slight hope that she goes out shooting.

Wherstead

Sunday [21 December 1823]

Yesterday nos fiers chasseurs were kept at home all day by the badness of the weather. Today we are expecting two Dukes, the Arbuthnots, C. Greville and Henry de Ros.

We mean to be here again the 9th or 10th of January till the 20th, and then in town till we go, which I hope will not be before the beginning of February.

Wherstead

Monday [22 December 1823]

We got over our dinner and soirée very well. His R.H. is as happy as a King with his whist and his chasse. They started at half past ten this morning. The day has been quite beautiful. I expect the return to be something quite enormous.

Mrs Arbuthnot and the Duke of Wellington are innocent à

[175]

force d'étre scandalous, it must be harmless or too bad. She is a pretty woman and not a foolish one but uninteresting and unattractive (to me, soit entendu) to the greatest degree. The dandies all behave very prettily.

They are just come in, in raptures. Never was there such a chasse, 900 head, 12 guns. The Duke of York is really ranting with joy as he has killed more than he ever did before, 128 head.

Pavilion
Saturday [27 December 1823]

I have been all this morning on the Chain Pier which is quite delicious. Granville has been cantering with the prima donna [Lady Conyngham]. Last night we had musick again in the Red Room. Mrs Hope came and engrossed the sparks, namely H[enry] and C[harles] Fox. Great enquiries about you and yours. The Duke [of Wellington] went to Althorpe this morning, he of Montrose is to supply his place.

Sunday

I think la régnante out of spirits. The King's kindness is quite moving. He wanted me to send for my girls and said he would lodge them in the Pavilion. It is not feasible but I expressed my very proper gratitude. There is one very distressing novelty, owing I suppose to his improved health: we stand till we are all ready to drop. He scarcely ever sits down himself and forgets to bid us. The Duke of Clarence has a soupçon of gout in his knee, Lord St Helens ditto, the King ditto, Granville occasional twinges, the Duchess of Clarence a des crampes, fat lazy Lady Erroll who is a great dear, aches all over and is ready to die of it. The rest of us have over eat ourselves.

We are to have Rossini tomorrow evening. The King told Lady Cowper and me that he cries for joy when he thinks how pleasant it is.

Pavilion
Tuesday [30 December 1823]

We had Rossini last night. He must have been very much pleased with his reception. The King was quite enraptured at hearing him.

[176]

His singing is delicious, so much and such varied powers of expressing whatever he pleases. He is a fat sallow squab of a man but with large, languishing eyes and des traits which justify his thinking himself, as they say he does, something very irresistible. We gave him in our turn lots of Handel, the Coronation anthem, &c.

Tonight we are to have a great assembly. Adieu dearest.

Pavilion
Wednesday [31 December 1823]

We dined in the large room yesterday. I was emancipated from my Dukes by the encreased number and the departure of York, and had Mr Luttrell by me. In the evening we had all Brighton, des figures incroyables. Lady Sandwich oppressively vivacious, Mrs Hope rather touchy, Sir Hudson Lowe with the countenance of a devil. Lady G[eorge] Seymour looking, as the King truly says, like an old soubrette in a play.

I am now going to walk on the pier. I am sorry to write you such dull letters from hence but you see my dear G, how little matter or vanity there is. Bless you, dearest.

[To the Duke of Devonshire]   Pavilion
1 January [1824]

I think you may like 'Nine days at Brighton, by Viscountess Granville'. So here goes. We arrived here on the 24th in time for dinner. The King received us more than graciously. I never saw him in such health and spirits. He scarcely ever sits down or is still for a moment, but allows us. No legs but royal ones could otherwise endure. The company assembled were the Duke of York, who adores us, breakfasts en trio with us every morning, says Wherstead is the best house in England, and my toilette the most perfect. Partiality could no further go. The Duke of Clarence, the Duchess, a very excellent amiable, well-bred little woman, who comes in and out of the room à ravir, with nine new gowns (the most loyal of us not having been able to muster above six) moving à la Lieven, independent of her body. Lord and Lady Erroll with faces like angels, that look as if they ought to have

[177]

wings under their chins. She is a domestic, lazy, fat woman, excédée with curtseying and backsliding. Lord and Lady Maryborough, a very agreeable woman, with a fine back and very plausible ugliness. The usual Dukes and gentlemen-in-waiting. Lord Exeter, who pays no attention to Lady Exeter, who, nevertheless, is as handsome and as delightful as ever.

On Christmas Day we processed into the chapel, where the service was really divine, but what with heat and emotion very over powering. I went after it to Lady Conyngham, and saw her Christmas gifts, which made my mouth water, and made me almost wish for a situation. A magnificent cross, seized from the expiring body of a murdered bishop in the island of Scio. An almanack, gold with flowers embossed on it of precious stones. A gold melon, which upon being touched by a spring falls into compartments like the quarters of an orange, each containing different perfumes. I returned like Aladdin after the cave, only empty-handed, which, I believe, he was not.

Our evenings have since passed much the same. The King has almost given up cards. The Red Room is always open and the band always playing. On Monday we had Rossini. The King all graciousness to him. He sang, which went to our musical hearts, 'Otello' and 'Figaro', &c. but the courtiers and the rest of the society were indignant at his familiarity. Being fat and lazy, and consequently averse to standing, he took a chair and sat by the King, who, however, gave him the kindest reception, and, less petit than his suite, understood the man, and treated him as his enthusiasm for music disposed him to do. I hope to hear more of him, for it is an unspeakable pleasure.

We have had one assembly, all Brighton. To-night there is a child's ball. Nothing ever equalled the King's kindness. You see I am quite touched.

Now, my dearest brother, for our plans. The first of February probably, not a day later, Granville, I, Ralph Abercromby, and Mr Jones, the private secretary, start for Calais. From thence we shall move leisurely to Brussels, and then go to the Hague to an hotel. Adieu, dear, dearest brother. The King does nothing but regret you. He says you are the life and soul of the Pavilion. La Marquise raves of you. The Duchess of Bedford comes with her children for the ball to-night, if the Duke is well. There is nothing like the zeal of a Whig lady. Lady Tankerville wrote a delightful letter to Lady Cowper. 'Lady Jersey never writes to me. She writes every day to the Duke of York, and would give her eyes, the only good thing she has left, to write to the King.' True woman's parenthesis.

[Bruton Street]
3 January [1824]

We landed here at half past three yesterday, dined tête-à-tête without dressing upon partridge and rice pudding, read till ten, played at chess till near one. Balancez this with the Pavilion account et jugez. Our favour went crescendo to the last. He hopes to have another squint at me before I go, and if he is not well enough to encounter the opening of Parliament, -this I fear will be at Brighton again.

The child's ball was beautiful. Near one hundred of them, neither crowd nor heat. The King was engrossed with the Bedford children. He saw one of her boys looking at his order of the Golden Fleece, and asked him what he thought that order was. 'Chinese I suppose'. We did not look quite pleased.

[Bruton Street]
[early February 1824]

We are almost at the end of our labours, but now comes the taking leave of every body, answering letters of those who write and do not come to town. I am half distraite in my shift, having had Lady Stafford, malgré the shift, for an hour, carriage at the door, Lady Harrowby waiting, three letters to write, Lady Holland just come. Plaignez-moi. Bless you.

[Bruton Street]
[mid February 1824]

I never saw Granville as well as he is now, in such spirits, and looking so brisk and clear. Our journey will be luxurious, and to the great happiness of the darling girls we take them with us. Mr Jones and Ralph will go in the britscka every morning to air the inns for us.

[Bruton Street]
[late February 1824]

We are just setting out, my beloved sister. I do not know how my nerves would have stood parting with you. I feel quite well and calm this morning, but the fatigue and worry of these last days have been very *unstringing*. Lady Harrowby and Georgiana [Ellis] were des mauvais moments. I love the latter as if she were my child, and I think her one of the most perfect of human beings. I look forward to writing to, and hearing from, you as the great pleasure in store for me. G, as always, yours with the most devoted affection.

Calais
26 [February 1824]

Half past two. We breakfasted at Dover between six and seven, and here at eleven. The sea very rough and the wind very cold. Granville and I in high health on the deck, all the rest in the cabin as sick as dogs. We have since been walking over this pretty, gay, little town. I could not resist shopping, and send you the result — a fairing from Calais, price two francs. We are all as well as possible, the sick all the better for it.

The Hague
Thursday [4 March 1824]

The hotel we are in is not very comfortable, but it is a pied-à-terre. We are all so well that nothing appears to me a grievance. Were it not for this, we should be somewhat discomposed at finding so much etiquette and ceremony expected from us immediately. Granville must go in a coach-and-six, with State liveries, to present his credentials. I am to receive the Hague world tomorrow and sit like a queen, having them all presented to me. I hope we shall, after these two killing duties, be allowed to go our own way for a time, as we have our house to prepare.

Friday

We are all bent upon getting into our house as soon as possible, as this hotel is almost too bad to bear, as noisy as the 'White Horse' in Piccadilly. Bad dinners, worse beds.

[180]

The English society is soon disposed of. My comments are entirely between ourselves. Lady Francis Osborne, who has been more than kind and useful to me than I have words to say. She knows every body, every custom, every shop, every Royalty, and every drug. She seems excellent and amiable, bearing wretched health with exemplary patience; but (fatal word and pray secret) she is tiresome, in a fever about trifles, and talking incessantly about nothing, with great confusion in her own ideas, and always taking hold of mine by the wrong end.

Mr Chad, merry, intelligent, devoted, the idol of the Hague, and a great addition to our little dinner Diplomacy.

The authorities of the town, and their wives. What shall I say of them? Broad, respectable, matter-of-fact people, that can never offend or please one.

Granville has been to Court. They were gracious in the extreme, but a degree of form! He went in one coach-and-six, the attachés following in another, with an escort of cavalry. The whole (His Ex. excepted), looking very ginger bread. I go on Thursday, then come three days of grand representations, all Holland pouring in.

Ten o'clock, Thursday evening

I have had lots of them tonight, the Nuncio with his gold cross; all the maids of honour. I am quite parched with talking, I am the pink of civility, but I remember Lady Harrowby's advice and do not let myself go to any likes and dislikes, but, like the sun (rather a dim one by the way), I shine on all alike. Granville acquits himself à ravir, talks incessantly to the Dips., bows them in and out, looks uncommonly well. I wish you could have heard us at dinner today, how we chattered and laughed by the waters of Babylon. Mr Chad is really extremely amusing.

My Court gown has been tried on and fits, my new shoes ditto, and I am consequently in particularly good sorts. I will send you a sketch of my presentation tomorrow.

This morning I went all over diamonds and black satin to Court. A little grand-chambellan leads me from the door to an ante-room, where four dames d'honneur receive me, till the folding doors open and I walk in alone to the Queen, standing in the middle of a very large and handsome salle d'audience. She is a shy, quiet, well behaved woman, in miserable health and thinner than Mme de Lieven. We talk of our Royal family, of the size of my house, and of the weather, a little back door opens and the King [William I] drops in. Five minutes more small Royal talk, and then I back out with a train five yards long, squiddle a little with the grand-maître, and that is all that belongs to my duties vis-à-vis the Court.

On 30 March 1824 the Duchess of Devonshire died at the Palazzo Spada in Rome where she had been living for several years. The Duke of Devonshire, who had liked her and had been extremely kind to her, was with her at her death.

[The Hague]
Sunday [11 April 1824]

My brother's letter, with an account of the poor Duchesse's death, arrived this morning. It has shocked us very much, she had so much enjoyment of life and I feel so unhappy and anxious about poor Mrs Lamb, it will be a severe blow to her. It also brings back past times to one's mind, and many nervous and indefinable feelings. This is a bitter cup, dearest sister. Of course for some days we shall not stir out of the house, or see any one in it.

[To the Duke of Devonshire]   [The Hague]
[? June 1824]

I will plunge at once into my subject but telling you that one word breathed would be the ruin of me, and thus I throw myself upon your generosity. What is not known must never be known – Mr Canning's intention of removing Granville to Paris, probably this autumn, certainly next year. But it is of the utmost importance that this move should appear, when it happens, to be an unpremeditated one, and in fact we are here for the purpose of making it appear so. I know I may trust you and think I shall please you; the united strength of these convictions no woman was ever known to resist.

For my own feelings, they are selfishly fear of any change of a place and life I like so much, dread of all the worries and duties of Paris, late hours, grande parures, visits, presentations, all my favourite aversions. Then comes the thinking Granville will prefer it, that my children will have better masters. Then mingled pleasures and pains. Sir Charles Stuart's house and gardens, the laxative nature of the Seine water, English physicians, French ladies of distinction.

Summing up – sufficient for the day, and a most sagacious resolution to enjoy the present and resign myself to the future.

God bless you, dearest brother. When you hear of the appointment you must act surprise to the life or I am undone.

Lord Francis Osborne, his wife, son and daughter, were living at The Hague, perhaps for reasons of finance. Their son, George, fell in love with Harriette Stewart. There was some hesitation on both sides of the family, prompted by lack of money and Harriette's ambiguous birth. The couple were married on 21 October at The Hague. George later became eighth Duke of Leeds, but by then Harriette was dead.

[The Hague]
[? June 1824]

Lady Francis puzzles me to death. I am tempted to pencher to the admiring side. Granville (who likes her extremely) has been arguing the point of her superiority of character. He says (and I three quarters agree with him), that her conduct is regulated by an uncontrollable determination to follow all her inclinations. That she is born with good ones is no *merit* of hers. She does what she always does, following her inclination. She is a person who dreads *scenes*, and would rather arrive when everything is a little subdued; no consideration out of herself gives motives to her actions but we wait to see her, sacrificing her own tastes for those of others (not to think her excellent, good tempered, attaching and free from all humbug) before we think her sublime.

Now for an example. Granville gave it. I have no wish to be Ambassadress in Paris, am quite insensible to the éclat of the situation, had rather potter on here. Well, this is not *character*, this is not *merit*. I am born so, my tastes are made that way. I may be all the better and my friends may like me more for being so constituted, but it is no effort, consequently no virtue, in me. I consult my own happiness and set my wishes by it. Now supposing that I go to Paris, overcome my regrets, combat my inclinations, perform all the duties of the situation with cheerfulness and good temper – that is *character*, that is merit as far as it goes because it is making self give way and acting in that manner for the sake and bien être of others.

This is the way that en bien et en mal admiration and applause are dealt out with so little fairness or measure. Do not think me insensible to Lady Francis's perfections. I love and esteem but I cannot *quite* admire her. Now supposing there was a question of visiting a divorced woman. If we went to see the black sheep, there would in such an act be more of kindness and dread of giving pain than a laxity of real moral principle. If Lady Francis stayed away, there would be more of its being a bore to go and the not caring two pence if the woman was vexed or not than of real morality. Yet the world would set this down under the head of principle and chastity, and judge us accordingly. I could go on upon this theme for ever. She is made of such excellent stuff, that coldness given by nature and selfishness by education lead to no worse result than preventing a very close examination of her character, magnifying her blameless life into a heroic one. When Francis went to Spain she was as comfortable as an old shoe, yet how many people looked upon her as something little less than an Indian widow burning on the pile?

[The Hague]
Thursday 15 [July 1824]
We have had a trying time of it these last three days. It has only been a stronger proof to me how very much they do like each

[184]

other; she has been crying her eyes out, and he is worn to the bone. The answer cannot come till Saturday,* perhaps not then. I trust to his naturally buoyant spirits and her wonderfully happy, easy nature to carry them through if it is an unfavourable one. I shall be the wictim dearest Lady Morpeth. I do love him so much and he has behaved so perfectly throughout. I think it will certainly be, they are both so happy, so sanguine, so contented with their prospects, that it has won Granville over to the cause, and you will see how entirely Lord Francis refers the decision to us.

My dearest of all dear sisters, I pray I may keep my little mind. I see nothing but you stepping out of the steamer. It is such vast, such overwhelming delight to me and you will find us all, I trust, povera sì, ma contenti. I can write no more. I can think no more my head is quite gone. Kiss Lord Morpeth for me – see how entirely demented I am.

[The Hague]
[Probably 20 July 1824]

I am only going to write you a few lines. I never saw any thing like the happiness of Osborne and Harriette, excepting mine when I think you will be here to witness it. What will it be to me to see you and yours and the little Governor† on the 31st. George Stewart brings him here and they will probably cross with you. Dear dearest G, is it possible.

The Morpeths stayed at The Hague for about four weeks.

The Hague
Sunday [19 September 1824]

I miss you more here, than I did in the bustle of perpetual movement – regret is the same every where. I try and fill up the

---

* A letter, asking leave to marry, had been written to Lady Francis at Spa. The reply, which was received about 20 July, was in the affirmative.
† The Granvilles' eldest son.

immense aching blank the loss of you makes in my day. The impossibility of being as happy without as with you is in fact a blessing, so I merely try to take from it its bitterness, without minimising.

The news of the King of France's death arrived this morning.[*] I have seen the Osbornes – very gracious – and Lord Francis has made Harriette a most beautiful cadeau, a writing desk magnificently worked in green tortoise shell and silver, the implements in fillagree. The best news I have is that the necessary arrangements for the marriage will all be made on the 2nd. This is an unspeakable comfort.

We are all going into rusty mourning for the King. I am in despair at the necessity of buying fresh mourning. It is not however bombazeen here; ten days moyen deuil and ten days petit deuil, rather impolite meseems to have no grand deuil at all for him.

The Hague
Friday [? 1 October 1824]

Granville set out for England at six o'clock this morning! It seems to me like a dream. He is to see Mr Canning at Walmer, to return to town with him, remain there two or three days, go to Paris to congratulate[†] and hopes to be here again on the 15th. What our further and immediate moves after that are to be I cannot know till I hear from him after he has seen Mr C. who still enjoins secrecy as to our final destination as he wishes Sir C. Stuart not to hear it announced till he has received his recall in form from the F[oreign] Of[fice].

The Hague
Monday [11 October 1824]

The last letter I had from him [Granville] was written two hours before he left London. He had been dining at Windsor, sitting

---

[*]Louis XVIII died on 16 September.
[†]This was to congratulate Charles X on his accession as King of France.

over écarté and Patience with the King, Duke of Wellington, Mme de Lieven, la Marquise. He had been to Cartwright who gave him a raging tooth ache. Now my dearest G, I am desired not to tell any body what I am going to tell you. I must entreat you not to tell or write it to my brother as Mr Canning is particularly anxious that (however expected) the fact of our immediate departure from Brussels should not be known in England from authority till Granville has communicated it to the King of the Netherlands. The fact is we are only to stay in Brussels long enough to take leave and Mr C. wishes us to take possession of our house at Paris on the 1st of November. Have the goodness to say that our plans after Granville's return are not fixed and only to write the fact of the special mission.

We are going on very happily here. Osborne and Harriette, happier every day. Lord and Lady Francis all kindness and graciousness.

Caroline Lamb is in a much calmer state at Brocket and under the surveillance of two nurses. William is with her de temps en temps but lives chiefly with Lord Melbourne at Whitehall.

The hope of seeing you next spring is the bonne bouche of my avenir.

[The Hague]
19 [October 1824]

No words can describe my happiness at having Granville here again. I think I suffered more from nerves during the last fortnight than I ever did before in my life. In the midst of today's excessive joy I have a shattered, worn feel in consequence.

I have been looking over the plans of our house in Paris. It seems an incomparable one. He has secured boxes for me at the French Opera, Italian Opera, and Théâtre Français. Mme de Gontaut* has promised me advice about all Court matters.

*Governess in the royal household.

The Hague
Friday [22 October 1824]

I have been hurried to death but today I feel all my troubles subsiding. Granville has felt the fatigue he went through. He has suffered with pain in the face, head, and a degree of languor. Every moment I have [? been away] from him, I have been with Harriette. [The] marriage went off beautifully. I never [saw] her look so pretty, in a wreath of orange flowers and her muslin and lace gown. I went to her this morning and found her rayonnante. Her house is the prettiest thing I ever saw, full of comforts and ornamented with her presents. Your tea chest the middle one of her drawing room chimney. I leave them with a perfect conviction of their happiness. Lord Francis was all kindness. Lady F. (after being so) relapsed into such selfish ungraciousness during and after the ceremony, yet they are very good friends.

Brussels
Monday [15 November 1824]

We are just setting out, my dearest sis. We hear the house will admit us, but that it is in a terribly délabré state. Sir Charles having emptied the rooms to fill innumerable large packing cases, which are all standing about in the ante-rooms and passages. The dining room is supported by props, having had a tumble.

When they arrived in Paris, Granville was fifty-one, Harriet close on forty, and they had been married fifteen years. The house was in a bad state of repair and they would have to move out the following spring to allow for renovation. The garden was a constant happiness to Harriet. But for one who had never bothered overmuch about dress, she now had to contend with the daunting frivolity of the élégantes, *that group of women predominantly of high birth and little brain – with what there was of it largely concentrated on dress,* coiffure *and theatrical entertainment.*

[188]

Saturday [20 November 1824]

How shall I begin, where shall I begin, dearest of sisters? I am delighted but then I have as yet plunged into nothing but a luxurious house, a delicious little garden, and the Théâtre Français. I have not seen a soul, and pass my days with Granville and the children. Were you to see me in my new apartments you would not believe in me. We have a luxe of rooms, all looking to the garden with the bright sun of l'Eté de St Martin shining upon them. If the repair was equal to the space and the beauty of this palace it would be perfection, but there are holes in the floor big enough to let me through, props to keep them up. All this must be set to rights in the spring.

We arrived to dinner the day before yesterday, and spent the evening in exploring and admiring. Yesterday morning I got up early and had an hour or two of unqualified bore, measuring and ordering. Heaven help my pocket! The first thing to be done was my court dress, then a barege gown for dinners, a blouse made of épine for soirées, a merino redingote, chapeau de velours, turban de joie, bonnet de blonde, in short my dear a complete trousseau. The result is that I am already half an élégante, and my person is like those molodrames got up at Covent Garden – no merit in the piece but saved *from* being damned by machinery.

At twelve I went into the garden with my girls who are in a state of enchantment. At two I went with Granville a delicious walk in the Champs Elysées. This morning I tried on the articles and have been out ever since walking and returning my visits. My only fear is expense, and think what dress is alone. Lord Hardwicke gave [his daughter] Lady Elizabeth [Stuart] 1,000£ a year, which she spend in bedecking herself!

I vary twenty times a day. Sometimes I am in transport, sometimes in despair. On Tuesday my toils begin with my presentation. My dress is come home, the size of the head dress composed of black gauze and jet, the gown barege lined with silk. I should lose cast were it an inch shorter or narrower. My evening cap is come home, black silk currants and tiffany leaves au naturel, my new bonnet d'une élégance rare, the feather of the heron, the veil of the blonde. If you can imagine me a gig it is your ignorance my dear.

I am to receive Paris three nights running after my presentation. I am then asked to a great dinner at Court and desired to name my company, which is to consist of twelve English of the highest rank. Lord Granville cannot go if I do not name him.

[Paris]
25 November [1824]

Private and most Confidential

My dear, French people are – what shall I say? – what I don't like, as most comprehensive. They now show themselves to me at their best, for they are extremely civil and prévenants, but there is a fond of ill breeding, insolence, conceit, and pretension qui se fait jour through all their countenances, manners, and attentions. Now let me say that I believe the exquisite set to which it is my good fortune to be admitted is the worst specimen of the kind. It is the pendent to Ladies Jersey, Gwydyr, Tankerville, Mrs Hope &c. They begin by thinking themselves ce qu'il y a de mieux au monde. Their conversation is all upon dress, the Opera, Talma. There is not as much mind as would fill a pea shell. They are pedantic and frivolous, with the most outrée consideration of rank and character accompanied with something – only like their houses – into which you grope your way, in the dark, with no body to show it you, smelling of onions and gutters. The fact, they will scarcely look at an English man or woman out of their own peculiar set, will not admit a French one who is not à la mode. I walk in, am put on a couch. Up comes a jeune duchesse or an old marquise and gives me five minutes, such as I to my shame have sometimes given to a country neighbour.

Now for a few of les phrases d'usage, which from their tone and manner give me a wish to hurl the cushions of their couches at their crêpé'd heads. 'Vous aimez Paris.' 'Vous-vous plaisez parmi nous', neither as doubt or question. 'Lady une telle est bien, même charmante: on ne la soupçonnera pas d'être une anglaise.' 'Vous avez des enfants: vous êtes bein heureuse de pouvoir les former à Paris.' 'J'ai passé chez vous' (with a 'Think of that' look), and a hundred such – nothing in the letter, all in the spirit.

[190]

But, O Lady Morpeth, it is the woman made by Herbault,[*] Victorine and Alexandre, the woman who looks to see if you have six curls or five on the side of your head. The woman who talks, dictates, condescends and sneers at me. It is odd that their effect upon me is to crush me with the sense of my inferiority whilst I am absolutely gasping with the sense of my superiority. What a thing to write, but it is only to you. But the truth is they have an aplomb, a language, a dress de convenance, which it is as impossible for me to reach as it would be for one of them to think five minutes like a deep thinking, deep feeling English woman.

I have not time to put half my thoughts together, but I wish you to know them. It has done me as much good to write them as it would have done to be blooded in a high fever. Let me wind up by stating that house, garden, my husband, my children, the clear, exhilirating climate, the animating gaiety of all out of doors spectacles, the endless amusement and variety of the theatres (Pasta alone is, whilst she lasts) a happiness. The sort of enjoyment it will be to have you often with me, are more than compensations for occasional vexation and weariness of spirit. Remember it is only to *you* that I shall ever unburthen myself.

I will tell you what is comfortable here. Today, and all post days in future, I send word to the outer gate that I am out. This is quite understood here. They think a great deal of expédier le courier, and I have had hours of solitude which have restored my health and temper. This house, too, is as quiet as the depth of country, not a sound to be heard.

[Paris]
[8 December 1824]

Our state presentation is put off on account of the grand deuil – for six weeks, and I had today my audience particulière of Madame d'Angoulême.[†] She is as plump as a partridge and quite merry, uncommonly gracious, asked a great deal after Lady Morpeze, how many children, the names of your married daughters, &c &c. Where did you gain her affections? I am to go

[*]The fashionable milliner.
[†]Madame Royale and Dauphine, the only daughter of Louis XVI, married her first cousin, the Dauphin, Duc d'Argoulême.

[191]

to the Duchesses de Berri and Orléans* and then a holiday I hope till the great affair.

I have seen two or three little bits of élégantes at Mme de Gontaut's, all cut after the same pattern. Every body looks alike, and like nothing but the scene in Richard the 3rd when all the widowed queens meet to rail at the Lord's annointed. At the present writing I have two long crape weepers dangling down to my knees, from a huge black crape cap. I have not seen a soul here today as I was obliged to shut up and rest between the acts of my duties.

[Paris]
Monday morning [13 December 1824]
On Saturday we dined at a sumptuous feast at the Rothschilds'. He has married his niece, a pretty little Jewess, née coiffée (a very good thing in Paris), for, just out of her nursery big with child, she does the honours of her house as if she never had done any thing else.

Mrs and Miss Canning come on the 20th; I am delighted. They will be a great comfort to me, for going about alone and *unsupported* is tremendous. When you come Paris won't hold me, and I look to May literally as the month of promise. You will soon get into dress (it, alas! is essential) but there are invariable rules, which is a blessing; never to mind the effect, but to sit still and have it done right, as to a dentist.

[Paris]
[c. 17 December 1824]
I have been going on as usual, innumeral soirées, all much alike. The Government have agreed to repair us. I think they ought to furnish us also. Perhaps Mr Canning may say, as Lord Westmorland did in a large society of French here, 'Je voudrais si je coudrais.' And now let me tell you that your letter about Lady E. Stuart was as amusing to me as a new novel. I am sure, from what

*The Duchesse d'Orléans was the wife of Louis Philippe who would become King in 1830.

I hear, your account is quite a correct one, but her faults were blessings and I could learn as a trade her defects. Save the wig, my success would be à la longue as unbounded as hers. To avoid intimacy of communication and create none, all this will rub my back up the wrong way, but I think over my part so much that I must end by learning it.

I believe Lady Elizabeth at the end of ten years was not told so often as I have been already that she was charmante, remplie de grâce et d'esprit. I have not time to mince the matter, but shall I at the same or half the period have everybody's good word as she has? We shall see.

You are much altered if it does not give you pleasure to hear that Mme Magrini has just sent home my presentation gown, chosen by Juste, and a model of all that is most elegant. I think I shall do, for my last gown has been asked for as a pattern, which at Paris is the sort of triumph that gaining a battle is to a general.

Harriet's official reception as Ambassadress, her traitement, seemed to her a formidable hurdle with all that it meant in the way of precise length of dress, of headdress, of detailed instructions on curtseying and conversation.

[Paris]
[December 1824]

I cannot for the life of me help feeling nervous about my presentation, and why, because they all make such a rout about it. If I can but go on, but I know I shall. My only dread is that there is a sort of zest in novelty which makes exertion easier, and a sort of pleasure in success, which is not with me a very potent stimulus, but sufficient to keep off the mortal flatness of trouble, civility, dress, and unwearied exertion without it. The truth is that there is such a strong tide in my favour just now, that if it turns I am worse than a puddle. I hope in the character of the French. They are not exigeants – too full of themselves to depend upon another, too intent upon amusement to have leisure to bore their neighbours. I am like Princess Charlotte. If I were to die at the end of my first year I should be handed down to posterity as an exemplary ambassadress, but if I live, as I trust I shall, to give time to the natural faults of my character to come out, I tremble for my good name.

I found myself this morning feeling annoyed at my Court dress being too short on the sides, and very much pleased when Frédérique dressed me en cheveux today (as a rehearsal) to think it looked very well, and to hear Granville's compliments upon it. Is this the woman who would not have cared if she had been seen in an old tattered garment, with a masquerade red silk petticoat under it? Do not think en cheveux is my own idea. It is de rigueur for a presentation, and even old Madame [d'Angoulême] receives me with her old grey careworn head bristled up by Frédérique.

However here I am not wholly discontented with myself. I never taught my children so much and so regularly as since I have been at Paris. I have made myself rules with regard to them which I do not allow myself to transgress. William is becoming a very good little Latin scholar. I am not utterly lost to every thing but dress and dissipation. I am aware that dress has been a grievance and occupation to me that it would not have been to another. I saw the imperious necessity of it, and am learning it as a trade.

Now, Lady Morpeth, for a few facts. Mrs and Miss Canning and little Governor arrive on Monday. We lodge the two former in two of our drawing rooms below. I found such difficulties and impending storms attending my naming of English ladies to meet me at my traitement, that I was obliged to take the line of peeresses. The Duchesse de Damas presides at the dinner of the Dauphine's table and enacts her, making me sit on her right hand, Granville on her left. I go from the presentation at five to the dinner. I wish it was over to a ridiculous degree. I am to make a little phrase to the Dauphine about honour, and her virtues, and my gratitude, twelve ladies standing behind her.

Granville is to be presented tomorrow. The ceremony more formidable in proportion as his speech must be longer. He is looking uncommonly well and how beautiful amidst the little ugly Frenchmen it is not for me to say. I always knew what he was, body and mind, but both shine forth here like lemon juice before the fire.

Monday morning

You will be glad, my dearest sister, to hear that I feel well this morning. I shall be nervous till the ceremony is over. And now for my toilette. Diamonds are my weak point, and I have been obliged to borrow some as they tell me a quantity *must* be worn, and those who have not enough must and do borrow.

[Paris]
[21 December 1824]

I am now in such a bustle that I can write but one line. My presentation is thought of such consequence, how I dress, how I behave, how I curtsey, so commented upon, so discussed, that I feel I was going to be hung and all my reputation turning thereon. You would have laughed if you had seen my Aunt William's astonishment at me. 'My dear Lady G., when I recollect you at the Hague dressed like a housekeeper. Forgive me – just like a housekeeper.'

[Paris]
[23 December 1824]

I think you will not be sorry to hear that my labours are over, that my presentation traitement went off very smoothly. I was foolishly nervous and forgot my compliment, for which Madame was waiting, but I am assured I did not disgrace myself, and the delight of having it over, is beyond expression. The King is adorable and looked as if he disliked ceremony as much as I did. Madame gêne à force d'être gênée. The dinner was magnificent. I never can describe ceremonies but I hope you will be glad to hear that I never can think any thing formidable again.

Harriet having been officially received at Court could now settle down to her work as Ambassadress. It was said of her that 'Quietly determined and dignified, she was already showing the élite of the French society that she intended to hold her own, and that she refused to be dictated to or patronised by the fine ladies who were ready to despise her because she was English . . . On

[195]

*the occasion of her presentation to the French Court the train
which she wore was five yards long, it required no small
cleverness to manage it with grace . . . Lord Granville, when
presented, wore his hat, but whenever he said the words, "Le Roi,
mon Maître", he took it off, but replaced it immediately.'*[24]

[Paris]
7 January [1825]

The *thick* is over pour le moment. I have had great dinners to go
to every day – about four or five soirées every night. Madame and
the Palais Royal in the morning, my jour de l'an visits to return,
and in the midst of this I contrived to give myself a violent knock
on my head one day, and to tumble *up*stairs luckily on another,
and bruised myself all over.

Monday morning

I am now writing whilst Marie is lacing my stays, on my way to
Mme de Gontaut to see les Enfants de France* taking their
lessons.

Three o'clock.

Now this is comfortable, Lady Morpeth. I have taken off my
negligée, put on my bed gown, have nothing to do but a little no
how dinner in a close cap to meet a dozen dabs and then to bed.

I saw the darling Monseigneur and Mademoiselle at their
lessons, as naughty as possible and great loves. Did I tell you that I
took the little Governor on a Friday to a child's ball? He was
delicious, danced like a little Frenchman, and behaved like a little
Ambassador. At ten he retired into a boudoir to dress, attended
by about.a dozen little boys. I asked him how he got acquainted.
'Oh, as you all do. They say, "This is Lord Granville's son", and
then we shake hands.' I was amused by a conversation amongst
them yesterday. I took the three boys to Isabella Chabot's room;
as we were going in I heard Freddy say to Granville, "Brother, is
this one a prince?" "No, she's a common woman." "But what
must we do to her?" "Nothing, unless you like it."'

*These were the four-year-old Duc de Bordeaux and his five-year-old sister, Louise
de France, Mademoiselle, children of the widowed Duchesse de Berri and grandchil-
dren of the King.

[January 1825]

Now let me come to the pith of my story. The Earl of Clanricarde[b] is aux pieds de Miss Canning, and we are in daily expectation of the question. He is immensely rich, quite good-looking enough, clever and very gentlemanlike. The girl is determined in his favour, but if you mention this to any body, I am quite undone – that's all.

[Paris]
17 January [1825]

At Mme de Noailles' last night about twenty women came in, out of mourning for a noce. I wish you had seen or heard them, all as gaudy as peacocks, and screaming like them – red velvet toques with pink feathers, cherry coloured gowns covered with emeralds.

Mrs Canning's evening was more paisible. She went to the Italian Opera with Harriet where they had Lord Clanricarde all to themselves. He did not propose, but all but. He has, however, to our delighted knowledge, bought a magnificent set of diamonds, and is ordering a d° service of plate. De notre côté we have not been idle. Mrs Canning has provided lace veils, gown &c. so the ornamental part of the concern is in great forwardness.

[Paris]
7 February [1825]

Now, my dearest, for the great news of the year. Lord Clanricarde proposed and was accepted yesterday. I never saw any two people look so happy and radiant as they both did during the decisive conversation. I felt convinced, *only* from their countenance of the truth. His only flaw is said to be his fondness for low company, and this is in the power for the wife to correct. He is perfectly gentlemanlike himself, and takes to high company in the most promising manner.

I went to Court yesterday. The Duchesse de Berri had the gout and did not receive. The King and Madame were gracious and short – two good things.

[10 February 1825]

There are ebbs and flows in my tide, dearest. The last three days have been unusually severe. I wish you could see a diamond wreath Granville has given me. Lord Clanricarde and Miss Canning are the people I envy. They send excuses every where, and sit cooing in my drawing-room. I like him extremely, and so does she, which is more to the purpose.

[Paris]
Saturday 19 [February 1825]

I find as I proceed that Lady Elizabeth was much more popular with the French than the English and her great anxiety was to be well with the élégantes. Now this is my least – well with them, yes; but much with them, no. When they call I am all civility but I never think them the least necessary to my well being or in any way court their society. They are very much talked about and by some made up to, but every body agrees in thinking their parties and themselves the least pleasing part of the society.

I understand Lady Elizabeth's excessive culte of them; they had *made her* and if they had left her she would have fallen back upon home, something worse than having no husband, and to make her society sought she was reduced to bait her hook with these fashionables – and quite right to do so. Now whatever may be my faults or failures, I have not to work up the ladder to make myself une grande dame and I have a fonds of English society – shall continue to have – of the crack kind. The difference in short between us is that it put her into a fuss when [Prince] Leopold went to see her and I *see* that he is quite grateful to me for being very kind and gracious to him when he comes in of an evening. Dearest Sis, I am thinking louder than loud, more secret than secret, but I trust to your understanding and discretion.

Now my plan is this: to make my usual society of the best of the English here, the English that come d°, and any of the French who show a very strong propensity to come to me. In short the best and the most empressé of the grand ones. I mean to give many and large dinners, drums, and visiting cards to the mass of the English and if they complain, honestly and fairly to state that my small society is composed of my intimate friends. I find from many of the English this complaint of Lady E. that she asked them but sat apart with her own little set. Now I mean to be general in my general society. I think she must have done this in order to conciliate the élégantes. Perhaps she did not do it, but be that as it may, I am quite certain my plan will be the best for me and as she was popular to the greatest degree, hers was the best for her.

And now, dearest, our grand worry is about the house. We are in terror lest the Government should decide upon selling it. Granville has written a strong and most eloquent dispatch, deprecating it. The bare idea puts us into despair. There is none to be had half as good. It is the plum in the cake and the losing it would quite alter the whole footing of the Embassy.

I have now a most delicate piece of business to put into your hands. I would write to Hart *straight*, but it is easier for him to refuse you than me, therefore I wind about. I have a diamond wreath, necklace, chain and earrings. What would a woman have more? Why, variety, or something to dangle or to wear as a sash, or twist in my flowing – that is imprisoned – locks. The Sacre, my dear, the Sacre. I want to cut a dash, near my sister Excellences. Now the means. I cannot buy, to borrow I am ashamed – from any body but his Grace. I want to know if it is possible for him to lend me whatever it is the [late] Duchess left me conditionally, for the whole of my public career, or if that is not possible, for the Sacre only. Whatever I may be when I cease to be Ambassadress, these jewels would only be more than I want. Being Ambassadress they would be invaluable to me; every grain of finery is a blessing.

There goes. If he says Yes – I own the folly – I shall be enchanted. If No, I am an easy creature my dear, and shall not give it a second thought.

[Paris]
[March 1825]
But one line for I have been walking with Hart till this moment and am now going to look at the hôtel d'Eckmühl with him. It is a delicious day and I enjoy myself amazingly tho' we do drum on, as if there was no carême in the world.

Fassin came to see *my* diamonds yesterday. He was thunder struck and says the earrings are the finest but one he has ever seen in his life, but he laughed and said 'Mon étonnement est extrême car trois differentes dames ont passée chez moi (une d'elle duchesse) pour me dire que Monsieur le Duc vous avez apporté une parure bien brillante mais sans valeur car ce n'étais pas des vrais diamants, mais des pierres tirées d'une de ses terres dans le Derbyshire.' Thus my dear they conjectured that Hart had brought me large bits of Derbyshire spar, which I fobbed off upon them as diamonds!

I intend if any body questions me as to my *eternal* right to them, to say they are family jewels, that I believed he had always the intention of leaving them to be divided between you and me if he did not marry, but that he had brought them now, supposing they would be more useful to me here than at any other time. This is true as well as a pretty version. The only difference being that these will be yours and those meant for me are, I find, made away with. I am richly repaid for this, by being in possession of le gros lot now, and towards the end of the century (I hope), George's wife, a middle aged woman at that time I also hope, will appear in them. I send you a sketch of the addition I am going to make to the earrings as they are now. I hope you approve. The two diamonds en poire hold the large lower ones.

I must add one word more. I said to Hart yesterday, 'It is all very well now, the diamonds are mine now and G's hereafter if you do not marry, but if you do in the course of my stay [in Paris] I shall instantly send them to Her Grace.' He said, 'You are quite safe, but if I do, I protest I'll buy her a new set.' This is only to show you his kindness for alas, there is no danger.

Burn this letter. I should not like him to think I had repeated this last bit.

[Paris]
[March 1825]

With regard to the diamonds, dearest, I do assure you he has given them to me and they are mine, so much so that they are going to be added to and embellished today à mes dépens. The only embarrassing question that could be put would be: can you leave them to your children. The answer – no, they are entailed upon my sister, after my brother's death. The story is this but need not be stated, out of a court of justice.

The Duke had always the intention of leaving (according to the late Duchess's wish) his diamonds between his sisters. Chain and watch to me, necklace and earrings to you. He has trifled away the chain and watch (which Guilleret observes requires some compensation) this compensation I consider fully made by the possession of the diamonds (eventually yours) for they smart part of my career. If a body asks you: I hear the Duke has given your sister a magnificent parure of diamonds – Yes. Then how can he give family jewels? Because if he does not marry he had always the intention of leaving his jewels between us, instead of which he takes them to her now when they are more useful and acceptable than they could be at any remoter period. If he never marries he will leave them between us. By the word *between* is understood – I have them for the present, you for the future. If this is not (as I see he thoroughly understands it) giving us both his diamonds, I do not understand English. He wanted to send for four notaires to sign that if (however improbable), he marries, he will buy a new set for his wife, and thus my dearest you can see you are equally a gainer by his generosity, for in that case you would have the jewels all the same, to leave to the heirs of your body.

If instead of three loving relations we were three jews, this arrangement could not exist. I should be saying – but where is my lot in hard money? You would be saying – But how are you to ensure no damage being done to the stones? He would marry and cheat us. He sees it so entirely as I do, that he has written as follows to Abercrombie père: 'I meant to lend her the jewels, but I have thought it better to give them to her.' If he was to give you Chiswick to live in and enjoy as long as he lived, should you not look upon it as a present even tho' at his death it was entailed upon his heir?

At the beginning of April the Granvilles moved out of the Embassy house so that repairs could be carried out. They would not return to it until November. Meanwhile they settled in the hôtel d'Eckmühl, a hôtel particulier belonging to the turncoat, Marshal Soult, which Harriet thought magnificent. 'It is on the very utmost limit of the Faubourg St Germain,' she told her sister, 'with a large garden opening to the Boulevard.' The Coronation of the French King, endless entertaining, and her sister's visit now occupied her.

[To the Duke of Devonshire and Lady Georgiana Morpeth]
[Paris]
Thursday [31 March 1825]

We move on Saturday but now my dearest brother, to you upon real business. I have had long talks with William Lamb; he is kindness itself and (seas over) firmness personified. He thinks no body would have so much influence over Caroline as you, that you would be more likely to persuade her to a quiet submission to the plans now in contemplation than any body. *I* feel that for her own sake she will be inclined – for the alternative in resisting it will not *now* I am certain, bring William to yield, but must be a resource to harsher measures.*

I think you might hold out to her the different impression that her resigning herself to a separation and behaving well about it will make upon us all however she may have disgusted, offended, and estranged us. There never were a set of people upon whom *him*† and the remembrance of early days held such a clinging hold. I feel it by myself, she has a great deal still in her power to regain, but if she now defies, resists and exasperates, she is lost.

Sister Morpeth, the Coronation is now irrevocable for the 29th May – but what of that. I am beginning to be quite pénétrée with the kindness of the French ladies of distinction – va crescendo, daily. Dear adorable sister, how happy I shall be when I have you here.

*Lamb had come abroad leaving his brother Frederick to arrange a separation from Caroline to which she eventually consented, though not without fierce opposition. She had turned to her cousin, the Duke of Devonshire, for advice.
†Lord Byron.

[? Paris]
[6 June 1825]

The procession today was beautiful.* A bright sun and bright blue sky. Crowds of people but a broad space found for the procession.

First, myriads of priests, all in their full costume, walking in two rows and chanting. Then the Cross, with the higher orders of the clergy. Then the Duc de Chartres in uniform, a handsome boy, walking with his father and aides-de-camp. The Duke of Orléans† looking like thunder. Then the Dauphin and suite, looking hustled, his eyes fixed on his book. Then the King, pale, old, adorable. Then Madame, white hat and feather and pelisse. Then Berri, all over ermine. Then the Dames de la Cour, outrées, blown by the wind, overwhelmed by the crowd, fasting, perished, fatigued.

It is the first time this has happened in France, and the sensation is extreme. I thought it a very imposing spectacle, but the folly of supposing it a virtue.

[To the Duke of Devonshire]   [Paris]
[June 1825]

We are now in the very kernel of the fêtes and I notch them off as a prisoner does the days of his captivity. We have weathered the King's entry and the great affair at the Hôtel de Ville. The last was very splendid. Thousands of people, an immense locale, brilliantly lighted. The whole Court en grande tenue. The Duchesse de Berri dancing quadrilles in a space squeezed out of the multitude, and asking people, 'Fondez-vous comme beurre?' which she evidently did herself.

Here is Granville come home, dubbed Knight of the Bath.‡ The King wore the Garter at the Hôtel de Ville. I am dying for tonight's post to hear of adorable Lady Morpeth actually in motion. I am sure she will be happy here.

---

*The Coronation of Charles X took place in the Cathedral Church of Rheims. Granville attended the ceremony but Harriet makes no mention of being there, and it seems more likely that this letter refers to the *Entrée du Roi* in Paris and Notre Dame which took place on 6 June.

†The Duc d'Orléans would later succeed as King Louis Philippe; his son, the Duc de Chartres, was fourteen years old.

‡Granville had received the Grand Cross of the Bath. On 9 June the King of France invested him with it at the Tuileries.

[203]

I shall have tomorrow about twenty or thirty visitors not aware
of my plan and this is a sketch of what they will find. Myself and
Lady Gower in bottle green with capotes upon our heads.
Comtesse Morley in a white muslin negligée with d°. Theresa
[Villiers] in a tea coloured pelisse, white bonnet with pink buds.
The whole suite of rooms open, furniture uncovered and I must
say for Eckmühl it is the most beautiful suite I know. Orange
trees and all the flower pots arranged on the terrace. The garden
(for today real summer is in) is in the greatest beauty, full of lilac
and all sorts of blossom. In the small dining room will be a
round table, on it a Baba, six plates of sandwiches, two bowls of
sallad, fruit, wine and what Lady Morley calls fancy waters. She
says such an idea never entered into an Ambassadresses head
and that cela fera fureur. If it takes I see in the horizon a buffet
in the large dining room, benches and chairs (as the summer
advances) in the garden and a band of musick; brilliant déjeu-
ners, in short once a week with no trouble and little expense.
The great advantage of this is that numbers do not signify for
what will not a garden hold. It negatives the terrible anxiety
about weather; when it is fair they will come pouring in, when it
rains they will stay away. Then the novelty of it. Breakfasts
being unknown here, and the refreshment of it in the dog days –
for this garden is now quite like a villa.

The only extravagance we are guilty of is having my usual
evenings brilliantly lighted, but I see the effect. I am complimented upon 'le luxe being l'habitude de notre vie', &c., and it
contrasts well with the Stuarts (I find this is beginning to be said)
– she went to every soirée she was asked to but never received
chez elle except on great occasions – or in a dark room. Forgive
the endless detail. Lady Morley tells me she had heard in
London my génie applauded and Lady E[lizabeth] blamed for
having slaved to go every where instead of admitting more
generally. At the bottom of this was dread of expense, it is
cheaper to go to four assemblies than to light a lustre and drink
fancy waters but it is buying enjoyment – and what a purchase.

[To the Duke of Devonshire]   [Paris]
                                                                    [June 1825]
I seize an idle moment, as a cat does a mouse.

Lady Morpeth! Oh, could you but see Lady Morpeth! Corset by Vachey, gown by Duchoiseul, head dress by Alexandre, at Berri's ball last night. She looked better than I ever saw her in a gold gown. I had hard work to prevail upon her to relinquish the bits pinned across the shawl. She had my diamond chain, second-best earrings, the girandoles, and second-best necklace, and a fine woman she was. The Royalties most polite.

Tomorrow we give a grandissime dinner. Here is how. The house all open, teeming with flowers. When we come out from dinner at eight we shall find chairs arranged on the terrace and steps, and the duc de Grammont's band, who play divinely, will strike up behind the orange trees, all in full bloom. Coffee at nine. The rooms all lit, and twelve globe lamps put amongst the orange trees, with quinquets [lamps] against the walls and at entrance of each avenue. I have tried it once, and it is the prettiest illumination for a garden you can conceive. I am dreaming of a souper dansant in ten days, when Paris will be thinned.

                                                                    [Paris]
                                                                    [? July 1825]
I say, who should not say, that it was a very pretty days pleasuring. We opened at a quarter before two on a hot summer's day and yet no glare, Grammont's band playing 'Robin des Bois', and the garden by three o'clock was swarming. At four the garden music moved to the Boulevard end and the ball began in the house from two till six, *all the time*, really my dear; gobbling in the great room, my plateau my own invention (for God's sake show this to no one but Hart), large basket and small baskets of tiny orange trees and flowers round them mixed with the vases and candleabra of the plateau. At six I sent away the fiddles till eight. The generality went home to rest and refit, about forty remained, tea and coffee, Grammont's band, races, leaping, petits jeux. Amongst those who remained were the drest quadrille. They were drest in wreaths of poppies and corn flowers with long yellow sashes. Alexandre upstairs to *re*coiffer them. At eight the house

and garden blazed. They came flocking back, set to and danced (lovers and Dows. walking about the garden) till twelve when I was obliged *literally* to drag them out of the ball room to supper where they sat eating, drinking, shouting, till half past one. I must say that during the whole time I did not see one moment of flagging or cessation from the most glorious enjoyment; and success as far as fête can go was brilliant. The élégantes are dying for more.

[Paris]
14 July [1825]

The Berrys are come. Mary is really charming. She is couleur de rose and more agreeable than I ever knew her. They dined here yesterday, and Granville was pleased with the virgin. They sat in the moonlight till after past ten, like a pair of lovers.

[Paris]
1 August [1825]

It is odd that you should have made all the reflections which have been lately crowding into my mind, and that you should have begun occupying yourself more at the precise time I have. I have begun reading the Bible with notes regularly. I always liked what is called serious reading, to me so much more light in hand, than much that is called lively reading. But the conviction that study of the Scriptures, and prayer, gives to one's feelings the warmth and life which we attribute the want of, to very different causes, is stronger in me every day; and I think it is a beautiful and most delightful confirmation of all that the Bible is, that it should be not only the most interesting, but the most awakening pursuit, and that all that it is in the letter, when once read in the spirit, becomes the comfort and delight of one's life. I do not say *one* word yet as to myself. I am so very far from what I ought to be: but I am much better in intention, a little in practice.

The Earl of Carlisle died on 4 September, when Lord Morpeth succeeded his father. In consequence the letters from Harriet to

her sister are now addressed to the Countess of Carlisle. Caroline
Lamb, having agreed to a legal separation from her husband, was
coming to Paris.

[Paris]
[mid August 1825]

There comes a letter from Caroline Wm. She is coming immediately. I think this may be a terrible corvée but on the other hand I
feel just now a little quixotic about it and as if it were possible to
do her good, and also great compassion for her which however
she may very likely immediately destroy.

[Paris]
[late August 1825]

Today Caro Wm has desired the messenger to look for apartments. I hear she has been all this time lodging at an apothecary's,
running up large bills and sitting up to a late hour at night
drinking champagne.

[Paris]
22 September [1825]

I am disinterested enough to be sorry that Caroline is thinking of
returning fra voi. She would not be beyond a mark troublesome
to me, but to Lady Cowper, Mrs Lamb, &c, she is a calamity. I
had a few lines from her yesterday, ending, 'sometimes I think,
like Mr Brummel, I shall stay here for ever.' Why not?

[Paris]
[October 1825]

Sir T. Lawrence's picture of the King and Dauphin promises
perfection.* It is really admirable. He has seized the King's
countenance and given the Dauphin one. The Duke of Cumberland has arrived. He sits here a good deal of the morning, drops

---

*Painted by desire of George IV, these portraits are now at Windsor Castle.

into the Opera box, comes here this evening, dines here tomorrow.

We go on with our Cumberland fillip. Tomorrow we have a dinner of forty people for him.

O, that I had you with me now! I enjoy myself so much. Dearest, what an odd thing life is and how it ups and downs, and ebbs and flows, rises and sinks for human beings in general, Mary Fox in particular. You know in England she has short legs, looks a little gummy, is taken out as a good work and you find her rather a heavy shuttle cock. You are glad when sparks dance and speak. Here she is a Venus. In short, Mary is a sort of sky rocket in Paris. I see her with my London eyes. I see her, a clean, bright, good, amiable little thing, a little too go by the ground, and look and manner rather too precise, but a perfectly amiable little soul. But do you know, the divinity she is considered here makes me laugh. Seriously, it is delightful, a most charming specimen of les compensations de la destinée.

I am just come from the Tuileries. Think of dressing at five, swallowing dinner like pills, rushing out on a winter night, and all to find I had mistaken the day, and have it all to do over again on Sunday next. Yesterday morning I woke upon a storm of hail and snow, fine weather for a déjeuner, methought. However, nothing discouraged I had the calorifers heated, fires lit in the green and yellow drawing rooms, and luncheon prepared, expecting no body. Well, as it happened, it was the most brilliant matinée I have had. All enchanted. They dread the air as cats do water, and the beauty and warmth of the serre – imagine it with the geraniums and roses all blown, and occasionally gleams of sun, with the garden looking through the windows like a diorama – prove to me that my house defies climate as it does crowd. They stayed till half past five and licked all the platters clean, and talked of the jardin d'hiver till even I was tired of my hobby.

Sydney Smith preached a most beautiful, eloquent sermon this morning to a crowded, alas!, dining room. I like him better so than when in society.

What I meant about Mary Fox is that by nature a little gummy, she is so tied by the leg, watched by the eye, so regulated, so tamed, so told not to say this, not to do that, not to go here, not to stay there, to cut this man, to avoid that girl, that she has lost all effect in society but that of being gêné'd herself and a gêne to others. Her very beauty suffers from it. She has no spirits, no opinion, no expression, no conversation. Yet she is not low, she is not grave, she is not foolish. She sits by the side of our ladies, and answers very prettily when she is spoken to. I never saw so many natural advantages thrown away.

[Paris]
24 October [1825]

Only a few lines today my dearest, to tell you I have been suffering more or less from toothache ever since I last wrote. I had the traitement yesterday, today a dinner, tomorrow my soirée. Tuesday je subirai l'opération. Pity your cowardly sister. I do not spare *you* the details. It is my front tooth I must lose, but we part to meet again. My dentist tells me it will not be a very painful job, and embellira ma bouche d'une manière étonnante. It is now much longer than the others, discoloured, all shaking. He will extricate it with his finger and thumb, restore its hue, file it, and stick it in again, quite even with the others. Monsieur de Forges, a charming man, makes it quite pleasant. I am to sit with a false tooth in my mouth till he has prepared my own.

I am beginning to return my visits. I seldom (now I know their dear little habits and outings) find any body at home.

Hotel d'Eckmühl
25 November [1825]

Here I am, free from pain, with a gap in my mouth as big as the middle arch of London Bridge. The tooth is out, and the sensation of room and purity and aisance in my mouth is so delicious, that I cannot bear the idea of having it replaced. I return to my dentist who is to put in a composition model of the original in his possession. It is to be framed in gold which prevents irritation to the gums or the breath being affected. About Thursday I shall return to the world, new toothed and new furnished. I hope Hart will not arrive till the gap is filled up. He would swoon at the sight.

In November the Granvilles returned to the Embassy house in the rue du Faubourg St Honoré.

[Paris]
[November 1825]

The comfort and delight of being chez nous in this delicious house, everything so clean and warm, is not to be described.

My mouth is so comfortable without its tooth that I cannot bear to have the new one stuck in. Yet, tomorrow at twelve I go to the dentist. It is not to hurt at all, and I shall not be obliged to look demure, and pince up my ideas and mouth as I did yesterday. Unless I am *very merry* indeed, it is not very obvious. I have been out for the first time this morning, paying about fifteen visits. I only found two old ladies at home, both toothless themselves, so I hope not exigeante on that score.

[Paris]
29 November [1825]

On Friday I have another soirée dansante. What would the parlez-vous do without us? My Fridays are reception to the French and I have the dread of numbers. I trust in my house, which I believe could hold five or six hundred, even when but half of it is open. Madame Appony finds that many come without invitation. This made me determined to receive, and hitherto none but the best company have ventured; but I am aware of the danger, though assured by many that none will come without knowing me well, an invitation de vive voix, or some sort of encouragement. How these perplexities annoy at times ambassa-dresses, those poor drudges of society, and that are increased to me by shoals of English, furious at not being always invited, and all the better sort of English and French disgusted if they are.

[Paris]
5 December [1825]

Society is not the sort of puzzling maze it was to me at my first arrival. I do not think intimacy is either sought or to be found here. Their object is to be amused and received. They are like children, lively, troublesome children, without tact, without suite, noisy and rude – if you spoil them. If kept in order, gay and animated, easily pleased and rarely offended. I do not think as a nation false or capricious, or that they are to be measured by the same rule as any other people on earth. Their expressions of affection, admiration, delight proportionately strong. You deceive yourself if you reckon upon this, but it is your own fault.

[To the Duke of Devonshire]

[Paris]
14 December [1825]

There is an excellent batch of English. The Hollands have a good apartment and an excellent cook. She is very well and to me all smiles, but to her alentours rather more in the termagant line than common. To the awestruck world who frequent her house (the most strict, undivorced, and ultra-duchesses now go there) she appears encompassed by a solemnity and state of fan and elbow-chair and shaded light which makes them suppose themselves in the presence of Maria Theresa at least.

Lady Granville is still the people's prayer, the glad diviner's theme. From the most insolent of the French women to the vulgarest of the English her popularity runs through all the compass of the notes. And what is still more charming of her, she is exactly the same as she used to be.

[January 1826]

My house, which was opened last night with a dinner of forty-four English, looks more brilliant and enormous than I can describe. We open the rez de chausée, the serre with a carpet doubled of scarlet cloth, eighteen lustres with lamps and six divans, the same temperature as the rooms, with all the doors and windows taken off in the ball and drawing rooms. Three salons au premier, five whist tables in the salon vert, écarté, newspapers and books of prints in the State couleur de paille bedroom. A buffet below in the first dining room till supper. At one the large dining room open with hot and cold supper.

Your letter about George [Morpeth] and his address made me pipe. He is adorable in all he does. I think every body seems to think that for so young a man, and with such prospects of every kind, the giving up was right as to taste and policy. *I* hope whatever he does, *when ever* he does, he will always be perfectly independent, stand upon his own ground, act upon his own thoughts, because nobody has such sound ones, give his own vote, because it is sure to be the right one. All this may be slip-slop, or nonsense, or treason. Je vous le jette en passant. You need not pick it up, if you do not fancy it.

[Paris]
[January 1826]

I have been so busy about my ball that I have only five minutes. The sort of worry I have had about invitations can neither be said or sung. It is tomorrow and I long for it as one does at last for ones confinement. The English have behaved like angels, waiting patiently for their *inwites* and discreet to the utmost degree about making applications. The French are almost all satisfied because almost all asked but it is not to be told what those I am not acquainted with risk for the chance. They send up their servants without even their comps. 'They have not been asked and desire I will send their invitations immediately.' The answer to such applicants as these is obvious and easy, but the worry of the whole not to be expressed.

The house however looks like a palais de fée. The conservatory is quite beautiful. Antoine has bought oranges and fastened them amongst the orange trees, the effect of this little contrivance is quite enchanting. The conservatory now it is finished with its divans and carpet looks exactly like a very comfortable, liveable gallery. The little ball upstairs is a little device for the élégantes and as it is open to all an affront to none, but telling them of it they will seize upon it as their own and the Bulls and the herd of French will have a peep and then rush back to the great ball room.

At each turn of the stair case there is a looking glass as at Devonshire House and the whole lined with flowers, carpetted, and with a stove.

[Paris]
[February 1826]

At my ball I heard that when the French people came up to a quadrille, they turned from it with disgust if there were any English. 'Ah, mon Dieu, il y a des anglaises.' The fact is that the butter is spread upon a fonds of hatred and jealousy towards nous autres, and then we meet it with an undue degree of hauteur and coldness. I do not mean me. They are really in general civil and so am I, but it is in spite of our teeth.

Granville seems to have no thought of asking for leave this year. Will it bring you here? I have no philosophy for this failing me. I look to it as to heaven.

[Paris]
[February 1826]

I have a worried feel today, and I ask why, and I say =
I can't make my accounts come right
I have had a very cross letter from Lady Jersey, and though I can't abide her, I am sorry that her hats and pelisses don't fit her. I know the cap that does.
I went last night to a little soirée, and five little insolent élégantes gave themselves airs, and I felt angry, and am ashamed of the feeling.

[213]

My Fridays worry me. They are now below stairs and very pretty with the conservatory open, but on the last numbers of French came without invitations, and I hear (do not repeat this), that in consequence of the novelty and success of my ball, they *all* intend coming every Friday in the year, and I hear of several people I scarcely know pretending they have received a general invitation to cover the proceedings. Now if I get out of this scrape I make them furious. If I do not, my house will soon be like a bear garden. Granville says never mind, and I am sorry I do. The English are angels, never come unasked and charmed when they are, and such dears. My soirées are now whist in the yellow drawing room, écarté in the first green room and English priests and buffet, which they devour, in the end room. The middle windows of the white and gold drawing room and the furthest of the two end rooms open to the conservatory, which is like a long gallery, full of flowers, divans, chairs, &c.²⁵

From this being so unlike any thing else, you can have no idea of the fuss made about it, and from this springs my woe. They all tell me I have spoilt them for any thing else, and I hear people go about the balls saying, 'Ah, mon Dieu, il n'y a pas de serre ici.'

[Paris]
10 [March 1826]

You cannot conceive with all your powers of conception what a delight it is to me to have him [Duke of Devonshire]. Nothing ever was so perfectly kind, so perfectly amiable. He enters in to all my pleasures, worries, understands the one and doubles the others. He tells me of all I love and hears all I have to occupy me, with a patience that is exemplary. He tells me he is pleased with a room near the sky, consequently airy, with a view of the gold dome of the Invalides, which has been backed by an Italian blue sky from the moment he arrived. He allows my little pretension of comparing my villa in the Faubourg St Honoré to Chiswick, and dear Sis, if you could see me at this moment. I am writing in the end of the conservatory. Behind my soft comfortable divan is a little grove of orange trees and lilacs and a large basket full of moss and violets upon the table, and all along the gallery I look down every flower of the spring. My garden will in time double my enjoyment. But pour le moment I shut it quite out, as the grass newly sewn and the bare bones of the trees form only a contrast to the hot glowing summer within.

We have given [Augustus] Clifford a room in the house. He is such a good amiable creature and fit to die of pleasure and laughter.

[Paris]
[March 1826]

We have been spending a delicious morning at nursery gardens, and what do you think that dear kind, magnificent brother has done – seeing that my garden is my hobby, and aware of what use the beauty of my conservatory is to me, how it enhances the Saturday mornings[26] and to have élégantes o'ershadowed by camelias &c, he has spent an enormous sum ordering for me the finest plants you ever saw. The pivoine en arbie, double red camelias, twenty-three hundred franks apiece, and some more things that people go to see as a sight which will all be found flourishing in my serre. I am pleased beyond reason and diamonds. A minor but great satisfaction is that my grass is already beginning to grow and will be green for my breakfasts. Did I ever tell you that my garden was like a ploughed field. When shall I see you sitting in my bowers, beloved sister?

[Paris]
2 July [1826]

I have this moment received your long letter, and the hope of seeing you drives me quite wild. I think of it, plan it, rejoice over it all day long, and at a moment when earth, sea and skies will all be so propitious for enjoyment. I have nothing to add but that it is a delicious day, and that I have been settling which two chairs in the garden we should sit and talk upon, and what a talk, oh, Heavens!

Friday [6 September 1826]

The Jerseys arrived here on Tuesday. Granville called upon them
in the evening. They dined here Wednesday. Thursday we met by
appointment at the fair at St Cloud in the morning. I took them in
the evening to Romeo. This morning I called upon her and she
comes here this evening. Now you see I have done one of each of
all the civilities (I forgot the box at the Français to see Tartuffe
and Valerie.) Tomorrow the Cannings arrive and I cannot then be
expected to payer ma personne. She is in excellent spirits, very
good humoured and as at present there has been nothing to cross
or irritate her she has been what the nurses call as pleasant as
possible. (Remember what the nurses call pleasant.) She talks a
great deal more than ever. Since she arrived nobody has heard her
stop once. I apologize for the figure of speech. He is lower, more
languid, more *undone* than I can describe, but he is going (peace
be with his bones) in a week. I do not know how long she means
to stay but if she continues as she is now it will be no grievance.

[Paris]
22 [September 1826]

We have a dinner of forty-five, no women but Mrs Canning, Lady
Clanricarde, and myself. The Cannings are both of them most
amiable and seem delighted with their sojourn here. Her health is
still very uncomfortable at times; I took Mr Canning to see Pasta
for the first time in 'Otello'.[27] He was very honest about it, which
is all I can say; she does *not* appear to him better than another.

[Paris]
9 [October 1826]

The séjour of the Cannings here has been most prosperous in
every way. The King's asking him to dinner en famille was as
flattering as any thing of that kind can be. People of all sorts have
been civil and empressés beyond measure, and no bitterness on
any side has been strong beyond suppression. *He* is in spirits that I
had never seen, *she* in unequal health, but most kind, friendly,
leaving me to go entirely my own way; she is out or in her room all

morning. Often in bed by nine o'clock, but when I have society exerting herself and behaving very prettily.

La figlia is apparently very happy. The sposo goes his own way but she never appears to require or miss any thing but what is. Perfect good humour and indifference de part et d'autre. I should not like it but they do which is luckily tout ce qu'il faut.

[Paris]
[October 1826]

I am every day more convinced that any amalgamation of French and English society is impossible. The only time when Lady Cowper was bored to death was at a partie fine at Madame de Noailles', and Mrs Canning nearly died of it. The French show no prévenance; they keep apart and eye the intruders, and the English, not paid for it, like me, will not make the quarter of the step towards an amelioration of this state of things.

[Paris]
[October 1826]

I am nervous, worried. Conceive my astonishment to find that when I had done more for Lady Jersey than by any person who has been at Paris, thought her more than satisfied, I found she was in a positive fury. The grievances are, like herself, unique, and she tells every body that we have not shown her a single kindness. She is in a state of nerves and irritation that defies all description. She says she has always loved me with the greatest affection and that I returned it. That she came here under these impressions and was received with the utmost *neglect* and *unkindness*.

These are our attentions: Granville went to her the evening she came. We asked them to dinner the next day; appointed her to meet us at St Cloud the next. I took her that evening to the Opera. I called upon her twice and found her at home both times, went with her to the Variétés, have lent her boxes repeatedly. She dined with us again; we asked her a third time, when she was engaged.

These are her grievances: I did not offer to bring her home from St Cloud. She was there with Lord Jersey and her three sons. I was in the *curricle* with Granville and all the children in the calèche.

That I never asked what her illness had been at Munich!! That I do not love her. Then the unaccountable untruth she tells. That I *desired* her *not* to call on me. That I was so fond of her in England that I gave her a lock of my hair!!!

I can give no better proof of what my reception of her was than by telling you that Granville was extremely pleased with me for it.[*] Mrs Canning laughed at me for it, and said my attentions to her were proof of how she could wind people round her little finger. In short, dearest, we were all thunder struck when the storm burst. I saw a great friend of hers this morning who came to remonstrate upon my having, tho' not liking her, received her so ill. I never saw any thing like his astonishment when I told him what attentions we had shown her.

The French were annoyed when in December in his famous speech Canning as Foreign Secretary, referring to the secession of the American Spanish colonies, called the New World into existence to redress the balance of the Old.

[Paris]
19 [December 1826]

Mr Canning's speech, *stronger* in the newspaper than in his mouth, has made a prodigious uproar here. Pray do not repeat *one* word *I* say. *Me*thinks it is all the better to take a high tone and alarm and awe them, *but* that one or two sentences were imprudent. I am convinced however, that no mischief is done by it beyond irritating them violently pour le moment; but I felt rather nervous at walking into an assembly last night of all the most furious. However, they were all gracious and civil to us, and a country may do what it pleases if its ambassador has des violons chez lui. I dance next Friday and have no qualms. Almost all the French demoiselles are not allowed to dance so near Christmas Day, but all the young married women do, an odd nuance.

[*] Six years before he married Harriet, Granville had made rather more than 'a leg' for her favours.

[Paris]
22 [December 1826]

There has been an immense sensation made by Mr Canning's speech, given as it was in the French papers, *quite* wrong. It is all now explained, pretty generally understood, and Damas made a manly, judicious, friendly, and pacific speech in the Chambre. The fury of the Faubourg St Germain is all turned against him. They say he is faux frère.

In December 1826 the Order of the Garter was conferred upon the Duke of Devonshire in recognition of his mission to St Petersburg to represent the King at the coronation of the Emperor Nicholas I. Besides taking with him a large suite and twenty horses, he had spent £50,000 of his own money. He was Lord Chamberlain from 1827 to 1828.

The following year got off to a sorry start. The Duke of York died on 5 January 1827, followed in February by the resignation of the Prime Minister, Lord Liverpool, owing to a paralytic stroke. Following several months of political intrigue Canning took office as Prime Minister but was obliged to turn to the Whigs for support and form a Whig-Tory coalition. The Granvilles were in London from March to May, the Duke of Devonshire having arranged a portion of the ground-floor apartments at Devonshire House for their use. There was a profusion of immense dinners, a concert, suppers, a ball.

[Paris]
6 [January 1827]

We have this moment heard of the death of the Duke of York. I felt a great regard and liking for him every day at breakfast at the Pavilion, and more so now when every body agrees in the perfection of his conduct in the last trial of all. All the accounts received of his illness and the admirable patience and consideration for those about him add to the pity I feel for his friends, to whom his loss must be quite irreparable.

We shall now have a week or ten days of perfect rest and quiet, as we do not mean to go out any more till after the funeral, and then I hope black gloves will be an excuse for balls &c.

We have not been told the length of the mourning, it cannot be short, and whilst it continues dancing is out of the question, and when it is over Lent will be begun.

Dover
Saturday evening [12 May 1827]

We have had a delicious day for our journey, my own dearest sister. The country looking beautiful and smelling as sweet as Chiswick all the way. We dined at Sittingbourne, have been drinking tea here, and just going to bed, as we are to get up at half past five tomorrow.

Give my love to my dearest brother. Tell him that I am sorry to say it, but London with all its perfections is hot and heavy, and one feels at about the fifth milestone, whatever may be the spirits, that one's health improves. Dearest, dear sister, I have been so happy with you, that it is hard work to reconcile myself to a fresh separation. I was glad to see the lilacs all sticking fast upon the trees as I came along.

[Paris]
28 [May 1827]

On Saturday we had Pisaroni[b] [at the Italiens], magnificent, wonderful, entraînante, electrifying Pisaroni. Hideous, distorted, deformed, dwarfish Pisaroni. Add it up, dearest Sisee, divide, subtract, multiply, it is capable of all for it is marvellous. She has an immense head, a remarkably ugly face. When she smiles or sings her mouth is drawn up to her ear, with a look of a person convulsed with pain. She has two legs that stand out like sugar tongs, one shorter than the other. Her stomach sticks out on one side of her body, and she has a hump on the other, not where stomachs or humps usually are, but sideways, like paniers. With all this, she had not sung ten minutes before a Paris audience was in ecstasies, forgot all its notions of tournure and grâce, and applauded beyond all hope. I cannot *describe* her singing, her recitation. I came home quite enchanted. Mme Appony never can sleep after she has heard her. This is perfectly conceivable, though I had a vulgar comfortable night's rest after it.

[Paris]
Sunday [22 July 1827]

I was in bed when dearest Hart arrived, and received him à la française. I am sorry to tell you that the last day at Windsor, the rapid journey, a hot walk and unwholesome dinner at Dieppe, have made him feel very poorly. He did not of course get up in time for church. We have been for the last two hours sitting in the shade in the garden. Politics, gossip, everything, you, Kings, Ministers. There is no end of talking, and he is the most wonderful person for keeping up our spirits.

Canning, who was in poor health, had gone to Chiswick on the Duke's invitation two days before the above letter was written. Soon after, Harriet was writing to her sister: 'The accounts of Mr Canning's health make me anxious. I hope Chiswick will be of use to him.' Canning died there on 8 August.

[Paris]
Friday [10 August 1827]

I shall say nothing of what I feel, beloved sister. I received Granville's letter on Tuesday at Dieppe.* I arrived here on Wednesday evening. I found Granville in deep sorrow, but still sanguine, still hoping, because not to hope was despair. Indeed I only wonder for a long time past that we none of us had so little fear of its coming to this. It is a calamity of so fearful a nature, the loss is so irreparable to his friends, to the world, it is impossible to look at its consequences or to define the change it may bring, the happiness it destroys, the misery it may entail, that one feels bewildered as well as grieved. In sorrow and suspense I look forward. My brother and Lord Carlisle will have felt this blow, with all its private bitterness and anxious and perplexed agitation. I think the situation of the King is one of unparalleled difficulty.

I can write of no other subject, yet I have the comfort of leaving my children [at Dieppe] well and happy. Little Granville is a

---

*The Granvilles spent part of several summers at Dieppe with their children.

[221]

comfort to his papa. He is all that is exhilarating and buoyant in a child, with consideration and tact that makes him at such a moment a real blessing.

[Paris]
12 [August 1827]
Last night, after little Granville (who is an unspeakable comfort) went to bed, we read over some of Mr Canning's letters. We scarcely talk on any other subject, and when not so occupied I think dearest Granville's depression is much greater. When the couriers return or go, there must be for a long time such a renewed feeling of the total change, and today, when he has no business to occupy him, nothing to force him to exertion, he is more low than I have yet seen him. It will be much better when he is again obliged to occupy himself with political business or that the change in every thing is complete.

As far as we can judge, the greatest sensation has been made here, and to us the greatest sympathy and kindness shown.

Not only were the Granvilles stricken by Canning's death, but the political scene at home was one of confusion. No one appeared capable of taking his place.

[Paris]
Friday [August 1827]
The post yesterday brought us all of pleasure that politically remains and the heartfelt delight of yours and my brother's kindness in giving us so much of your time and all your thoughts at a moment when we can only live on our accounts from England.

I feel for my dearest brother, who has again been worried and perplexed, and as he says, 'without all that gave charm and interest to what he was doing.' His letters written daily from Windsor, and as he alone writes, made us pass the day there with him. Granville has no wish but to see *his* memory honoured in the arrangements of the moment and his course pursued for the future.

I hope all the young and promising men on our side will now

come forward, and that we may see all that, like your dearest George, were enthusiastically attached to Mr Canning tending to fill up the void he has left. In so doing they may work for his fame. I cannot at this moment see any other motive for ambition.

[Paris]
22 [October 1827]

I went to the Duchess of Hamilton who with a hoarseness and an appearance of great souffrance is going immediately to encounter a journey into Scotland. Lady Susan [her daughter] is not very pretty and receives and kisses one like a young princess. The Duchess talked much of her education, the terrors of trusting the girl out of her sight, and her over scrupulous fear of who, what, &c. During this conversation Lady Susan had been sent out to walk in the streets of Paris with an old snuff-taking Marquis de Villeneuve toad eater and honourable companion – tête-à-tête. 'I like Susan to be with him. He is such an excellent old creature'! They are by many degrees the most absurd people I ever met with.

[Paris]
[October 1827]

Our two young sparks create much sensation. 'Est-ce là des dandys?'. Lord George Bentinck is much admired. The Duchesse de Rauzan came yesterday evening and shot all her darts. 'I like your Benting; he is a very good boy, dear Ambassadress. I love you so much, I shall come again on Friday.'

I wish I could describe the court paid to Flahault.[*] Margaret is still on her couch. He pays her the greatest attentions, and left many an anxious sufferer after dinner yesterday to go and sit two hours with her, and the sufferers waited for his return with the most patient devotion. He really is charming in society, gay, sociable, flirting, whist-playing, general, particular, monté sur tous les tons, but when he *cuts in* at whist there is universal gloom.

[*] He had married 'Poor dear', the Duke of Devonshire's old flirt, Margaret Mercer Elphinstone in 1817. She was still known as Baroness Nairne and Keith (in her own right) which must have foxed the French.

[Paris]
1 November [1827]

I will give your love to Miss Berry, who is as happy as the day is long, made much of by me and habituées dropping up three pairs of stairs to sit with her. The William Russells are gone I believe today. I saw her here one morning but she would not come out of an evening. She is prettier than ever, and as ever like the Tower of Babel, tall, unbending, and gifted with tongues.

Lady Keith's house is delightful. Talking, singing, whisting, and, as he is acquainted with all sorts of people, one meets the curious added to the pleasant, and his popularity makes people too happy to go. I think Lady Keith is much more popular than she was, and she deserves to be so, for she is very civil and very sensible, and is always delighted to open her house; but her manner is hard, and the French part of the society evidently go to see Flahault and not her. Some of the pretty women treat her with a perfect neglect that makes my blood boil. The other evening I went there to a small soirée of about a dozen people. One of these impertinent women came, shook hands with Flahault, came straight up to me with a profound curtsey and pretty speech, and then sat down by the pianoforte with her back turned to Margaret. It was so marked that Lady Keith had the good sense to burst into a loud laugh, which made the woman turn round and apologise, during which Margaret nodded and laughed at me as much as to say, 'You see now all I told you is true.' Madame Sobenska fait fureur, she has about fifteen lovers. Madame Flahault has an engouement for her and they are seldom apart. The ill natured say that Flahault always contrives this when he throws his handkerchief. The role he plays here is most brilliant; one should say he is a little too old for it, if his success in every way did not justify him.

[Paris]
[December 1827]

I went last night with Granville to see Pisaroni [in Rossini's *L'Italiana in Algeri*]. She sang admirably, but the principal scene consists of her looking at herself and dressing herself at a long glass, praying – that is, singing – to Venus, madre d'amore, 'rendimi piu bella.' I thought the audience would have joined in

[224]

chorus at so reasonable and desirable a request. She sang it, however, like a sensible woman with all the confidence of youth and beauty, and respect for her wonderful gosier repressed every expression of derision.

With Canning's death home politics muddled through, moderate Whigs giving their support to the Canningites, until with no outstanding statesman to lead them the Government foundered and the Ultra-Tories with the Duke of Wellington as Prime Minister came into power. Granville handed in his resignation. Lord Stuart de Rothesay (formerly Sir Charles Stuart), who had been given a peerage, was reappointed as Ambassador to France by Lord Aberdeen, now Foreign Secretary. After a few weeks in England the Granvilles returned to their rented house at Dieppe where they had left the children. By the end of September the family, which included George Stewart who had become Granville's secretary, were back at Bruton Street where they would remain until the beginning of 1831.

[Paris]
Monday 5 [May 1828]

I have never had one moment's uneasiness upon the principal subject of your letter. Granville has never once been out later than three, almost always at home before two and this equally when the run of luck has been good or bad. For about three months it was bad, and he lost a *few hundreds*! It has now been for some time good. He has won back what he had lost and about as much over a few hundreds. He now plays three or four times a week at ten franks stake. He [Montrond][b] told every body here one day that Granville had played the night before till seven in the morning for which I gave him a most hearty scold obliging him to render up the fib with 'oh, mais alors c'était Flahault . . .'

You ask me what I think of Lady Hunloke, she is a very good tempered, sociable, facile à vivre woman – devoted to her girls and to their will and amusement, all her own little sports are quite secondary and submitted. I miss her in society – most extremely – not in intimacy for I know no one with whom I should so little count it as her failings are being worldly, bustling and gossipping which are for me three cose da morire. Of all the graver accusations against her I can as far as my experience of her goes – pronounce *not guilty* upon mine honour – that is, I think her honest and decent. This esquise is quite confidential as I should particularly dislike to point out her little flaws to any one but you.

[To the Duke of Devonshire]   [Paris]
                                                          2 June [1828]
I need not tell you what Granville's intention is, but I beg you not to mention it till his official letters upon the subject have been received. Of our plans we have of course scarcely had time to think. Your kindest of offers is an immense comfort to us, as, whatever we do, the possibility of seeing you and G for a moment is invaluable. My girls go to Dieppe on the 15th. We have our house at Caudecote* till October.

                                                              [Paris]
                                                        12 June [1828]
I think upon leaving Paris, our first move will be to Dieppe but whether we shall spend the winter in England or Italy cannot yet be decided. I am happy the decision does not rest with me, as between all the pours and contres I should go distracted. My longing wish to be with you would combat painfully what I think most desirable for Suzy. We shall know by the next courier the probable date of our departure from hence. Nothing was ever like the kindness of the regrets expressed here, and I shall have some, but there are immense compensations. The worry and packing and settling are fearful, and I long to be wound round the card, what ever it may be.

I have begun the great task of paying bills, burning and settling papers, and I take a great deal of exercise and have much occupation with the girls.

                                                              [Paris]
                                                      [Summer 1828]
In the letters acknowledging Granville's letters of resignation no

* At that time two and a half miles west of Dieppe.

[226]

time is mentioned. I suppose it will be three or four weeks more before we leave Paris as Lord Cowley must be sent for. He will, I suppose from all accounts refuse and then other proposals must be made. Of course nothing of future plans has yet been thought of. The excessive kindness of people here and the way in which Granville is talked of and appreciated is most gratifying.

[Paris]
7 [July 1828]

Granville has not had any letter from Lord Aberdeen announcing Lord Stuart's appointment, but the diligent young Lord has written himself to say that he shall be here in a fortnight. We are therefore as busy as bees. We shall go straight to Dieppe, remain there two or three days with the girls, and then, my own dearest sister, we shall go to London. Hart has offered us Devonshire House. After a few days there, we shall return to Caudecote, but our plans for the future are quite en l'air.

I love the people here for their excessive kindness, and for the universal and strong feeling of admiration and esteem felt for Granville. I have the delight of seeing how entirely his character is appreciated, and his departure lamented.

[Paris]
[First half of July 1828]

The sort of worry that packing and paying and starting will be is untellable – the more so as we are so little of *bustlers* in general that we go on as if we were never ever to go.

[Paris]
[14 July 1828]

Here am I, writing in an empty drawing room, all my packing done ready to go. Granville is *very* sorry, but sorry like an honest, noble minded man – no repining, no irritation. He stands by his own conduct, without one shade of bitterness or unfairness. In short, I think more highly of him than of any human being – happiness enough for any woman, Lady Carlisle.

[Royal Lodge] Windsor
29 July [1828]

The drive here was delicious. I sniffed up country air and felt better and better every mile. We found the two luxurious, large pink rooms, with blazing fires, a pleasure beyond all moral ones. Nothing ever was so gracious, kind and amiable as the King has been to us both, and he talked to me with such affection of all those I best love that I was charmed, Lord Carlisle, Hart are his two favourite. There is nobody to gêner or awe me. I enjoy the luxurious comfort, the themes, veranda, the conservatory, the prospect of junketting.

The King and Lady Conyngham both asked if you were not gone, said they knew you only waited to see us and therefore had supposed you had left London. We are going to the Castle and the Virginia Water.

Devonshire House [London]
Thursday [31 July 1828]

Our last day at Windsor was delicious. The Virginia Water, which I had never seen, and which I think almost prettier than any thing I ever did see. Dinner at 5 o'clock, short irregular dinner, the band in the boat playing all the time and after eight arriving at the cottage with an order from the King *not to dress.*[28] Oh gracious dispensation! He parted from us with a redoublement of kindness to both. We had no addition but Lord Bristol to the last day. Yesterday we went with Polignac and Lord Amhurst to see the Castle and Wyatville.* The latter amused me most. *It* is magnificent and beautiful beyond description.

We called at Holland House on our way here. Lord H. much better, Lady H. souffrante. We found Mme de Lieven here anxious to pick up the crumbs. Lady C. had been (luckily) very civil about her, praising her agreeableness and saying the King had wanted to have her but he was so afraid of being ill that he would not extend the party beyond necessary invitations. Of you, Lady C. talks with enthusiasm – the most perfect of human beings and her *best* and *dearest* friend. Of Morpeth also she raved.

*Sir Jeffry Wyatville (nephew of James Wyatt) had undertaken the alterations and had transformed Windsor into a Gothicised castle.

Brighton
3 [August 1828]

Here we are.* On Friday we found Hart looking better than I ever saw him. Yesterday we drove in flys, walked on the pier and all over the town. After dinner we went to tea with Lady Hardy, where we found little Johnny Russell. Bad as the weather is I cannot say how much I enjoy being here. My brother is extremely kind to little Granville, which doubles my pleasure. He is such a delightful little companion, so independent, docile and full of natural tact and instinctive civility, which prevents his ever being de trop. We hope to be able to cross over to Dieppe on Tuesday but at this moment the sea is impossible.

Brighton
Monday [? 4 August 1828]

How amusing these windows are, three look down upon the beach, two to the Pavilion. Here is Walewski. How to dip, driven down to the sea from his hotel two hundred yards off in a cloak in a calèche with his chasseur. A secret to enliven my letter, little Johnny Russell is making a prodigious leg to Miss Louisa Hardy. He never leaves her. I know not if he will propose or she accept, but it is the most decided flirtation I ever saw.[29]

Brighton
7 [August 1828]

Now this time we are really going. The morning is fine, very hot. It is very great happiness to think of being with the adorable children again. Hart is quite well, and I think he has enjoyed having us with him, as we have been with him. How happy I was to hear from you! How ten times more happy to be at Castle Howard! I think it will be soon, Lady Carlisle.

*The Granvilles had taken rooms at the Albion Hotel (now the Royal Albion) which had opened in 1826.

Dieppe
Monday [Summer 1828]

Lord Stuart has made several alterations to the house in order to restore it as nearly as possible to what it was.* I am delighted to hear that she is to be at Paris in ten days as I have a feel about the house that it ought not to be spoilt and he does not care or heed any thing that is economical and she understands and would hold up its perfections. He has taken down the looking glasses in the back room, put up in the gaps his old pictures of the King and Queen and [Princess] Charlotte. He is going to sell the glasses to Lord Caledon [his brother-in-law] and others. Do not quote my Paris gossip.

[Bruton Street]
Tuesday [16 September 1828]

I hear Mrs Norton*b* is to be at Chatsworth. I am sorry we are to have an original amongst us, somebody impossible to like and ungracious to dislike.[30]

We dined at Holland House. Lord Holland is uncommonly well, and I think his crutches are more a habit than necessity. So thinks my lady. 'Put away your nasty crutches, Lord Holland; you look as if you were in prison.' 'Oh, dear woman, pray let me have them; I like to have them near me.' 'Impossible. Mary, take away your papa's crutches.' She is in high spirits and, as you see, in force.

[Bruton Street]
[Autumn 1828]

You never read any thing so warm and kind as Lady Stafford's *acceptance* of us. I promise myself pleasure *even* with her if she is in good humour. I have a love of the place Trentham, a longing to be in English country again, a great wish that Lord Stafford should be pleased.

But Chatsworth and above all – Castle Howard!! God bless

*The familiar tale from a departing Ambassadress is only equalled by the exclamation of dismay over lack of taste, neglected house, by an incoming one.

you ever dearest. George Stewart and the girls are bellowing for joy and raving of the charms of London in my ear.

Trentham
19 [? October 1828]

Lord Stafford is better than I have seen him, stouter and much more alert. She is also in robust health and in perfect good humour, and their reception of us has been most gracious.

No words can say how I enjoy the beauty of the place, the charm of the country in England. They were out when we came and I rushed to the potager – you know my weakness – and walked up and down between spinage and dahlias in ecstasy.

This is in many ways a beautiful place, but the tenue, the neatness, the training-up of flowers and fruit trees, gates, enclosures, hedges, are what in no other country is dreamt of or to be seen for love or money; and then there is the repose, a freedom, and a security in a vie de château that no other destiny offers one. I feel when I set out to walk as if alone in the world – nothing but trees and birds; but then comes the enormous satisfaction of always finding a man dressing a hedge, or a woman in a gingham and a black bonnet on her knees picking up weeds, the natural gendarmerie of the country, and the most comfortable well-organised country. Then at home, if the people are those one loves, the whole day is passing from one enjoyment to another; if not, one escapes, follows ones own inventions. Oh Sister, when I get to Castle Howard! The idea of being at Chatsworth! with dearest Hart is transport mixed with awe and timidity.

Chatsworth
[November 1828]

I am quite charmed and *bewildered* with all that I have seen, it is so immense, so magnificent, the improvement is so great, some things so inconnaissable, some so exactly the same that it makes one feel giddy and in a dream. Granville is still a little pulled but getting quite stout. Hart is in roaring spirits, most amiable and kind.

[To the Duke of Devonshire]   Westhill
                                              8 [December 1828]
What a delicious letter yours is, dear adorable brother!

Westhill is dissipated. We found here the Gowers, and the Poodle running tame about the house. This morning, a warm, spring, ravishing morning it was, arrived on foot Agar and Agress [the Ellises], both fat and healthy, and he in raging spirits, bringing us a good piece of news that, strange to say, was news to us – namely, that our goods have sold in Paris at an enormous value, the piano forte at double its original price.

                                                               Westhill
                                       Monday [8 December 1828]
One moment. Lady Stafford, Granville, and Poodle are finishing their breakfast. Coach and four at the door to go and see York House† and shop. Lady Gower sitting in beauty over her toast, a delightful admirable charming creature she is. The beautiful children in white beaver hats and scarlet coats running about.

We go to Panshanger tomorrow.

[To the Duke of Devonshire]   Panshanger‡
                                            [13 December 1828]
All our possible friends and children are here brought together. Yet the flatness is infectious and our tails are between our legs. To give you an idea of the way here. I am at near two returned to my room, fire out, no house maid having been near it, not a single morsel of writing paper in either of our rooms, one bad pen and a drop of ink.

The year 1829 was an uneventful one for the Granvilles. They had their house in Bruton Street but nothing in the country and much time was spent as usual staying with relations and friends.

---

*Lord Stafford's country villa at Wimbledon.
†Built for the Duke of York and acquired by Lord Stafford after the Prince's death. Subsequently it became known as Stafford House.
‡The Cowpers' country seat in Hertfordshire.

A trifling preoccupation was Lord Ashley's devotion to the Cowpers' daughter, Lady Emily. In the past he had shown no inclination for Harriet Canning, who had been more than ready for a proposal, and now, head over heels in love with a fascinating and spoilt girl, he was prepared to wait indefinitely for her to make up her irresolute mind.

Brighton
30 [March 1829]

I do so long to walk in a nursery garden with you. Let me tell you a little tale. This morning I woke with a rheumatic pain in my shoulder and neck. I put on a merino gown, a shawl, a wadded cloak, a fur tippet and walked up and down the Esplanade as fast as I could peg. Returned home in a violent perspiration, sat in my things, peeled them off by degrees and ever since have felt perfectly well without a twinge.

Tunbridge Wells
Sunday [23 August 1829]

We have had most agreeable, delicious little repasts at the Lievens. The first day the Cowpers and Lord Ashley. Emily was in the most captivating beauty. Lady Cowper very much in love with Lord Ashley and I too, we agreed, much more than the girl. However, I think her pleased with him and that she will like and marry him. He is quite willing to wait and hope and try every thing to gain her affections. His manner of making up to her is so exactly what we all like and admire that every body was in astonishment at her insouciance. So passioné, so devoted, yet so manly, so noble, nothing of the common place role in it. It is hardly possible to judge of her, she has been so indefatigably and perseveringly spoilt, but she is natural, gay and good humoured.

Brighton
Thursday [27 August 1829]

I received a letter today from Lady Cowper, begging us to go to Panshanger, which we shall not be able to do. She says: 'We are still in a great state of irresolution about Lord Ashley.' I shall really break my heart for him if she decided against, yet I should break a dozen, if I had them, for him if she married him without loving him.

[Bruton Street]
Wednesday morning [2 September 1829]
I hear Emily says she is not in love, never was, and never shall be; that she supposes she must marry some day, and hopes when she does she shall love her husband, because it is right, but the later the better. Lord A. knows this, and Lady Cowper begged him to consider how much his love and grief would be augmented by coming to Panshanger, but he persists. He does not care what risks he runs for the slightest hope. The girl, I know, was so rude and revêche that Lord A. was wretched. Then Lady Cowper, in an agony of pity, scolds and tells her she has a heart of stone, and writes a kind note to the spark. She said to me Emily said to her one day: 'You tease me so, you talk of nothing else. Let me forget it, and then, perhaps, I shall like him better.' The reason I think Emily a poor concern as a wife is that she is so spoilt, so self-willed, so humoured, that her own way whatever it be, will never bend to any influence and that I think is in a word the beau ideal of a bad marriage.

[Bruton Street]
Wednesday [7 October 1829]
At Devonshire House we met George Lamb and Caro. They went off [to Chiswick House] to see the elephant[31] – we to Fanny.[*] It is better to make you all faint away at once. We are grievously disappointed. She is a little better looking than her print but the want of nature is the calamity! The whole is laboured and artificial, voice, action. The only good moments are the strong expressions of anger or contempt – a faint copy of Mrs Siddons.

[*]Fanny Kemble, niece of Sarah Siddons, made her début in *Romeo and Juliet* at Covent Garden on 5 October, to great applause.

On the balcony she makes me sick and she [illegible] a large wide mouth into the shape of Mlle Sonntag's. Granville thinks she may become a good actress by long study and practice. I do not.

Lilleshall[*]

20 [November 1829]

We have been this morning driving and walking. Mr Sneyd is just arrived. He looks very pretty and manly in a fur coat and seems uncommonly amiable. Very low and flat, which I think such an improvement to him, as he has quite enough in him to afford to be below par, and it is so much pleasanter than when he is all becks and wanton smiles.

Bruton Street

12 [December 1829]

Hart and I very cross – within an inch of staying at home over the fire – to see Venice Preserved. Miss Kemble is infinitely better than in Juliet. She certainly will be in time a very good actress but there are all the faults, the monotonous voice, forced attitudes, curling nose – yet with it some very fine moments, some very well imagined and new effects, and her countenance at times is very striking especially when tenderness is not required.[†]

The popularity of Brighton had greatly increased in the reign of George IV and the Duke of Devonshire was one of the first to establish himself at the newly developed Kemp Town, at the eastern end of Brighton. In 1828 he had purchased the shell of 14 Chichester Terrace and in 1829 the adjoining house built by Cubitt, 1 Lewes Crescent. A small indoor spiral staircase at the back joined the two houses together. By December the house was ready for entertaining and it was thought to be pretty and well

---

[*]Now the home of Lord Gower and his wife.
[†]Fanny Kemble's first appearance as Belvidera was at Covent Garden on 9 December.

furnished. A small ball was given and there was 'much galloping and waltzing'. However, Lady Holland, who had been bidden to dine, thought his house 'too distant for timid persons after sunset. There is no back road to it, and I always fear the cliff.'

Except for the early weeks of 1830 when Harriet was in Brighton, the Carlisles and Granvilles were mostly together so there are no letters concerning the death of the King in June, when the Duke of Clarence succeeded as William IV; nor is there any reference to the coup d'état in France in July when Charles X was supplanted by the Orléans family, and Louis Philippe, Duc d'Orléans, was proclaimed King and crowned in August. At home, however, there was increasing demand for Reform.

[Brighton]
Sunday [10 January 1830]

My beau rêve is to come here, some times, you, I and the girls, to Kemp with my brother for four or five days, in real fine weather, with all the joy of escape from London, my brother's own place.

Are you not shocked at Sir Thomas Lawrence's death – it quite haunts me, so sudden, so fearful, and what a loss.

[Bruton Street]
[February 1830]

My pain in my face is quite gone. As I have no lover, the only calumny they can visit me with is that I am with child which I mention (as Holly* is painstaking upon the subject) that I may say that I am not.

[Bruton Street]
[February 1830]

I have nothing new. Lord Ashley behaved most beautifully last night. How that girl can help liking him, seeing his devotion for her, with something so noble, so manly in his whole manner and conduct! He danced all night with the girls, did not follow her at

*Lady Holland.

all, and his spirits appeared good without being forced, though I, who know, could have cried over him.

[To the Duke of Devonshire]   [Bruton Street]
                                   12 [November 1830]
Lady Gower and the Duchess of Buccleuch dine at Court today. G and I, both in the last stages of decreptitude, rush there at eleven, yet I think she rather likes the thought, having a more junketous soul than me. Morleys not asked, she who lodged and fed them. My girls enchanted. Eight hundred friends.

[To the Duke of Devonshire]   [Bruton Street]
                                   13 [November 1830]
Well, last night was the completest failure.* Elbowed by the navy, numberless queer figures, and at eleven, in the midst of a dull rout, with scarcely any dancing-men, an impromptu was got up, and two reluctant serious quadrilles performed to one or two squeaking instruments taken out of the band and playing out of tune. Talleyrand† crawled past me last night like a lizard along a wall.[32] Dino dined there, gracious of Billy [William IV]. The Queen enquired most graciously after you – in detail.

Matters had now reached a crisis in Parliament. At the end of the year the Duke of Wellington, and with him the Ultra-Tory Government, was obliged to resign over his vacillation towards Reform. The Whigs came back into power and Granville was once again in possession of the Paris Embassy. The Duke intended lending his diamonds again to Harriet.

[To the Duke of Devonshire]   [Bruton Street]
                                   20 December [1830]
You are most kind and adorable, but are you sure this time there are not objections you may feel when the moment comes, some

*This was a party at the Palace under the new reign.
†Talleyrand had been appointed Ambassador to England by the new French King. The Duchesse de Dino accompanied her uncle and acted as his hostess.

grand affair at which you would like them to hang on Blanket [his niece, Blanche], or a wish to show them to the future Duchess of D., the morning after your proposal? A Revolution and a wish to sell them. Think this over and say, 'Send them back' – without scruple, if my logic strikes you.

I have had letters from Madame de Flahault, and some parlez-vouz, most flattering. Nothing yesterday from Lord Stuart, but Mrs Hamilton* writes, evidently, I think, begged, to deprecate our coming soon, yet go we shall.

Calais
10 o'clock [2 January 1831]

We had a passage of three hours, the sea very rough, till we got near the French coast. Granville and I perfectly well, on the deck all the time. The weather was fine, very cold as we got here. We walked about the town, smelt the peat, saw the National Guard en frac with his gun, the merry noisy people all over the place, in this cold weather on round-abouts, the women in caps as usual. Going abroad, any how, any where, is such a lark; not more, not less, but a lark, neither comforts nor grievances are as substantial as in England. I am tonight in the humour that I like being on the road so much more than being arrived in Paris.

[To the Duke of Devonshire]   [Paris]

[Early January 1831]

I must begin a letter fresh from the mint. We are just come from the Palais Royal – a dinner given to the English Embassy. Our reception was beyond measure gracious. The King and I talked without ceasing. He gave me a detailed account of all the terrible days. The Queen† was très souffrante, and is more low than her relations. Madame Adelaïde very sprack and delightful, sitting by the King. I was very fine, in a grey satin gown, my diamonds,

---

*Her husband was Secretary at the Embassy. The Stuarts, after leaving the Embassy, remained on in Paris – an infliction to a new incumbent.

†Queen Marie-Amélie. Madame Adelaïde was sister to Louis-Philippe.

which make my fortune, and a Herbault all feathered and bowed – very fat, but squeezed in to a tournure.

[Paris]
Monday [10 January 1831]
Let me now try to settle my thoughts, and give you a sketch of my four days. I have done immensely in them, yet I tremble when I think how much remains; but this is our May and June in London, with all the labour of dressing and visiting, for Paris is Paris still, swarming with English, and the French rising from their ashes every day. Balls beginning, dinners constantly, every French woman at home three days in the week, ten of them I am told on Saturday. Yesterday I went at two to the Palais Royal, desired de me faire bien belle. I found to my despair that the great wish is that one should dress a great deal and very fine to encourage trade. I accordingly went in grey satin trimmed with blond, a Herbault white hat and feathers (the fashion is that the latter shall stand upright like a sentinel's). Dearest D's diamonds and most of my own.

We have had our attachés to dinner. Ashburnham rheumatic, languid, and upon my word I doon't kno-o-ow genre, which is not useful or efficient, but he seems sensible and gentlemanlike. Magennis well meaning, good tempered, would be a puppy, if he knew how, rather prosy. Waller, good natured, vulgar little man.

[To the Duke of Devonshire]   [Paris]
14 [January 1831]
The housses are on; the room, the green beauty, looks just like its old self, with the sun broiling upon it. Quiet is the word for this great town, dearest; one must savourer it, for it can not last long. If you could know how like a dream it seems to me, to be so perfectly settled here, as I now feel!

[Paris]
[January 1831]
The house is deteriorated, yet not as much as I expected, but Granville is quite right. He will not go to the expense of setting it

[239]

up again so we shall tread on Pauline's old swans and have a matting in the conservatory where we need to have a scarlet cloth carpet. I called on Lady Stuart and was as civil as I could be but she was, I thought, quite agitated and talked incessantly in a loud nervous voice. I have not seen him yet. One sees that she is a strong minded, sensible woman who behaves very well, but that she has lost all she values in life, that her soul was in the set out of it all, that l'Ambassadrice d'Angleterre was a sound sweeter than a shepherd's pipe when given to herself, that curtsies, 'Madame, un fauteuil je vous prie', out first, handing, placing, preceding, were her intense pleasures. He is, I believe, much happier grubbing about Paris like an old clothes man.

[Paris]

[January 1831]

Granville is extremely busy. I delight to see how he is considered and valued here; my only regret is, entre nous, that he has such a man as poor Mr Hamilton, who, as he grows older and less sanguine about his own affairs, is left with the outward man entirely unstuffed, not one idea or qualité of understanding, that can make him of the slightest use or relief in any one branch of diplomacy.

[Paris]

[21 January 1831]

The Stuarts dined here and yesterday I took Betty [Lady Stuart] to the Opera with me. She is good, sensible, has behaved perfectly well in a difficult situation but she is, à mon avis, the least interesting, the least attractive woman I ever met with, talks too much, too loud, is too absent, too busy – huffy and vulgar notions of all kinds about civilities and ceremonies. This makes the *pleasure* less of endeavouring to make the self imposed awkwardness of situation as little irksome to her as possible. To paint her in one word. Do not tell. Mrs Hamilton hinted to me that what would console her most would be being considered as a cut above the general society here, first in all times and places. So I see it is. She even likes a nod and a smile occasionally, in the midst of the things, and, in short, would like to enact with me ex-Queen and régnante. So, when she comes, we play at Ladies, and all is as smooth as possible. Lord Stuart and I are, tout autre, as happy and as little dignified as need be.

My only grief and care is economy. I flatter myself there is an immense difference, but it is the eternal subject of lighting that vexes me. Granville does not care a straw about the thing looking less well than formerly. It is all in reasoning perfectly true, but I find to my shame that I have not a mind that can raise itself above dark rooms and an ill-lit ball.

[Paris]

[January 1831]

The new mode of all is a tiny mat of hair or a tiny black velvet, not thicker than a Venetian gold chain or two round the head, in front sewed on it a small *coloured* stone or an enamel or a turquoise set round with little diamonds or gold, all ones old little odds and ends of jewels come into play, nothing is too small. Today we go to the Appony ball; the girls wear white net gowns over satin with a fringe of satin, a large bouquet in front, white flowers in their head and little emeralds set round with diamonds (presents of Lady Duncannon to me on my marriage) on their black velvet cordon.

[Paris]

27 [January 1831]

The ball at the Palais Royal was splendid and beautiful: four immense rooms, dancing in each. We sat all night, the Queen and I, with our girls on either hand. We supped in state also; I between Suzy and Madame Adelaïde, Ad. and I eating poularde au gros sel and asparagus and very jolly. My girls were drest in pink crape gowns, my pearls (Suzy the necklace, Dody the bracelets, across their foreheads) and an immense pink rose with white bruyère stuck up aloft and monstrous well did they look with lean tailles déjà allongée d'une pouce, their real bodies, Lady Carlisle.

Do you see me, Lady Carlisle, in my dressing room – hartshorn and oil on the chimney, cloves in a saucer, a piece of flannel airing at the fire, Michaud – do you remember him? – and Richard arranging paravents in the bedroom to keep out the blustering wind.

I must not write more, for I have got all sorts of business relative to my ball. It was very different autrefois, when I had only to say like children – more, more – as to light, flowers, &c. Now, most laudable it is, we are all a retrenching and vexatious public can wish. This makes me foolishly nervous and anxious, especially as I must say the Stuarts (who saved in every day life) gave splendid balls. I have, however, obtained dearest Granville's consent to light much more, and have dancing in two rooms, the long and the middle one. Think of Betty's spirit who had it in three; double lamps in the conservatory, seven or eight hundred francs' worth of flowers, and yet called stingy because she put up some pretty white moreen instead of hideous red silk! Ainsi va le monde, and who would fear its criticisms, but those who have taken calomel and starved!

[Paris]
[? February 1831]

I can conceive of nothing more odious than Fanny in Beatrice.* A playful Kemble is my non plus ultra of what is offensive.[33]

[Paris]
Monday [21 February 1831]

Your letter last night delighted, and above all, touched me. You are a kind angel and make me most happy. I sometimes feel a tight pang come across me, head and heart, when I feel that I am away, but I have much to console, to please me, and next year, even if nothing hastens it, we must meet.

I have just been sending out notes for a fatal dinner [for] the Queen's birthday. Myself and forty nine sparks of high degree. Granville will not let the girls dine. In the evening I shall have a stuffy drum, but that they like.

*Fanny Kemble appeared in *Much Ado About Nothing* at Covent Garden on 17 February.

I cannot let my thoughts dwell on Betty. She runs in and out when ever she likes. I shall be sorry when she goes; to lose a very pleased happy person, miss her in my society, always glad to come early, stay late, talk without ceasing and bonjours and how-d'ye-dos all the visitors much more audibly and busily than I do myself. She is esteemed and popular, and what ever was amiss in the doings here was, and is known to have been singly and wholly his work. I do not feel as if she was here, never think of her but when I see her. No body feels the least gêné at finding her always sitting near me, and all her toads toad on because they see that I toad to her too.

[Paris]
Monday [28 February 1831]

Your life is too vivacious, and you are more dissipated than we are. My own throat is gone. Sister, how does yours do?

I like Betty *much* better as we go on. Her faults of manner or at least the impression they make, wear off, and she is become happy, easy and is constantly here, and *sometimes* very droll, always shrewd and clever. She is amazingly liked and respected here, people have left off looking the least surprised at seeing her here in the evening, when they drop in, with their best speeches, which is a great comfort to her and to me. He comes rarely, prowls about among the douairières (as he tells me).

[Paris]
[March 1831]

I know you will forgive me, my dear sis, for only writing a line today. My ball is tonight, and I think you will pity me when I tell you that I and my girls have, for the last three days, done nothing but receive and write notes, and I with so bad a cold and sore throat that I have for the last two been doing nothing but gargle, and the night before last was obliged to blister my throat. But your sprack sister, being well dosed and entirely starved, is in perfect good trim for the hop, and I do not mind appearing in a negligé of velvet and flannel.

At home, Parliament was restive, Reform being still the watch-word and Lord Stuart became a kind of barometer: a happy countenance would indicate that the Whigs – and the Granvilles – were out.

[Paris]
24 [April 1831]

On Friday at my hop, it was known that there was a majority against us. I had an *out* feel, and the natural antipathy to being beat, independently of larger and finer feelings, but I talked big and confident of dissolution. My spirits rose upon Lord Stuart's coming in as cross as a lap dog and as rude as a bear. I thought this promised well. Mme de Flahault sat like a thunder cloud, and her friends declared that when spoken to she could not or would not answer. We hope that during this falling of the sky we shall catch larks. Susy says: 'Uncle Duke will certainly come.'

[Paris]
29 [April 1831]

How it delights me to hear that Granville is so appreciated. It is true he slaves, and slaves alone. The place of Secretary of Legation is filled, but not occupied. Mr Hamilton, harmless, inoffensive man, can neither comprehend nor reply to even a question about etiquette or the news of the day. 'What sort of weather is it today, Mr H.?' 'God bless my soul, it never occurred to me to make an observation. It seems to me, I may err, I would not pronounce rashly, but I'll step out and make a point of ascertaining it'; a nervous, bilious, conscientious, pauvre sire.

Lord and Lady W. Russell are arrived. She is really beautiful, grown in to a very large woman, brighter and clearer than any thing I ever saw.

[Paris]
[2 May 1831]

What you call election gossip is read like a sentence or reprieve by your devoted relations. We savourer every line, and when we

[244]

have done, begin again. Why, sister Carlisle, what times? I have no doubt of the elections going well.

Granville is a good deal better, but very languid, and unable to walk. I hear him now laughing with Pozzo. You know, they never laugh so much with us, Lady C.

[Paris]
[Late May 1831]

I have been this morning in full enjoyment of the local happiness of this place. The garden is radiant with beauty, freshness and sweetness – flowers, singing birds, green grass and inumerable orange blossoms. My two darling boys are delighted to have me as their play fellow, being better than none, and we have been gardening for the last two hours. In the middle of all this came recollections and regrets, and an *intime* wish for you and Hart – both alive to my enjoyable existence here and more than doubling it, and yet dearest G to whom I talk (it is my greatest comfort) in a light hearted way – there is much more of melancholy than of bitterness, it is not anxiety and careworn look and gnawing at my heart. I only lament over the absent and cry a little and sigh a great deal. I am delighted to see Granville here again – it is his element.

Dieppe was again a refuge for the Granvilles in the summer.

Dieppe
12 [July 1831]

I have just received your letter, my very dearest sister, and wish you joy a hundred times of your birthday, and of its being a year less than I thought, and mine also in consequence.

I expect Willy and Freddy per kettle on Saturday.

Friday.

Well, here's an event. Who do you think came in the night, is now asleep at Clarke's, fancying himself known only to me? I shall not tell the girls. They shall have all the surprise of seeing him walk in to my room. My dear, adorable brother crossed in the night in a pelting rain, which still continues. I will not direct my letter till I have seen him.

Here he is, looking so well. I have not a moment. We dine with him tonight.

[Dieppe]
[July 1831]

The steam boat came very empty last night. Freddy writes, 'As to politics I don't care a pin about Prince Leopold.* Reform is my principal aim.' He is rather a prig, but an amazing darling.

[Paris]
[16 August 1831]

The Conynghams dined here yesterday, and we had quite a brilliant soirée. Madame Appony sits by la Marquise, as Lieven used, and her *beauty* is much admired. She is wonderful!!, as fresh as a daisy, bouche comme une rose, in a light blue gauze hat with white feathers and a salmon coloured gown made *extremely* high, with long sleeves; looked infinitely handsomer than when in a satin frock, swaddled in jewels. Lady Maria is perfectly good humoured and inoffensive but idiotic. Lord Alfred idiotic with pretension and mauvaise langue.

[Paris]
Saturday [20 August 1831]

Lady Conyngham and her cubs came last night. She is so much better than her brood. The foreigners are much excited about her, Madame Conyngham, and think her, as she is, still beautiful. I thought Paul of Württemberg would have screamed with curiosity and excitement, and Madame de Vaudreuil with anxiety to

---

*Leopold was proclaimed King of the Belgians in July. Frederick, the Granvilles' youngest son, was aged twelve.

see which had conservée'd herself best; not having met for twenty years, the result must have been mortifying.

My plans all in uncertainty, but I feel that I ought to do some thing wholesome. Aix en Savoie! Granville consented. But I gave it up. I am morally quite unequal to a journey of six days without Granville, when if any thing was to go amiss I should go in to a nervous madness. St Germain? Very easy, still on the cards, but hardly enough, as I want bathing and sea air. Boulogne? Sea air, sands, the journey with Granville, to wait for him there and come back with him. Very tempting, though it is a hideous place. What would make me think it a Paradise would be if you would join me there. I could give you a room in the excellent inn; we would drive and dawdle all day long. It would be too delicious. You will perhaps say, Why not come to Brighton, Lady Gran? I will tell you, dearest Sis, it would alter the whole thing. What I want is perfect repose. If I went there I must prepare dress for self and girls, go to the Pavilion, struggle against dinner and balls. If you come to Boulogne, a gown, cap and a bundle will suffice.

Susy sat between Lord Rivers and George Villiers on Friday at dinner, and talked most to the latter, whose agreeableness is entraînant to the greatest degree. Lord Rivers seems amiable and pleasing, but he pays us no court. She is in tearing spirits, the most adorable darling that ever lived, and really doated upon by all who know her. Dody is a dear girl too. It is not the same cloudless, radiant nature, but full of goodness and intelligence, and she will be a very delightful person.

On 'Friday at dinner', 2 December, Lord Rivers had seemed recalcitrant. To Suzy, the Granvilles' eldest daughter, now twenty-one years old, it was love at first sight, and now that the sisters were to enjoy a London season, the young man in question proved no laggard in his devotion. They met often; engagement followed proposal; marriage in 1833. It is perfectly apparent from Harriet's final letter of 1831 that although Dody (Georgiana) aged nineteen was 'a dear girl too', she did not measure up to her sister in her mother's affections. In her marriage (also in 1833) her 'Uncle Duke' seems to have been the strategist. He chose as her suitor a young man in the Blues, Alexander Fullerton, 'gentleman like' and with expectations, finding in his person some resemblance to his own mother, Duchess Georgiana. The couple were well matched and devoted and eventually joined the Granvilles in Paris, he acting as his father-in-law's secretary.

But politics were still the dominant theme of 1832: the Whigs sat uneasily until the Reform Bill was finally passed in June and the Granvilles were able to feel secure.

[Paris]
Friday [20 January 1832]

I know I have been meagre and unsatisfactory in my letters of late, but I shall improve. I also live in the hope of going to England when Granville does, and then I can talk of a hundred things I can not write.

We have now only George Villiers who, charming as he is, does not dance or talk to any one but married ladies of distinction, and therefore is no lark for us. Lord Yarmouth[b*] has taken to good company and appears at the drums and balls. He is the *greatest pity* that ever was and such powers of being delightful and captivating, grandes manières, talents of all kinds, finesse d'esprit, all spent in base coin, and he walks among us like a fallen angel, higher and lower than all of us put together.

The Miss L Gowers dress in white, blue and pink crape when they hop; when they dance, in white moirée gros de Naples. Pea green dº, lilac grenadine and a [illegible] of white organdies. Their heads are crowned with wreaths, Lady Carlisle, or a tress

*Lord Yarmouth, who never married, had a reputation for keeping disreputable company.

with one large dahlia or cactus, or at home a bunch of brown, pink, or blue broad satinée ribband so [sketch], with one bow and high comb.

Monday [February 1832]
Breakfast: A cup of Bohea, huge piece of roll. Luncheon: Broth with vermicelli, no bread. Dinner: Two mutton cutlets, macaroni or leg of fowl. Rice or tapioca pudding or one veal cutlet, one quail, or one wing of chicken, half a partridge, an artichoke.

Then comes the pith, a wine glass of sherry in a large glass of seltzer water. Cup of coffee after dinner, if hungry some roll with it. I eat very slow, chewing uncommonly and you can have no idea of the improvement in my health. You see vegetables and fruit, fish and pastry are all banished.

Paris
Monday 6 [February 1832]
Lord Yarmouth goes every where and is by far the most agreeable man I ever talked to. You will hear of him and Miss Morris. She is very pretty, very intelligent, and he is always with her and her chaperones, talks to the girl for hours together, but there is something in his manner convinces me he means nothing, as the phraze is, and I am sorry for it and interested for her, never having seen any body of any sort, size or shape, so desperately, so deplorably in love as she is. It is like reading a very high wrought novel to look at her. Perhaps with all the misery she must go through, it will be happier for her to love than to win him for one must live in Paris and talk of him to his intimate friends to know how entirely perdu his reputation is.

[Paris]
[12 February 1832]
Lord Yarmouth set off for London! Every body astonished, some say it is to avoid *her*, some to make settlements, the less romantic, that he wishes to be made a Peer, but I was happy to see Miss

Morris at the ball on Wednesday just as gay and blooming as ever and looking less like a victim than any body I ever saw.

[Paris]
[February 1832]

Lord Hertford offered Miss Strachan to Lord Craven,* but that he declined. Lord Yarmouth being gone to his Papa looks as if he had intentions. I know he thinks her beautiful and he is said not to be insensible to the additional attraction of her fortune.

[To the Duke of Devonshire]   [Paris]
[25 February 1832]

I am dying to be off. Yes, my opinion is exactly like yours – be temperate, clean, charitable, starve, work and give, but oh, neither Lord Palmerston, you, or Granville say one word of *when*. Granville will not budge from his post till it is absolutely required of him.

Tonight your uniforms dance and mine walk, as the parlez cannot endure hopping amongst the dress coats. I try to make up with flowers, candles, and food for want of better sport. Champagne et des poulardes truffées versus waltz and quadrille. I have asked all the English I know in Paris, only two hundred and fifty after all. The diplomacy come full fig, all their swords and diamonds. French as they please – not at all or in uniform or not. I have humbly imitated your famous Chiswick breakfast; my buffet half a mile long is great in the joy of the parlez at seeing the oranges grow out of the table. We have no fears. But oh! dearest Brother, the numbers, the Carlists, the hideous, the anxious. Well there are always the Miss Levesons. Suzy in a blue wreath and diamond épi in her hair, Dody ditto with your turquoise branch in hers. Lady G. in all her borrowed splendour.

---

*Charlotte Strachan was the ward of the 3rd Marquess of Hertford, her mother having been his mistress *en titre* for a number of years. Lord Craven had started Harriette Wilson on her notorious career when she was fifteen.

[March 1832]
I can hardly reckon on the delight of being in London this spring, yet Granville for the first time admits it as a possibility. This is such happiness that I forget the only two drawbacks, health and money. But the happiness of being amongst you, the vision of Grosvenor Place, * to live perhaps a whole month with D., the rapture of the girls, and the escape from a good deal that worries and bothers me, such as shoals of inconceivable English, half of them in a perpetual rage at what some call 'taking pleasure in wantonly mortifying and insulting' – all this, although mixed as it has been with a great deal of exquisite pleasure and enjoyment derived from my adorable children, makes me look with the feelings of a bird from its chain unbound to England. And I should then return to what is delicious, Dieppe and autumn here.

[To the Duke of Devonshire]   Kemp! [Brighton]
                                               [19 April 1832]
Thursday 2 o'clock
More beautiful, more luxurious, more delicious than ever dearest of brothers. How happy you are to be able to dispense such happiness. I never enjoyed any thing so much – the repose, the delight, the cristal air. The pavement where I air six times a day – *shall* at least.

                                               Brighton
                                               [22 April 1832]
Though the wind is east again today, it is delicious, blue, gold, soft, and we have been since church basking on the platform under the cliff. I hear of many people here but do not see them. Kemp is too charming, it is a little kingdom of one's own.

                                               Dover
                                               Thursday [26 April 1832]
The weather as fine as possible, not too hot, not too any thing. Talleyrand just going to be put on board in his carriage – *no*, he is

*The Carlisles had left Park Street and now lived in Grosvenor Place.

first going to be put in a chair by my side in this room, so I shall have to squiddle with him before. I have settled all his affairs, what he was to give the Guard of Honour, every thing I don't understand. All the authorities came in to see him. The whole bore, with none of the pleasure of having dearest Granville. I believe I have made him give twice more money than he ought.

Dearest dear brother and sister, I have no words for what I feel at having left you. I must write a line to Granville by Monsieur de Talleyrand, who goes on without stopping.

Paris

[May 1832]

Yes, Mrs Cavendish is delighted, and really enjoys herself and is very happy, but let me laff a little only to you and Hart. She can not be light in hand or pleasant, though essentially I think better of her than I ever did before. But the conducteur at the Cimetière du Père Lachaise was worn, as we occasionally are. We went there yesterday. The day divine but without sun. She was enchanted, but asked him who first thought of it. That was well. But of the people (one and all the buried), every particular. Were they poor, were they rich? did their relations come and water the flowers (who should?) *every* day, (who would)? Did clever people come and water Molière's flowers? It does not look written as it sounded said, and it was sans relâche. To me, Should I like to be buried there, should I like to have *my* flowers watered, did I mean to buy ground?, should I water *her* flowers if she were buried there? I almost began to dig the hole.

[Paris]

29 [June 1832]

Did I tell you Talleyrand paid me a long visit. I never knew before the (as Mr Foster says) power of his charms. First of all it is difficult and painful to believe that he is not the very best man in the world, so gentle, so kind, so simple, and so grand! One forgets the past life, the present look.* I could have sat hours listening to

*He was known, of course, as the greatest intriguer and most unprincipled man in Europe.

him. I am certain nothing will persuade Talleyrand to remain here, or to give up London, and indeed what a position to quit, and what a position to gain!

You are an angel, dearest G. There is but one certain means of happiness. I have the greatest pleasure in reading religious books. I find that I *understand* the Bible better than I ever did before, that I know much better what I am not and what I ought to be, that the subject interests and occupies me deeply, whilst I am employed on it. But I am dissatisfied with the want of warmer, stronger feelings and power of weaning myself from the clinging, aching interests of the world. I do not mean as the question of living in it or retiring from it. If my idea of what we ought to be is a right one, the whole feeling and character would be so changed and *dedicated* that it would be indifferent where, how, or when. And it is to attain this that appears to me such terrible difficulty, because just the chain that must be broken is the one that binds and fastens one down.

I hear Lord Yarmouth is fitting up a house and furnishing it in London, where he means to live. When this Lord left Paris he said he was going to look for a wife, to Madame de Flahault and others. He deprecated violently marrying a pretty or a young thing, says what he wants is 'some thing nearer thirty, some body he could not have a jealous feel about.' Well, one is also told that, odd as it is, money is his great object, being his idol.

Guinea* is all gratitude to Mrs Gibson, 'found her airing my bed with one hand, and holding out a mutton chop in the other.' A little physic also she has administered and is in short a darling.

---

* A pet name for Granville (the Granvilles' eldest son), which had displaced 'the little Governor'. Mrs Gibson was the Carlisles' housekeeper, having been nurse to all the children.

The marriage between Suzy Leveson Gower and Lord Rivers took place at the beginning of February in the drawing-room of the Paris Embassy. 'Uncle Duke' had lent them Chiswick for their honeymoon. At about this time Granville seems to have had a very slight stroke, or else a recurrence of a particularly violent attack of gout.

[Paris]
[mid February 1833]

All I hear of my darling adorable child fills me with delight. Few people have had such happiness as she now has. He was her idéale from the first moment she saw him she thought him the most captivating of human beings. I sometimes have moments of anxiety for the future – fear almost from the very brightness of their present bliss.

Private. Will you tell me what you think D will wish. To be bent upon having them in London? How long does he mean them to bide at Chiswick? Tell him to tell you when ever they do, or do not, any thing just as he likes. I feel positively *loaded* with my gratitude to that dearest brother – for all he has been – and is now to them. I trust to my *admirable* little woman to act as she ought always – yet I some times think her devotedness to her husband, may make her careless, forgetful in little things.

[To the Duke of Devonshire]   [Paris]
23 [February 1833]

Our plans are still en l'air. Granville better, but still walking with a stick and thrown back by the least fatigue or over exertion.

Chiswick is such a Paradise to those two darlings, that no wonder they wish to remain there. When ever they go to you, if I am not there, let me say one little word to you, but promise me sacredly secret from them and dearest G. Do not fear his sauvagerie, and never encourage a London going-out life. It would endanger that happiness for which I would gladly pay the price of my own, to which I have already with delight sacrificed its brightness. To live at D.H. with you and your society, all that line is well; but the wearisome, heartless round of what is called going out, where people can not be devoted to each other, and are bored in to being devoted for the time to others, would expose him to the only danger I could envisager for him. He is so much the creature of entraînement, impulse of the moment, with an artless, innocent warmth of feeling for those who by kindness or by design get about him, that any thing that separated him from her, from her immense and hourly influence, might unconsciously to himself lead him in to mischief. He is excellent and adores her, but that has nothing to do with what I mean. If I did not think your understanding as good as your heart, your finesse and tact as perfect as your feelings, I could not venture to say this. G would think I meant more. They would laugh me to scorn, but I give it you with perfect confidence. You will measure my meaning in its true sense; and, having told you this, I care not where they are, so that you are looking on. You have made their happiness and you will guard it. God bless you, most dear.

[Paris]

[May 1833]

I am so happy, coming, most dear relations, coming, and Granville so improved and improving. He rode yesterday, said he felt almost as well as ever. I have been very busy launching darling Suzy's court dress today. I think her going on Thursday an excellent plan; we may not be in London for the next drawing room and I think Lady Rivers will like to present her. I always think things of that sort pleasant without me. I do hate and dread them so, that it must damp my companions, and my own bright and most adorable lark will so plume her feathers, going upon her own bottom with her new family.

Granville was created Earl at the beginning of May. As he and Harriet were in England there are no letters to her relations concerning the death of William, the Granvilles' seventeen-year-old second son. He was mentioned only rarely in the past but

[255]

there are indications that he was an invalid almost from birth,
though whether from a crippling accident or disease is not known.
The Granvilles were back in Paris for Dody's wedding, again at the
Embassy, on 13 July; a week later news came of the Duke of
Sutherland's death (Lord Stafford). Again there are no letters.
Lord Gower, the once flirtatious Govero, now became 2nd Duke
of Sutherland. Other deaths in 1833 included Agar Ellis, now Lord
Dover, who had married Harriet's favourite niece.

Before the summer ended the Granvilles took a short holiday.

Aix en Savoie
27 [August 1833]

I am most happy at this place having been so useful to Granville,
and he is so well, and we are, in spite of our rude habitation, so snug
and comfortable, that I shall leave it with much regret. Our life
suits me so perfectly – up before eight, boating, walking, driving in
char-à-bancs, the lake smooth, the boats flat-bottomed, without
sails, like Robinson Crusoe's rafts, the roads good or impassable,
the coachmen, peasants en blouse, drag the horse up and down by
the mouth, such a nice safe way, all cheek by jowl together. Our
breakfasts and dinners are excellent; such butter, mutton, and
greengages as never were seen before. We have had delicious
weather, our post three times a week brings me letters from my
girls. As to you, I am delighted to hear of your enjoyment of
Chatsworth, your being able to go about in so many different
ways. Your life till the company comes must be ecstatic.

You have no idea how much more worthy I shall be of sharing it.
What with spectacles, mineral waters and courage, I am a new
woman.

Every evening we have a little woman of Colmar singing on our
balcony, Monsieur, as she calls her (I hope) husband, playing on
the guitar. It is enchanting.

[To the Duke of Devonshire]   [Paris]

[23 September 1833]

Your beautiful and magnificent present has turned our heads.
Dody tells me she was overcome at the first sight of it. It is of

real use, for how is Lady Georgiana Fullerton to meet the King and Queen of the Belgians, who arrive on the 4th and will do nothing but dance and drum, without jewels to bedeck her? Is not the white satin gown, trimmed with blonde, intended for the first great occasion, with your gift to relever it, a dainty dress to set before a King?

[Paris]
Friday [? 22 November 1833]

Courage, dearest Sister, courage, air to talk to oneself about ones nerves. I had the most *violent* nervous sensations in bed the other night and I can hardly bear to think of them. I felt as if every thing was giving way – *shrinking* in me, under me, round me. I felt terror, I said 'Oh, this is it. Here are the nervous sensations belonging to the time of life, here is the blood rushing here and every where – well – I know what it is, never mind, it will soon be better, courage.' I got out of bed with a fear that the *sensations* might make me fall down (they did not poor dears, they are gigantick, tremendous, but they never do one the *least* harm). I drank a glass of camphor julep with fifteen grains of sal volatile.

[To the Duke of Devonshire]   [Paris]
[12 December 1833]

Silence means to bide at Nice during the winter. She continued peaceable and harmless to the last, went with me to the Tuileries. The King admired her beauty loud enough for her to hear, and she was, as she always is, avec des gens en place extremely happy.

I hope Suzy will arrive before snow or real desperate weather sets in. The Carnival makes me sick, and I want her as a pull against the disgust of giving and going. I do hate society, dearest Grace, more than ever, as a friend told me last night. 'C'est terrible de s'attacher aussi fortement à *sweet ome*, milady.' I was puzzled at first and thought he said 'sweet wine'.

George Lamb had died at the beginning of January. In March Suzy was confined of a son in Paris and was subsequently very ill, to her mother's great alarm.

[257]

[Paris]
[End of March 1834]

I write with a mind in a great degree relieved. I cannot feel as those about me do – not yet satisfied and sanguine – now *you* will be my comfort, for you will understand me. I never have undergone such agony of mind as for the last three days. Every terror, nervous feeling, impossibility of exertion – of hope I have undergone – you never can have suffered as I have done, though you will know its shape and power over one – for I feel now my nerves have made me exaggerate. She has been *very* ill indeed – oh sister sister, I have suffered even unto death. I can not even yet enter in to detail.

There were changes at home in the Ministry and it was touch and go whether Granville might be offered an alternative post.

Private.   [Paris]
[3 June 1834]

I was happy to hear from you yesterday, and all your thinks at this interesting moment. I am glad Lord Carlisle has the Privy Seal. It takes the *scrub* look from the present Cabinet, and is honour to whom honour is due. I can not say how glad I am that the exchange of situation was not offered to Granville. He not only likes Paris best, but would have disliked the Admiralty particularly – no knowledge of Naval affairs, no turn for scraping and economising people, and a necessity of speaking. Yet it would have been extremely painful to him, if had it been asked as a convenient and useful thing, to have refused. *England* would have been purchased at a price that I should have been grieved to see him pay.

[Paris]
Monday [June 1834]

Miss Berry dines here today, she is at times excessively disagreeable with a fond of some good and friendly qualities that make one get over it. But one thing is increased with age – no civility or attention does – it is always complaint, comparison, and scolding. I went to see her on her jour. 'Ah, ah! none the better for you.' 'What do you mean?' 'I might have died yesterday with a wretched cold, for any thing you thought of the matter.' I appealed to the young ladies present if it would not indeed be a miraculous degree of attachment that would have made me guess by instinct the day before that Miss Berry had caught cold, and this followed by two or three smart raps, has done her a great deal of good. Her *self* has become so exigeante, that people are positively angels or devils as they call on her or not, and Granville and I who have been uncommonly polite, are just let off with sighs and groans. 'Nothing surprises me here; no attention seems wonderful to me, remembering what I used to receive.' To give you an idea of it I offered her a very pretty cactus, which she had admired excessively. 'Ah, ah! send me a plant indeed. I used to have as many and more than I wanted without asking, only sending to the conservatory for whatever I chose.' 'You did not marry *us*, Miss Berry', [*] another rap which has been salutary to the virgin.

The Granvilles went again to Aix and from there to Carcassonne, Bordeaux and Angoulême.

Bordeaux
Saturday [13 September 1834]

I found a letter from you at Carcassonne, my own dearest sister. It made me so very happy. Only your delightful accounts of Castle Howard made me pipe, gave me a mal du pays to be there, to help you hang up the prints, to walk with you to the dairy, see the setting sun, and rich tints, and a thousand sights I have never seen and loved as I have at Castle Howard.

Bordeaux
Tuesday [September 1834]

If you will but come to Paris, I engage to give you a thousand and one ways of combating fear. Fear is such a coward. Face it, talk to

---

[*] She held the view that she had arranged the marriage between Lady Elizabeth Yorke and Sir Charles Stuart.

[259]

it, say 'What are you?', and you will find what large unreal shapes it takes and how they vanish before energy and resolution. I have felt terror (for example, I was twenty thousand times more afraid of cholera than you were, of tooth drawing, cattle, carriages &c), well, I have constantly (especially lately) entirely conquered my terror by strong determination.

You will say yours is more a matter of health. I can only answer to this by reminding you of Chatsworth, and urging air, society, interests, amusements, change of scene occasionally. St Leonards with poor Mrs Lamb, a glaring sun and a lodging never seemed to me a lark of the first magnitude – Paris, Lady Carlisle, Paris.

Paris
[End of September 1834]

You are a darling old woman (as Lady Morley says to me) and you are so well and so sprack, and so certainly intending I trust and expect to come and pay us a visit. Spend your fine autumn where you are, then come five in number – Earl, Countess, lord and two ladies – and give yourself a little quiet dissipation and amusement in la belle France.

The King was very gay last night. We are to go to Fontaine-bleau for three days the week after next, and the Fullertons are to be asked I believe. It will be a great comfort to me to have her there, and he likes it, so she tries to be pleased. We both equally shrink from it in perspective, but I bear it better when plunged than she does.

[Paris]
Monday [29 September 1834]

We find many English here. The Berrys run up and down. Tuesday they go to Fontainebleau till Thursday.* We go from Friday till Tuesday. We all think of nothing but dress, with different shades of interest and emotion, and different results to our thoughts as you will judge when I tell you that the Fullertons

*Louis Philippe, his family and Court, were making a ten-day visit to Fontaine-bleau. This was the first time it would be opened up since the days of the Empire.

dined at Bellevue on Saturday and Mary [Berry] received them in organdi with long pink sash, the end floating in the breeze. Do not tell. It is an extraordinary but harmless weakness. She is in very good looks, subdued, very kind, and often as you know friendly and true, and has left off all her disagreeable ways and hootings at me.

[Paris]
Friday 3 [October 1834]
We are just setting out for Fontainebleau and being fine brisk weather, Mme Appony to join us tomorrow, I look forward to it with some pleasure and less of dread than might be expected. There are moments before which my firm nerve shakes, such as four-long hour dinners (there is a collation at five *after* the drive, luncheon is *during*) and being in time for dinner.

I see Berry has been at breakfast in the forest and sailing on a pond. We shall meet these fortunate girls screaming their way back,[34] and Naples, Russia, and Prussia, who return today. Appony is classed for this time with Spain, England and Belgium.

[Paris]
Thursday [9 October 1834]
Our last day at Fontainebleau was the bouquet; in the morning a junket on the Etang de François I in a very large sort of barge boat, with circular seats and an awning, from which we saw the château as if it grew out of the water. We stepped in to a pavilion in the middle of that étang where the massacre of St Bartholomew was finally settled – because, Lady Carlisle, what is whispered on the water can not be heard on the land. (I told the King this, and he was much edified and surprised – very glad to hear it, no ways doubting, only had never happened to hear of it).

The ball was magnificent, the gallerie de Henri II lit in a blaze, and a banquet after it, which lasted till half past two, the whole thing grandiose, magnificent and luxurious, and I liked it of all things. To come home is pleasant in its way. Italian opera three times a week, no dinners or drums begun, delicious mornings in this heavenly weather, in what is real country, the Bois de Boulogne. On Sunday we think we shall run in to the Tuileries, to prove our gratitude by boring them to death.

[Paris]
[14 October 1834]
We are fond of Berry. Since I have reflected upon her age,* which is not often present (vu the gaudy colours, noise and constant about-ishness), I think she deserves much excuse, égard, for what is disagreeable, much esteem and approbation for what is pleasant, sociable by habit, exigeante by situation and intimate by force. There is something goes against one in the process, but the result is great delight when she obtains (what she must naturally consider) her due in society, and an enjoyment of it, that neither the young nor the happy can come up to. Hear and hide your face in both hands. Berry had on a white crape hat with three or four little white feathers tipped with cherry colour, the last new shape which is lower, broader, rather more [illegible], a white muslin gown, broad white satin sash, bouclé par devant, a tulle scarf of stripes of cherry colour and white.

[Paris]
[24 October 1834]
Now dearest of sisters, do you know Miss Berry has made herself so pleasant and popular here that her going will be very much felt and regretted. I *never* saw any body upon whom success had so happy and softening an effect. All her bitterness and snapping up is gone, and she is more good tempered and easily pleased at this moment than any body in Paris.

[Paris]
Monday [27 October 1834]
You are a darling woman, Lady Carlisle, but you do not talk enough of coming to Paris. Miss Berry can not tear herself away. I

*Mary Berry was seventy-one years old.

found her yesterday (to shew you what we shall all come to) in a gown the pattern of which was a dark green treillage, roses and lilacs intertwining, a green shawl and bonnet, the bonnet lined with deep rose colour, yet she did not look absurd or too young, but handsome like Mlle Mars and gayer than 20,000 larks.

Quite unexpectedly William IV dissolved Parliament: the Whigs were out and the Granvilles left for England at the beginning of January.

[Paris]
[Mid November 1834]

I have but time for a line. How wonderful, how sudden! My reason and my wishes for him [Granville] make me very sorry. But the thought of being in London in less than three weeks, in Bruton Street, expecting you! Write to D. for me.

I can not write, and that is the long and short of it, my own dearest, best loved sister. I can scarcely think, so like a bomb has this news come upon us! and all opinions vary. The *soundest* think it will float, others think it will sink before three months are past. Of my own feelings I do not speak. First comes Granville. He likes being here, so I wish it; but then comes the overwhelming thought of you and Susy.

You may imagine our impatience for further news.

[Paris]
[1 December 1834]

I have but one moment. Brougham arrived in tearing spirits. I have not yet seen him.

We shall be in Bruton Street. People are kinder than any thing ever was. Granville must be more than gratified at the feeling about him here. He is really adored.

[Paris]

Friday [5 December 1834]

Brougham has caused an immense sensation here. He is in roaring spirits, not the least ashamed of his last extraordinary step, (his law request),* talking without ceasing, gold, copper, but as all is stamped the same people allow for its nature of the coin and fix its price, which prevents either doing the good or harm that might be expected. He goes to the Chambres, and to all the institutions, to all the theatres, to all the dinners and all the soirées, and I am told has, since his arrival, written as much as he has talked. He is a sublime quack, Lady C. Brougham, Sir F. Lamb, Mme de Flahault, good humoured, gay – liking to be all in a fury together.

What busy and exciting scenes we are returning to, most dear sister!

[Paris]

[January 1835]

We think of setting out the end of next week, to be in London about the 15th. We are very well and very *eager*. I delight in the thoughts of London. It will be to me a pleasant city. No assemblies, balls, operas, but dinners and réunions at my friends. Those who receive early – not smart – admit of cross-stitch and sketching, lists of elections, walks with Lady C. of a morning. Dissipation is the sting of life, and for the first time it will be no duty for me.

Once I shall go *with you* to Berry, and that's all.

The Government was short-lived. On 8 April Sir Robert Peel resigned. The Whigs would take over again, Lord Melbourne (William Lamb) as Premier, Lord Palmerston Foreign Secretary, and the Granvilles would return to Paris.

[To the Duke of Devonshire]   [Bruton Street]

[12 April 1835]

One line out of breath, most dear D.

I hear Johnny [Russell] is likely to be Foreign Affairs. I shall be

*He wished to be made Chief Baron.

[264]

very sorry for Lord Palmerston. He must have something and what will he accept? Now my dearest brother, look at this picture and on that. On one hand, you and Paxton,[b] sitting under a red rhododendron at Chatsworth, under the shade of palms and pines in your magnificent conservatory, with no thought of your country's weal and woe.

Now, walking up and down a terrace in Phoenix Park, arm in arm with Morpeth, your secretary, saving that hapless country, adored and worshipped. Think of the gratification to them, of the power to you of doing good. Damp but glorious. I hear they want you to go to Ireland. I cannot, intimate as I am with your intelligence, guess what you are thinking at this moment.

Che sarà sarà, for all of us.

[To the Duke of Devonshire]   [Bruton Street]
                                                        [13 April 1835]

Of course you know that Lord Melbourne is to declare himself Premier in the House today. Miss Berry has been agreeable, but I had the satisfaction of telling her that she was not a Whig at heart and that I always saw the Tory foot. Lord Palmerston. He talked most openly (*most* private), told me there was a report that Johnny was to be at the Foreign Office. He looked much ému when he said it and added, 'this I can not believe'. Then he muttered, 'I suppose I shall be shortly there myself', and then loud, 'in which case I hope you will instantly prepare and pack up for Paris.'

                                                                Paris
                                                        [29 May 1835]

One line, my most dear sister, to tell you that we arrived after a most prosperous journey today. We have had the attachés to dinner. Poor Henry Greville[*] straining every nerve to be useful; laborious and plodding, and making himself extremely agreeable during our repast. I feel more as if I had left you all since I arrived, than I did en route.

[*]Younger brother of the diarist Charles Greville, and himself a diarist of lesser reputation – though he excelled, according to Lady Holland, with his 'viper's tongue'.

[265]

[Paris]
[1 June 1835]

Tonight I go to the Tuileries. On Friday dine at the Broglie's to meet Talleyrand and Madame de Dino. When ever any body who hates me dines any where, I am always fetched for them, poor souls. The evenings I decline, as in London. I do not see in these summer days why I should not.

Paris
[4 June 1835]

Granville is gone a round of ministerial visits and I am with the window open, the orange flower smelling too strong, the nightingales singing too loud, and this in the middle of a city is very delicious. There is a beautiful passage in Mrs Norton's book* about that, the gifts so impartially granted to all and what ought to be our gratitude. How excellent, how beautiful I think some of her writing; but some how or other she does not fit in to her own frame, she is not in keeping with her own opinions and feelings, and it is impossible to bind her up with her own stories.[35]

Paris is full and gay. I am at this moment remorseful at not stepping up the Elysian Fields to Meg [de Flahault]. We dine at Court, full dress. I went the other evening and was most graciously received, though Dino sat to see us with her gas light eyes, but we all did as if she was not there.

[Paris]
Tuesday [June 1835]

Lady William has sent me a distressing cadeau, very beautiful – a white feather – all white, little dots and all – but a mile long and like a water work. I shall look so very like Mrs T. Fool in this singular and most remarkable ornament – and she is coming, we are told (like her tongue) incessament.[36] Get and read André† by George Sand, it is written by a woman who has written horrible things though all I believe wonderfully good, but *this* is beautiful. Poor Ada Byron,‡ who is going to marry the greatest bore I know.

*Probably *The Wife's and Woman's Reward*, 1835.
†A novel, published in 1835.
‡Augusta Ada, Byron's daughter, married Lord King, 1st Earl of Lovelace on 8 July.

[266]

[To the Duke of Devonshire]   [Paris]
                                           [7 September 1835]
Balzac is a fat, red man, whose locks flow. He sits in the pit at the
Opera, looks about him, and said Lady Jersey in a box aloft was the
vrai type de l'aristocratie anglaise. 'Le Père Goriot'* I have not read
but will, and will ask with a fan before my face if he is historical or
fabulous, ancient or modern, and let you know. I long to have G
here. Your details of them all, the way you tell me all I wish to know
and nothing I don't, the pound of flesh, no parler après avoir dit,
the best style of writing with no manner of doing it, makes your
correspondence one of the greatest pleasures in the world.

[To the Duke of Devonshire]   [Paris]
                                           [23 October 1835]
The [Russian] Ambassador Pahlen is a very handsome, fine
looking man, something brave et loyal, talks quick – not, I should
think, clever. Picks his teeth with his knife, scorns sugar tongs, a
grand specimen of a Russian soldier.

*Georgiana Carlisle and the Duke of Devonshire were in Paris in
February. In the spring proceedings were instituted against Lord
Melbourne by George Norton for misconduct with his wife.
Caroline Norton had many admirers including Trelawny, the
friend of Shelley, but her husband was likely only to bring a case
where the supposed lover was a man of fortune, whereby Norton
would profit if he won. The Prime Minister was acquitted on the
first day of the trial (23 June).*

[To the Duke of Devonshire]   [Paris]
                                            [25 March 1836]
I have been shut up for weeks,[37] as Granville has the gout, and
now there are the Easter holidays. How your account of the royal
boys amused me.† Is the second to marry his cousin?

---

*A novel (1835), skilfully uniting several interwoven stories.
†The Princes Ferdinand and Augustus of Saxe-Coburg-Kohary were Princess
Victoria's first cousins. They were in England for a few weeks.

Paris
[22 April 1836]
We are all excited about Norton – that is, all but me. I hear the great thing said against him is that he swallows the lovers or not according to their rank and position. Lord Melbourne yes, Captain Trelawny no.

Paris
Monday [? 25 April 1836]
I have had a most ravishing letter from D. Every body raves of his ball, and I am so pleased that he should see his endeavours to please answer. I agree with you so entirely in all you say about him, and the cleverness and peculiar charm which make frivolity, and sometimes a degree of want of proper consideration of, more than of feeling *for*, others, more attractive than the sense and savoir of others, who look down (and with reason) upon dress and dissipation.

Granville fell from his horse on Monday, but most happily was not hurt, though he felt a little shook by it. But how one does think, upon such occasions, of all that one is spared, of the mercies one ceases to dwell upon. The terrors one magnifies and amplifies that are not permitted to be realised and it seems to me that life ought to be spent on our knees, and how is it? carelessly, ungratefully.

Tell Miss Berry she will find much of the sort of society she most likes, every body at home always and out-of-door pleasures abounding. Mme Durazzo* is now taking a house here. She is a very great and universal favourite – she is here, there, and every where; abhors (I am told) Miss Berry.

[Paris]
Friday [May 1836]
We are much interested about the Norton case, for *his* sake. What is unlucky and alarming is this being the second case.† Ones hope

---

*Marchesa Durazzo, a member of a prominent Genoese family.
†There had been an earlier scandal in 1828 when Lady Branden's husband had bought an action against Melbourne for adultery with his wife, but the case had been dismissed.

of escape turns upon the meanness and total want of anything to excite sympathy in Mr N. *I* think F. Lamb a little nervous about the Norton story.*

I have not a word to say how much I think Miss Berry will be annoyed. Mme Durazzo is every where – every body intime, very popular, she cannot avoid her and I think Durazzo will set every one against her. At this time of year when every thing and every body come so much together – in the winter such an enmity might have managed its matters.

[Paris]
[13 May 1836]

So Miss Berry is really to be here on the 23rd. It will be a great embarras to society where Durazzo walks over the course.

Paris
[7 June 1836]

We sat after dinner, at half past nine in walks Durazzo. I soon saw Berry, her, the whole kit, Agnes and all, talking, bowing, smiling. Berry is all civility, and came boasting. 'Did you see us?' I do not think Genoa will be friends, but Berry is dying to be well with them, and pursued and was more gracious than I ever saw her. These girls are wonderful.

[To the Duke of Devonshire] Paris

[23 June 1836]

We are in breathless expectation of the verdict. Nothing even by telegraph this morning. So afraid of what he may have bleated about our Gracious.† Who could bear to have their letters ripped up for evidence?

The Turkish Ambassador has just sent me two beautiful écharpes for turbans – one painted, the other embroidered silk and gold – a scented purse, a necklace, a bottle of otto of roses,

---

*Frederick Lamb had such a reputation as a rake that Harriet may have wondered whether he too might be incriminated.
†It was feared that Melbourne might have been indiscreet concerning political – and royal – persons.

and a parcel of gilt and brown pastilles. We think this is a pretty custom.

We are still in suspense, harmless letters and awkward facts, but no verdict come yet.

[Paris]
[June 1836]

By the bye, as you sometimes take alarm at stories circulated, and as indeed it is difficult to believe in lies without any foundation, you may perhaps see and hear in the papers here that at our journée on the 28th Granville lost 48,000 Franks. For your own satisfaction and as an answer to the d – – – d good natured, it is amusing to have to state, that on that day, it so happened that from the receiving at all hours and the soirée ending at 12, Granville did not even play his usual rubber at whist. Ainsi parle le monde.

The Granvilles were in England in July and August. They made a short trip on the Rhine before returning to Paris towards the end of September.

[To the Duke of Devonshire]   Devonshire House
[14 August 1836]

Your letter, my dear brother, found me here yesterday. No flower arrived, cruel Paxton.

We dined with the Hollands. At the turnpike we met Landseer. He has painted the most perfect little picture of Lord Melbourne.[*] Rogers was looking very ill. It is a compliment to him to say so, one had thought he could have gone no farther. The Speaker[†] and Lady dined at Holland House. She, in green satin, with sleeves ornamented with bows, and a wreathed cap, looking at my blue silk bags and ribboned cap and said: 'We are in error, I see, we over-do a little; we ought to adopt on these occasions

[*]Now in the National Portrait Gallery.
[†]Hon. James Abercromby.

[270]

demie-parure.' We complimented her much on her husband's looks but she shook her head, 'You should look at his person', slightly designating her own upper leg.

[Paris]
Friday pm. [11 November 1836]
Where, oh where, are our letters? It seems to me that we do nothing but write, and you do any thing but hear.

We all dined at Neuilly day before yesterday. Sir Robert[*] [Peel] can scarcely speak any French. The King talked English to him but what was distressing, the Queen (under a natural embrouillé that being deaf to the language was the same as being deaf to the sound), bawled out every word to him as if he was stone deaf, loud and distinct. 'J'és – père que vous – vous plai – sez à Paris.' An odd effect, and made Sir Robert fidget on his perch next to her at dinner.

Repair and decoration in the Embassy were again essential but by January all was in order and Harriet wrote of the smell of paint going off, 'and we must begin again drumming and affronting'.³⁸ Louis Philippe's heir, the Duc d'Orléans, was to marry Princess Hélène of Mecklenburg-Schwerin and in consequence there were to be receptions and fêtes – spicing a natural curiosity about the bride.

[Paris]
[March 1837]
Every body seems to think the Duke of Orléans' marriage settled. They say the bride is tall, thin and plain, and perfectly well brought up. Bad teeth, red hair, amiable countenance.

[Paris]
Monday [May 1837]
The duc de Broglie who was to have gone tomorrow to meet the Princess has a fluxion and swelled face, and may be prevented,

<hr>

*Peel had resigned the Premiership the previous year.

which will be unlucky. The picture has come, and the Duke of Orléans has locked it up. I hear 'c'est atroce', but Monsieur Bresson sends word that it is a very unfavourable likeness, but that she, Miss Meck, insisted upon sending it. Wise, I think.

[Paris]
Friday [May 1837]

The presentations to the duchesse d'Orléans are to take place on the fifth and sixth of June.* We intend going on the 4th (if diplomacy is received apart); if not on the fifth. We take apartments at Versailles, one week before the fête from Monday week. We shall go there as soon as Granville is well enough to move for the benefit of the change of air, his first ride and the comfort of being on the tenth (the day of the great doings) within a stone's throw of the spectacle at night, the musée in the morning.

The duc de Broglie and all his suite write enchanted with Princess Hélène. They say she has perfect self-possession, the best manner, never the least put out, knowing what to do and say on all occasions. Lady Stuart came to see me today with her daughter,† looking less well than usual and rather stormy. Betty, too, in a fuss. Lord Stuart won't come. They both wish to stay to see the opening at Versailles.‡ Betty is puzzled, opens her mouth, hangs her paw, looks like a very hot red spaniel.

Princesse Hélène has black eye lashes and a fine complexion, Monsieur Bresson says she is the gentlest and most determined person he ever met with, that never *out of France* was such a manner and tenue seen. Her teeth are little black stumps, the foot very big.

[To the Duke of Devonshire]   [Paris]
[12 June 1837]

I was at the Reservoir Inn at three. At six we went to the château. At near three in the morning we drank tea, then put on our

*The marriage took place on 31 May.
†Louisa, who later married the Marquess of Waterford.
‡Versailles had been neglected over the last years. Louis Philippe had restored and altered it and a great fête marked the opening as well as the marriage of the King's heir.

bonnets and shawls again, and I and Mrs Foster [her maid] came
back to Paris, ventre à terre, and arrived at half past four. Versailles
was as beautiful as possible within and without. The Salle de
Spectacle is beyond description or imagination. Though entirely
red and gold, as light as day. The full dress, Miss Elssler's legs,*
Mlle Mars' conversation – 'spare me the details' –, you will say.

What I admire most is Versailles, the thing itself, human beings
streaming over all its glories and amongst the jets d'eau, clumps of
roses, and under, thanks to the late season, the lilacs, laburnums,
horse-chestnuts, and all the busy delight and bustle – a hum of
millions of people looking their smartest. Nothing ever was in my
opinion so perfect as the duchesse d'Orléans' manner, so calm so
quiet and still, yet always more attentive, more gracious and more
perfectly up to it all than any of those around her, a sort of tenue
that would make any defects of manner in others (were there such)
remarkably obvious. The diplomats much pleased with their box.
Mme de Flahault says we were degraded. We mean to enquire how.
The foreigners of distinction very indignant at a great gaucherie.
Stuarts, Staffords, Mme Durazzo, having been asked all to dinner,
the day before received formal printed un-invitations, desired to
consider their former invites as nuls et non avenus.

*William IV died on 20 June and Princess Victoria ascended the
throne.*

[To the Duke of Devonshire]   Paris
                                                          23 June [1837]
I hope Granville will be well enough to pay a visit to England, and
he much wishes it himself; but he cannot yet walk and it must be
some time before he can risk making any exertion or undergoing
any fatigue. We therefore remain here for the present, avid of news,
devouring newspapers, gasping for letters, and marking days by
the intelligence received; for it is history, fate, romance, all in one.
Every thing new, nothing to be calculated upon. Such a little love of
a Queen! Lord Melbourne must take care to throw a something

---

*Fanny Elssler (1810–84) was a celebrated Austrian dancer.

paternal in to his manner.* We pine to hear of the First Lady. All point at that other Queen, Harriet the First.† I alone say she never can, or will make such a sacrifice.

God bless you. If you have any pity, write.

[Paris]
[July 1837]

I feel so much interested about that little, wonderful, Queen and admire all I hear of her and Lord Melbourne's relative position. What a strong, anxious tie it is, that binds him to her service, so unlike any thing else of the sort that one ever heard or read of.

[To the Duke of Devonshire]   St Germain
[14 July 1837]

We think of being in England for a fortnight the very beginning of August. Dieppe and Brighton on the way.

We came here yesterday evening. The weather is divine, the air pure and bracing as at Kemp Town. How I hope I shall find you on the pier. Is the passage out of steamer, on to pier very unpleasant? I think I can recollect having it in horror, but if Mme St Clair has achieved it, carrying her fears and legs featly over it, I will give my alarm to the winds.

The Granvilles postponed their visit to England until the autumn. Their eldest son, Leveson, wished to marry a Roman Catholic widow, Marie Dalberg, Lady Acton, whose husband had died in January of this year. The great drawback was her insistence on any child born of the marriage being brought up a Roman Catholic. They married in 1840, there were no children, and she died in 1860.

---

* So soon after the crisis with Caroline Norton.
† Harriet Duchess of Sutherland, Lady Carlisle's daughter, was appointed Mistress of the Robes.

Leveson is unaccountable – and so is she. There never was any thing so decided as Granville upon *the* point. I have no reason to believe, and now Leveson does not think, that she will ever give way upon it. I am glad to find how few people seem to know about it as it spares one the inflictions of questions and interference.

[To the Duke of Devonshire]   [Paris]
                                                        5 August 1837

You have painted the Queen to me in general colours. What tact the little woman seems to possess! What determination! And how much security there is, I think, in her friendships, engouements and entourage, making her go on blowing in the right quarter. When I hear of Lord Melbourne looking very ill and worn, and see how neck and neck the election runs, I feel as if our great dependence was in her grace and favour, and I hope, as you say, we shall do uncommonly well with that.

[To the Duke of Devonshire]   [London]
                                                   [21 November 1837]

I found G at dinner at Court, in hat and feather and diamonds, gayest of the gay and in her element. You know she loves in Courts to shine. I find Queen Victoria perfect in manner, dignity, and grace, with great youthfulness and joyousness. I find a dinner at Court very curious to see, but my bad nature prevailed, and I got so impatient towards eleven that I hardly could bear it. It is so much more like a Court than any I have seen, and I am spoilt by bobbing in for ten minutes to the Queen's back and cross-stitch at the Tuileries. She talked almost entirely to the men, but very graciously and kindly to us. [The Duchess of Kent] at whist looks careworn, but all seems smooth.

In Paris the winter months passed in drumming and dancing and entertaining the English, relations, and friends. The Fullertons were usually at hand, living mostly in the Embassy with their children. Granville was not in good health, nor it seems was Harriet. (Princess Lieven who was living in France exclaimed at the bad health they shared.) Everything about Queen Victoria interested her – was there a likelihood of her marrying the Duke of Hamilton's eldest son, Lord Douglas?, she asked her sister. 'Oh, how I should like to perch on the wall with you. Easy sight seeing.' Her brother wrote her a description of the Coronation.

[To the Duke of Devonshire]   [Paris]
                                                    [2 July 1838]
You must know that it is quite impossible to make you sensible of the pleasure of hearing from you this morning. It was quite delightful and Lieven was allowed a peep at the sketch. She bids me tell you that you are the only person capable of giving a proper notion and vivid description of such things. For where is Lieven's heart and what is her absorbing interest? Why Precedence, my dear, who first, who last, who here, who there.

We go on Tuesday, the 10th. A new road, shorter, avoiding Lyons and the Jura, dipping perpendicularly down la Dent du Chat into hot little Aix bason. Oh that you could be tempted! God bless you.

                                                    Aix-les-Bains
                                                    [August 1838]
I think it such a great and important object that the Queen should have such people as *yours* about her.* The influence may not be as direct and as intimate, as would be most perfect, but it must always tell and out of doors and in doors give to both reality and appearance, a purer and higher stamp.

                                                    Aix
                                                    [August 1838]
You never mention a possibility of your Paris visit. If you wish for quiet, you can always command it there. If you wish for fêtes and

*Blanche Howard, the Carlisles' daughter, had married William, Earl of Burlington, Uncle George's eldest son and the Duke's heir. She had just been appointed eighth lady-in-waiting.

spectacles, there are to be many on the occasion of the christening of the child that is hoped for on the 15th. Mme de Lieven tells me today he is to be called Comte de Paris, and that his marraine is to be the Ville de Paris.

Dijon
[September 1838]

The Hollands intend being at Paris almost as soon as we are, and I delight in the thought of seeing him. I know not how she and Princesse Lieven will put up their horses together, but I hope well, and she (Mme de L) so pines for society and politicians to talk to that I think it ensures keeping the peace, especially if the trial is not very long.

[Paris]
24 [September 1838]

Now what have I got to say? Lord Holland is rather low, and she is suffering again, confined to her couch. She says it is the fatigue of the journey. I say it is such a dinner as I never saw any body eat before. Lord Holland had a long conversation with the King at the Tuileries, and I hear he intends a surprise to go to meet them the day they are at Versailles. I do not think the to-be-astonished are pleased in proportion.

The Dowager Duchess of Sutherland, the Duchess-Countess (Lady Stafford of earlier days), died at the beginning of February 1839. This closed the Paris Embassy doors for a short time.

[Paris]
[9 May 1839]

The Queen was enchanted with her dinner at Lansdowne House, examining every thing, lights, liveries, plates, knives, merry and inquisitive, uniting the difficult parts of a girl dining for the first time from home and a sovereign dining for the first time with a subject.

[Paris]

21 [June 1839]

Lady Jersey is as pleasant à vivre as she used to be rugged. Never comes near me but when I propose it, and then is as good humoured and pleasable as it is possible to be. Mr O.* gives her pineapples, boxes, and visits. Mrs O. takes her to the French play. Upon seeing these operations, many women, many minds. Madame Appony outrée. Mrs G.† pénétrée with reconnaissance and delight that such penances are only afflicted upon the silent.

[Paris]

[1 July 1836]

Leveson is in high spirits, in love with nobody. Very intimate again with Lady – [Acton], who is playing her on and off game with many of the unwary, but he is I think, aware and safe.

[To the Duke of Devonshire]   [Windsor Castle]

[? 11 October 1839]

It is delightful. I had forgotten the beauty of the place, inside and out. The weather is quite heavenly – every comfort and luxury. Lady Sandwich and Lady Clanricarde. The Princes of Coburg arrived.‡ A key to go all day long in to the garden. No driving required. I have been taking a delicious walk on the Terrace in to an embroidered garden. Lord Palmerston said that if my brother could but come here for six months en maître, Windsor would be the most magnificent thing on earth, and it is quite true.

The Queen looks lovely, much more delicate without looking ill. Lord Melbourne appears to be in as great favour as ever, and I think their relative manners in a difficult position perfect. We sat round in the evening, but had much to look at. 'My cousins' are both of them very unaffected and with very good manners, perfectly at their ease with her without gêne or familiarity; and Prince Albert the youngest is charming. Ladies Sandwich, Clanricarde and I are won. It remains to be seen who else will be.

Roast beef and potatoes with the Ministers and Maids. Going

*The Duc d'Orléans.
†Harriet herself.
‡The Princes Ernest and Albert of Saxe-Coburg.

[278]

in a real coach and horses to Virginia Water. Lady Sandwich says she idolises the Queen. Lord Normanby imagines that there is nothing actually en train as to marriage. Lord Melbourne sat by her yesterday evening as usual, did not sleep at all or talk too much. Prince Albert played at chess. Lady Clanricarde said, 'The trial is too great; if he wins he has a master mind.' He lost. H.M. asked Lady Clanricarde: 'Do you think my cousin like me?' She said yes, because he is, though much handsomer.

Windsor
11 October [1839]

You know the magnificence of Windsor – the charm of the Queen – add to this then Ladies Clanricarde and Sandwich, heavenly weather and 'my cousins' and you will imagine there is de quoi. The two young Princes arrived too late for dinner. They met us in the drawing room. Both with good manners, particularly *here*, steering clear between gêne and familiarity. The eldest well-looking and like Leopold, the youngest handsome and captivating, like Paris. Whether waiting at all, or for what, is yet to be seen. We *sat* last night but with all our eyes on. Tonight we dance. Lord Melbourne sat by her yesterday evening, not the least sleepy but they talked much less than usual. Only think of dancing tonight, Lady Clanricarde with a velvet gown and Lady Sandwich just recovering her health – are low at the prospect of the evening. It is easy to see what she does – adore – en tout bien et tout honneur – his manner perfect.

[Later] The dancing was prosperous inasmuch as the Queen is the prettiest most delicious thing. From the evening my conclusion is that there will be nothing in this visit.* I think the madre looks provoked – the boy discouraged. I do not think she shows him any attention, or rather much attention but no liking.[39]

Devonshire House
[12 or 16 October 1839]

We have been to the play. 'The Lady of Lyons' has beautiful

*However, the Queen asked Prince Albert to marry her on 15 October.

poetic passages in it. Macready admirable in the conception of his part – delectable in the execution of it.*

Lady Sandwich (the Dow.) has just been here. She tells me Prince Albert has been flirting the last two days, she was not sure, but thinks with Miss Cocks.† An odd distraction I think.

[Paris]

7 [December 1839]

Lady Cowper's marriage,‡ the early period fixed for the Queen's,§ all was news. Lady Cowper has courage to face her angry children. I cannot say how much I blame them for telling out what they feel, but I wonder she can encounter their antipathy.⁴⁰ What a happy mother she might have been and what an unhappy existence will she I fear have. Her understanding never has been of the slightest use to her.

[Paris]

[December 1839]

Lord and Lady Clarendon¶ dined here yesterday. They appear extremely happy. He does not give one the notion of being in love, but comfortable, settled and rid of the old loves – a great pull in such matters. She good, amiable.

[Paris]

[27 December 1839]

Madame de Lieven has had a letter from Lady Cowper at Broadlands. She seems perfectly happy at the decision she has taken. Says she was a sotte not to have had the courage to do it long ago. Foreign affairs will be more come-at-able, I suspect,

*Macready was acting at the Haymarket Theatre on both the above dates.
†Probably Lady Caroline Somers-Cocks, maid of honour to the Queen.
‡The widowed Lady Cowper married Lord Palmerston, her admirer of many years, on 16 December 1839.
§The marriage was fixed for 10 February 1840.
¶George Villiers, Earl of Clarendon, had married the widowed Lady Katherine Barham. One of his 'old loves' had been the mother of Eugénie, Empress of the French.

than they have been for a long time. Lord Palmerston's incivilities will obtain a varnish.

The Clarendons went yesterday. They have been very amiable. She is plain, but seems the best, most sensible, inoffensive wife that can be, extremely fond of him, and he looks happier, healthier, and honester than I ever saw him. Burn this.

The spring of 1840 brought a great sorrow. Blanche Burlington died in April and the Duke of Devonshire, who loved her as his own daughter, felt the loss deeply.

[To the Duke of Devonshire]   [Paris]
                                                        30 [April 1840]
I thank you more than I can say, my beloved brother. It would have given me intolerable anxiety not to have heard from you, and in that letter, in the midst of anguish, there is something that speaks peace. I feel as if, in that angel's departure, there was a sort of mission to us all to suffer, resign ourselves and hope. Your letter will always be by me. I love you my dearest brother. I never knew how much I loved you. You are never for a moment out of my thoughts.

                                                                [Paris]
                                                      [? 30 April 1840]
It is not possible for me to express my gratitude for your letter. Without it I never could have poured out to you all the devoted feeling of affection, of sympathy, that I have longed to write to you and dearest Lord Carlisle. I feel what absence is, not to be near you all now. What, however, could I be that you are not to each other in the midst of the blessings that remain and duties that occupy you, which you so adorably feel, and for which God will give you strength and grace. I feel that we are all left to endeavour to follow her in all that may await us in this life of trial. I only hope to be like you.

[Paris]
Monday [May 1840]

I long to be with you, to talk to you, to feel with you, to learn of you. I think it is a long time before we practically believe how much is given, how little asked. I do not think it is in man easily to understand the unbounded mercy of God. Come unto me, and that at the eleventh hour, as at the first, this (the only peace on earth) we shrink from till brought to it by fear and sorrow, terror and bereavement.

The question of the possibility of Leveson marrying Lady Acton is easily answered by your own thought. It is not the difference of religion but her irrevocable determination about children. That puts it entirely out of the question. I can not understand their going on as they do – both aware of the insuperable bar.

God bless you my angel sister.

[Paris]
[17 August 1840]

Mr Macaulay dined here yesterday, and as we had nothing to do but to listen he was very welcome. He told us all about every thing, and is I think prepared for any thing. I expect nothing.

[Paris]
7 [October 1840]

My love to all yours. Dear, beautiful Castle Howard. Autumn brings it so to my mind. There is no place of which my recollections are so vivid. At any time I can cry over its walks, its beauties and its pleasures. I can smell it and see it with almost all the ecstasy there is in all the enjoyment of earth, air and sky.

The year 1841 was one of affliction. Granville suffered a stroke in early spring and sent in his resignation although no successor was appointed for many months. The Government was dissolved in August and the Tories came to power. Lord Holland, the dear friend of so many years, died in October and that same month the Granvilles left Paris for good. In the summer they had rented a place at La Jonchère, near Versailles and the Marly woods, hoping that country air might benefit Granville's health. The Carlisles joined them for a visit. Few letters were written other than short notes concerning Granville's slow improvement, but plans were being hatched for a journey south.

[To the Duke of Devonshire]   [Paris]
                                        [12 March 1841]
I am very good for nothing after my long grippe, and on a day like spring am not to go out. But I am sitting with lilacs in my alabaster basket opposite my great cage. All your presents and my original ones living in harmony together, all coming under the glass, where they have a garden. In the middle, sand from Havre. Branches of millet in a dark blue vase and bulbs of light blue Bohemian glass.

                                        La Jonchère
                                        [15 June 1841]
I think my brother will approve extremely of this place. He does not mind a drive. We could lodge him, but I fear he would not like it, as the bedrooms, though very clean and nice, are extremely small. But what he would like is the dry, pure air and high situation. They are making hay, but there is no sting in it. I have not smelt it and I think it is damp brings out its sweetness and mischief so that it merges in this large atmosphere.

[To the Duke of Devonshire]   La Jonchère
                                        [August 1841]
One line without stopping to take breath. We hope to set out for Nice the second week in October. We shall spend the early months there till February, and then we hope Rome. Naples in April. What happiness if you are coming! But all turns upon one thing, of course, how Granville is at the time.

The Granvilles had spent the greater part of seventeen years in Paris. In October 1841 they set off for Nice with a short stay at

[283]

Lord Brougham's house at Cannes which he had put at their
disposal. Their party consisted of the Fullertons, George Stewart,
Till the dog, a cook, maids, footman, courier. The Levesons were
to follow and the Riverses would join them later on. After
wintering in Nice they travelled slowly: Milan and Stuttgart in the
early summer, Herrnsheim in August (the home of Lady
Leveson), Munich, Verona, and finally Rome by November
1842.

[To the Duke of Devonshire] [Rome]
[Early January 1843]

You will have heard from my sister of our proceedings, my
dearest brother. You will have seen that, after too great delight of
seeing Granville to all appearances perfectly well, we had a
lesson, for which I am deeply grateful. He is now going on quite
well, the only difference being that he feels himself rather less
strong in walking, and that he consents to give up reading, outing,
and all that can fatigue or excite. You are most kind about
Chiswick, but no. My great wish is our house in London, and
then to go to all your Palazzi and abroad again if necessary.

[To the Duke of Devonshire] [Rome]
16 [January 1843]

I have an irresistible wish to write to you, dearest brother,
because I can not vent myself to any body who quite understands
me, and I think you will. Little Till is dead after two days of very
great suffering. The servants are all in tears. We had made him
such a pet, amusement and companion, that we shall miss him
more than I can say. They are all sorry, but no body can quite
enter into my feeling about it, and my great object is to hide it. He
is linked with so many thoughts and moments. There never was
such an engaging creature. And then the very thing of not being
able to make any one understand, and therefore endeavouring to
suppress how very much I am grieved about it, makes it worse.
Pray do not answer this; I write it only for my comfort, and I have
the conviction that you will entirely understand what is reason
and what is folly.

[To the Duke of Devonshire]   [Rome]
                                                    [20 January 1843]
It is very odd. I felt, when I last wrote, ashamed of being sorry,
afraid of being thought to have been, which I was, crying all day,
and I have been comforted by the excessive kindness and
sympathy people have shown.

[To the Duke of Devonshire]   [Rome]
                                                 [Early March 1843]
What can I say, how begin, how end? I wait, best and kindest of
brothers, to tell you all that your gift bestows.* Granville's delight
is to alarm me, to tell me that it is still uncertain, that the
Reverend [R. Rhodes] may be taken ill and be unable to start.

                                                   4 [March 1843]
We see in the papers that between Calais and Paris there has been
forty feet depth of snow Oh! brother, brother, R.R.R. and his
precious freight! Every thing is prepared. Darling Till's basket
new lined, and a new red collar. His name is to be Tiber.

                                                  11 [March 1843]
Great news. Backhouse has had a letter from Mr R.R. on the
road. He expects him today or to morrow, and desires to find him
deux lits de maître. We think one must be for Tiber. Everything is
prepared, and a small negress to wait upon him and teach him all
Till's tricks, of which she is perfect mistress. Her voice, manner,
and shape exactly like Till's. We are extremely fond of her, but
she is not possible as a constant companion, as a drawing room
favourite. She is, to begin with, like a little hyena. We hope, that
as Tiber's maid, she may learn sweetness and decorum.

[To the Duke of Devonshire]   [Rome]
                                                      [April 1843]
I sing Tiber. There never was such a darling. Beautiful I think,
caressing, soft, helpless, and yet with a spice of the family temper,
which prevents insipidity. Oh! there never was such a love of a

*The Duke of Devonshire was sending out another dog as a present. It was being
brought by the Revd R. Rhodes.

[285]

dog. We do not attempt education; all our care goes to health, and the success is perfect. He is plumping up, his coat glossy, his paws beginning to flounce and furbelow.

In late April the party moved to Florence; to Arqui; Lausanne was reached in July, Devonshire House in August.

[To the Duke of Devonshire]   Arqui
                                                          23 [May 1843]
You can have no idea of the pleasure it gives us to accept your proposal of D House. Thank you a thousand times for that, as for so many acts of kindness that gild our life. Granville has taken the second mineral water this morning, and begins the mud bath for his leg and arm tomorrow. He is very well, but as yet the light air and perfect repose are the only remedies we have had time to judge of.

I think Chiswick an incomparable place, enjoyed on a bad day. What will the enchantment of the folks be on a fine one!*

[To the Duke of Devonshire]   [Lausanne]
                                                         1 [July 1843]
One does forget that one is not fifteen in moments of excitement, and after being become older, larger, more infirm and apathetic at Rome than I have words to describe, the sulphur baths and drink at Arqui have so renovated me that I am obliged to recollect I am not a mountain nymph, and to be hauled back to this hotel last night. Continue to let me know how you are. Change of air for ten days. You get this on the 6th, put on your things, as women say, step over to Baden, where on the 12th we hope to be, take a peep at Herrnsheim and steam back all together to our native land. Think and leap.

*The Duke was giving morning parties at Chiswick on Wednesdays. At the last one the weather had been wretched, the guests obliged to crowd into the house. 'Not very champêtre', according to Lady Holland.

[286]

[July 1843]
We have had two nights of a fairy tale in the new Trois Couronnes
on the lake at Vevay, too enchanting. A magnifique château with
every luxury and comfort, a large terrace balcony, with seats,
tables, and orange trees, overlooks the parterre, and then with
parapets upon steps down to the lake. Granville is so well that my
only fear is you will none of you be able to think how essential the
utmost precaution and regularity of life are to him.

[To the Duke of Devonshire]   Devonshire House
Sunday [August 1843]
Oh! Chiswick! dearest brother, Chiswick! What shall I say?
Chatsworth, be jealous. Charles Greville, who overtook us at
Hammersmith and ambled on, was in ecstasies. He had not been
at one of your breakfasts; it was an utter surprise. He said he
never saw any thing so pretty. Then your room! The carpets! The
improvements in the garden, the walk through the open room to
the Horticultural, the flowers, the perfect enamel of the parterre,
the pink passion flower. Landseer's picture.* Charles Greville fell
from astonishment to astonishment. He had not seen Landseer or
any thing. 'God bless my soul! Have you seen any thing abroad to
compare with Chiswick?'

[To the Duke of Devonshire]   Devonshire House
5 [September 1843]
You are a benediction to us all. Here we are again in gratitude and
clover. Can you imagine the scene at Eu? Louis Philippe; how he
will bow! – roll over perhaps.†

[To the Duke of Devonshire]   Kemp Town
[December 1843]
Your letters are sun and make my climate. Brighton is doing its
pranks – pouring rain and gales of wind, and yet we, ensconced in

---

*Probably Landseer's *Bolton Abbey in the Olden Time*, painted in 1834, and
commissioned by the Duke.
†On the occasion of Queen Victoria's visit to Louis Philippe at the Château d'Eu.

your charming house, and as comfortable as it is possible to be, and before I answer your letter I must detail its advantages.[41] The gaiety compared with other places from the wide expanse of light and broad spaces; no sopped leaves and wet paths – a trottoir and two lamp posts. In the bluster no smoking chimneys. At half past six sat down to perdreaux a l'Espagnole, emincé au gratin, and a leg of mutton. Now where can hopeless weather boast such antedotes as this?

[To the Duke of Devonshire]   [Kemp Town]
                                                    [26 January 1844]
Brougham has been sitting with us on the esplanade for an hour. A little low for Cannes. 'Upon my soul, this is not credible', and it is today almost the finest day we have had. He was comparatively tranquil and exceedingly droll. God bless you, my dearest brother. We are going to luxuriate along the cliff.

                                                       [Kemp Town]
                                                    [28 January 1844]
Did I tell you of Lord Brougham's coming on Friday morning, hallooing and bawling to us on the esplanade? He was very droll, stayed an hour and is gone back to London.

[To the Duke of Devonshire]   [Kemp Town]
                                                    [29 January 1844]
Quite beat down with summer, I sit down, no fire and the windows open, to say a word or two. Dearest Grace, will you indulge a whim of mine and do me an immense favour? My prizes for a lottery are all settled and I have more than enough, but I want an extraordinary one from you. Do you think Mr Paxton could contrive that I should receive on the 6th a covered basket, docketed, with fruit and flowers from the Chatsworth conservatory? Oh, what a catch for the Brightonian, fond of names and who never sees a flower! I will hope that in the natural course of drawing that prize might fall on a resident, and if not, exchange being no robbery, I could manage one with some winner of a

drawing or a paper knife. Brother! Mr Paxton! I do not breathe
my request to any one, only if you can't or won't, take no heed of
it.

[Kemp Town]
[February 1844]

I went this morning in a fly by myself to the forbidden fruit, the
Huntingdon Chapel* (Dissent, but the service seemed to me just
the same as ours) to hear Mr Sortain. Wonderful eloquence,
energy, ardent and overwhelming, conquering every sort of
natural disadvantage. In person like Thiers[†] and Lord Boscawen,
with a thread, wire of a voice, and articulation seeming Herculean
labour. But how new, how clever, what beautiful language – and a
conviction that rivets one.

London
Friday [29 March 1844]

The Queen cried all day long after Albert departed. How rare it is
for royalty to have such pleasant sorrows.[‡]

Bruton Street
22 [April 1844]

I see I have not said enough about the Drawing Room. Vic looked
enormous, she bowed and smiled and hoped I was well, but less
gracious in looks and manner than the unpopular Albert who
seemed inclined to embrace me. Leopold careworn; Kent civil,
very few people. Lady Wharncliffe entirely enclosed in a gold
frame work, just like barley sugar treillage one sometimes sees over
cream and strawberries in entremets, a great love, in ecstasies over
the darling cream coloured horses, as comfortable as in bed, and
Lady Jersey, a very good natured old woman. The Duke of
Wellington in radiant health and spirits. Ouf! dearest sissie, it
bores me almost as much as being there to fight it over again.

*The Chapel of the Countess of Huntingdon Connection (a Methodist sect) was
built in 1761 in the grounds of her private house in North Street, Brighton.
†President of the Council and Foreign Minister.
‡Prince Albert had gone to Coburg on 28 March for his father's funeral.

I went yesterday to St Paul's [Knightsbridge]. I never liked any thing so much as Mr Bennett's sermon; * never disliked any thing so much as the performance of the service, a sort of parody of what I do not like in Rome. The clergyman who read the service hurried it over in a monotonous rapid mutter, the new way I am told. The music constant, troublesome, lively, inefficient, so that the Litany was like charity school children divided by London cries. But then came Mr Bennett, admirable, simple. The soundest doctrine, warmest piety, and most practical result. So here were all the pours et contres of Tractarianism – excellence in fact.[42] We went to the Temple Church at three. Too long, nearly two hours, beautiful music and very bad preacher.

The rest of this year, 1844, was spent between London and Brighton. Harriet's letters consist mostly of names of friends she has seen, and of Granville's health.

Wood End, [Brighton]
Thursday [Autumn 1844]

Jephson† now recommends dandelion instead of coffee and people are drinking it so much that at Leamington and its environs it sells for 4s. and 6d a pound. Make some of your young protegées gather some roots, have it ground and tasted (by some strong and daring stomach) just as coffee is drunk. You need not be afraid. Dandelion tea has long been the favourite tisane of the French. Jephson says it has none of the acidity or heating properties of coffee.

Panshanger
31 [December 1844]

Beautiful beyond any thing. Entrance hall – the room that is not the drawing room – but that we live in. The dining room magnificent – and the whole house an equal temperature and as warm as your heart could wish.

*The Revd W.J.E. Bennett, vicar from 1840 to 1850, when he resigned owing to the odium caused by his obnoxious ritualistic proceedings.
†Dr Jephson was a well-known and successful Leamington physician.

1st [January 1845]

Outside yesterday a dense (a happy new year to you all) fog, today better – the sun struggling. Society – Ld Melbourne and the Beauvales – Cowpers and Vyners – Mr Sneyd, the Poodle, Ld Aberdeen. I wish I could speak as you like of Ld M. We found him by the fire in a state of great languor – he did not speak and appeared extremely below par. At dinner he talked incessantly but it only gave the notion of extreme excitement and he ate and drank fearfully. We have had a very snug breakfast. Granville is extremely well. I did not like the idea of coming which I kept to myself and I am rewarded by being very comfortable and easy. The fog has, alas, and at 12 o'clock, got the better. I think you will (perhaps) understand my pining longing (kept to myself) to be at Brighton again in pure chrystal air.

Panshanger
2 January 1845

I am happy to tell you that Ld Melbourne was quite another man yesterday, appeared in better health, and more natural in spirits. Granville was struck with the agrément of his conversation and immense stores of knowledge.

[To the Duke of Devonshire]   Wrest Park[*]
[January 1845]

Beauty, luxury, and comfort. The fog has kept us indoors almost entirely, some walking in a handsome Nymphenberg looking garden excepted. The dining room and library are beautiful, the drawing room not finished. The tapestry manqué in design, execution, and colouring. The weather is unwholesome. Granville bilious, Lady Cowper in bed with a sore throat, Lord de Grey very ailing, but cheerful and patient. Mr Sneyd has a cold; the Poodle well for all, opening their eyes wide to the narrowness of their vestibules and corridors. We live a great deal in our rooms. In the evening we work and talk. We go to bed at eleven.

[*]Earl de Grey had only recently built Wrest Park in Bedfordshire in the style of a French country house. It is also known for its eighteenth-century gardens.

In March Granville had a bad attack of jaundice which weakened him considerably. In October he suffered a serious stroke.

[Bruton Street]
28 [March 1845]

My own dear sister, we drove round the Ring in a brougham today. It was very reviving – a strong gale of southerly wind, the Serpentine like a rough sea.

[To the Duke of Devonshire]   [Bruton Street]
[May 1845]

First, flowers. An orange orchid in full bloom sits in the middle window, the wonder of all beholders. You are much too amiable. Though we are just returned from sitting in an alcove in Kensington Gardens in a half hour of radiant sunshine, the weather here, too, is atrocious. Wind east and north, west for moments to delude one, and then back. But Granville is going on delightfully well.

[To the Duke of Devonshire]   [Bruton Street]
[December 1845]

Excellent bulletin, most dear brother. We had an hour and a quarter's drive in Hyde Park. He said he never enjoyed any thing more. He is stronger and all things are improved, but I know I must not feel sanguine. Yet I accept with gratitude and adoration all that is sent to soothe and cheer.

Granville died on 8 January 1846.

Notes

1   B. Askwith, *Piety & Wit*, 11.
2   For seventeen years Lady Bessborough had 'lov'd almost to Idolatory the only man . . . who has probably lov'd me least of all those who have profess'd to do so – tho' once I thought otherwise.' *Granville Correspondence*, ii, 434.
3   *Ibid.*, 363.
4   E.C. Mayne, *A Regency Chapter*, 238.
5   Askwith, 11.
6   'Lady Granville has a great deal of genius, humour, strong feelings, enthusiasm, delicacy, refinement, good taste, *naïveté* which just misses being affectation, and a *bonhomie* which extends to all around her.' *Greville Memoirs*, i, 63.
7   M.M. Cloake, *A Persian at the Court of George III*, 148.
8   Writing to Granville Lady Bessborough spoke of '. . . eyes long cut, of a beautiful bright blue, unlike any I ever saw except yours . . . the same long look, and the brilliant light blue in the middle, with a vein of dark.' *Granville Correspondence*, ii, 494. In fact the 'occhi azzuri'.
9   'The Dutchess of Rutland [is] every day at home and when sure of seeing no creature is dressed at all points to keep up the habit . . . one day *alone* at breakfast with her little son dressed as if for company and the same care which the conscious sylphs would have paid to the drapery and ringlets – her Grace going to the glass to arrange the ringlets and looking back over her shoulder at the effect of drapery behind.' C. Colvin, *Edgeworth Letters*, 61–2.
10   See *Granville Correspondence*, ii, 360.
11   *Ibid.*, 364–70.
12   Until quite recently the only published reference to Harriette is in *Granville Correspondence* and probably went undetected by the editor of the letters. In January 1802 Lady Bessborough won a prize of a little locket 'which', she told Granville, 'I mean for H. Pray give me a scrap of your hair to put into it for her'. i, 318.
13   R. Edgecumbe, *Diary of Frances Lady Shelley*, i, 33.
14   'Lady Elizabeth Gower is beautiful and I think altogether the most engaging, graceful, unaffected person I ever saw with a great deal of

conversation and talents withoùt pretensions.' *Edgeworth Letters*, 156.

15   In this ballet version, choreographed by Louis-Jacques Milon, assistant *maître de ballet* at the Opéra, Bigottini, herself chief dancer at the Paris Opera, had her biggest success. Lady Shelley was overcome by the 'delicacy and pathos of her acting', which made her cry. *Shelley Diary*, i, 204.

16   Samuel Rogers, poet, wit and connoisseur made many enemies with his slanderous tongue. Maria Edgeworth had no good to say of him. 'Of all the backbiters *ever I seen* dead or alive Rogers is beyond compare the most venomous, audacious and universal and at last it can hardly be called backbiting for he bites before the backs are turned . . .' *Edgeworth Letters*, 510.

17   It was about this date that Baron von Neumann, Secretary to the Austrian Embassy in London, attended a reception at Burlington House, and finding such a crowd of old women he thought himself in the family vault. E. Beresford Chancellor, *Diary of Philipp von Neumann*, i, 24.

18   Maria Edgeworth thought him very clever but conceited; he 'bites his fingers from vexation when he is not talking'. *Edgeworth Letters*, 187.

19   The Misses Berry did not please Maria Edgeworth. 'French ton – French gestures but not well bred low French voices – 'Moi je dis' in every tone. We saw quite enough to know that we wished to see no more.' *Edgeworth Letters*, 184.

20   To the virtuous Mrs Arbuthnot Lady Bessborough was 'much the cleverest & most agreeable woman I have ever known. In her youth she had been *très galante*, & in her mature years she had retained those charms of mind & manner which, in her earlier life had rendered her irresistibly attractive . . . Her errors arose from a false education & the seductive examples of clever but unprincipled men; & were well redeemed by a warmth of heart & steadiness of friendship that rendered her dear to her family & friends.' Bamford and Wellington, *Journal of Mrs Arbuthnot*, i, 129.

21   *The Greville Memoirs* provide a sketch of this unseemly conduct. 'Agar obtained early the reputation of being a prodigy of youthful talent and information. Quick, lively, and had a very retentive memory – the most conspicuous youth of his day. He resolved to marry and as his heart had nothing to do with this determination he pitched upon a daughter of the Duke of Beaufort's who he thought would suit his purpose, and confer upon him a very agreeable family connexion. Being on a tour of the North, he intended to finish it at Badminton and there to propose to Lady Georgiana Somerset, with full assurance that he would not be rejected, but

having stopped a few days at Castle Howard, he there found a girl who spared him the trouble of going any further, and at the expiration of three or four days he proposed to Georgiana Howard who, not less surprised than pleased and proud at the conquest, immediately accepted him. There never was a less romantic attachment or more business-like engagement, nor was there ever a more fortunate choice or happier union.' ii, 389–90.

22 The King's prevailing subject of complaint is *old age*, at which he feels, of course, the most royal indignation.' Sir Herbert Maxwell, *The Creevey Papers*, ii, 48.

23 Writing to Metternich on 14 March of this royal command to the Pavilion, Mme de Lieven described Harriet as 'longing to see the end of this visit. She cannot bear to be embarrassed or bored; it is quite a new thing for her.' P. Quennell, *Letters of Lieven to Metternich*, 162.

24 A.M.W. Stirling, *Letter-Bag of Lady Elizabeth Spencer-Stanhope*, ii, 84–5.

25 'Tonight is Lady Granville's regular reception, and always the pleasantest thing in Paris . . . but there never are much more than three hundred people, with four rooms open'd, beautifully furnished and lighted, & opening into a conservatory which goes round all the inside of the garden front, also lighted and carpeted. It is lovely and the French are in *fits* of delight & admiration about it.' C. Grosvenor and Lord Stuart Wortley, *The First Lady Wharncliffe*, ii, 2.

26 Writing of Harriet's 'Saturdays' Lady Wharncliffe commented: 'They turn into little breakfasts, and perhaps little dances, which being a morning affair is perfect for *half out* creatures.' She also wrote of 'the green room, which is the drawing room *upstairs*, furnish'd with green, and much more comfortable than the more splendid room below.' *Ibid.*, 3.

27 Giuditta Pasta (1797–1865), the Italian soprano singer, had captivated her audience in Rossini's *Otello* and had taken Paris by storm in this opera in 1822. Stendhal had found her performance unforgettable.

28 'They [the guests] meet at three o'clock,' Lady Shelley recorded, 'at which hour five or six phaetons come to the door, each to receive a lady and gentleman who drive about the country until five. At that hour the whole party dine in a hut on the shore of Virginia Water . . . The party sit at table until between nine and ten o'clock, then they return to the Cottage, dress *presto*, and go into the saloon where they play écarté and other games until midnight.' *Shelley Diary*, ii, 41.

29 Louisa Hardy, the daughter of Admiral Hardy, Nelson's friend,

declined Lord John Russell's overtures to marriage. Lady Holland thought it the greatest pity that 'he has the rage to marry upon him, as he is so frequently repulsed.' Lord Ilchester, *Lady Holland to Her Son*, 89.

30 'Mrs Norton is so nice it is a pity she is not quite nice, for if she were quite nice she would be so very nice.' Lady Leconfield, *Three Howard Sisters*, 192.

31 Probably the Duke of Devonshire's 'particularly sagacious female elephant' which he kept at Chiswick House. W. Blunt, *The Ark in the Park*, 19.

32 'His long powdered hair hanging down over his shoulders, his cadaverous complexion and his deformed foot give him a most extraordinary effect.' Leconfield, 145.

33 Her mother accused her of playing Beatrice 'like the chief mourner at a funeral'. D. Marshall, *Fanny Kemble*, 59.

34 'We arrived at Paris from Fontainebleau before five, having stopped to talk to Lady Granville on her way thither.' Lady Theresa Lewis, *Journals of Miss Berry*, iii, 432.

35 Writing of Mrs Norton, Lady Gower (soon to be Duchess of Sutherland) commented that 'There is certainly a great deal that is in bad taste about her, which one wonders at not feeling more shocked with on recollection, and out of the influence of her extraordinary beauty.' Leconfield, 178.

36 'Pour le charlatanisme la Granville vous en offre sous les formes les plus séduisantes.' G. Blakiston, *Lord William Russell to His Wife*, 350. Perhaps the sympathy of these old friends did not go very deep either side.

37 Writing to Lady Cowper in January of this year, Mme de Lieven remarked that 'Lady Granville still remains seated in her big armchair. She takes very little trouble and has singularly simplified the duties of an ambassadress.' *Lieven-Palmerston Correspondence*, 109.

38 Mme de Lieven was again writing to Lady Cowper: 'Lady Granville is the same as ever, very original, very self-centred and very outspoken . . . The French ladies don't like it, and she is always in some difficulty or other.' *Lieven-Palmerston*, 121.

39 'November 8th. Our Princes go away on the 14th; the question is when to return? The general belief is that the Great Lady has made up her mind, & only waits for the convenient moment to declare it – his organe is reckoned very shrill & displeasing.' *Lady Holland to Her Son*, 180.

40 Harriet seems to have been at fault in her conclusions. Ten days after her marriage Lady Palmerston (as she now was) wrote to a friend: 'My children too are all pleased at the step I have taken . . .

Had any of them been annoy'd or made the least objection I could not have done it, nor would not; but their liking and approving has made every thing easy for me.' T. Lever, *Letters of Lady Palmerston*, 224.

41 Lady Palmerston too had a decided penchant for Kemp Town. 'Here I am in the Duke's house,' she wrote, 'which is most comfortable and like an enchanted Palace, with all its beauties & nick Nacks. Birds flying on India Papers, curiosities of all sorts, a clock with two Birds that sing a duet, Pastiles kept burning by invisible hands.' *Ibid.*, 212.

42 'The Rev. J.W.E. Bennett . . . began cautiously to raise the tone of the services in this fashionable church; preaching in a surplice, intoning the prayers, dressing his choristers in cassocks and surplices, and making them chant the psalms. Then he assumed the eastern position at the communion table (which he called the altar), bowed to it, and even went so far as to add a cross, candlesticks, flower vase and frontals.' P. Anson, *Fashions in Church Furnishings*, 84.

Bibliography

ALL BOOKS ARE PUBLISHED IN LONDON
UNLESS OTHERWISE STATED

Anson, Peter, *Fashions in Church Furnishing*, 1960.

Askwith, Hon. Betty, *Piety & Wit*, 1982.

Bamford, Francis, and the Duke of Wellington, edd., *The Journal of Mrs Arbuthnot*, ii, 1950.

Blakiston, Georgiana, *Lord William Russell and His Wife*, 1972.

Blunt, Wilfrid, *The Ark in the Park*, 1976.

Chancellor, E. Beresford, trans. and ed., *Diary of Philipp von Neumann*, 1928.

Cloake, M.M., trans. and ed., *A Persian at the Court of George III, 1809–10*, 1988.

Colvin, Christina, ed. *Maria Edgeworth, Letters from England, 1813–44*, OUP 1971.

Edgcumbe, Richard, ed., *Diary of Frances Lady Shelley*, i, ii, 1912.

Enfield, Viscountess, ed., *Leaves from the Diary of Henry Greville*, i, 1883.

Falk, Bernard, *'Old Q's' Daughter*, 1937.

Gladwyn, Cynthia, *The Paris Embassy*, 1976.

Granville, Castala Countess, ed., *Lord Granville Leveson Gower, Private Correspondence, 1781-1821*, i, ii, 1917.

Hibbert, Christopher, *George IV Regent and King*, ii, 1972.

Ilchester, Earl of, ed., *Journal of Hon. Henry Edward Fox*, 1923.

Ilchester, Earl of, ed., *Elizabeth Lady Holland to her Son, 1821–45*, 1946.

Leconfield, Maud Lady, ed., *Three Howard Sisters*, 1935.

Lever, Tresham, ed., *The Letters of Lady Palmerston*, 1957.

Leveson Gower, Hon. Frederick, *Bygone Years*, 1905.

Leveson Gower, Sir George, and Palmer, Iris, edd. *Hary-o, The Letters of Lady Harriet Cavendish, 1796–1809*, 1940.

Lewis, Lady Theresa, ed., *Extracts of the Journals & Correspondence of Miss Berry*, iii, 1865.

Marshall, Dorothy, *Fanny Kemble*, 1977.

Maxwell, Sir Herbert, ed., *The Creevey Papers*, ii, 1904.

Mayne, Ethel Colburn, *A Regency Chapter*, 1939.

Quennell, Peter, ed., *The Private Letters of Princess Lieven to Prince Metternich, 1820–1826*, 1937.
Sichel, W., ed., *The Glenbervie Journals*, 1910.
Stirling, A.M.W., ed., *The Letter-Bag of Lady Elizabeth Spencer-Stanhope*, ii, 1913.
Strachey, Lytton, and Fulford, Roger, edd., *The Greville Memoirs*, i, ii, 1938.
Sudley, Lord, ed., *The Lieven-Palmerston Correspondence, 1826–56*, 1943.
Ziegler, Philip, *The Duchess of Dino*, 1962.
Ziegler, Philip, *Melbourne*, 1976.

Biographical Index

Arbuthnot, Mrs Harriet, 1795–1834. Granddaughter of 8th Earl of Westmorland. Married Charles Arbuthnot as his second wife 1814. Known for her close friendship with the Duke of Wellington. 'Pretty but what is vulgarly called Pig beauty', the emphasis being on youth, according to Lady Charlotte Bury.

Ashley, Anthony Lord, 1801–85. 7th Earl of Shaftesbury 1851. Married Lady Emily Cowper 1830. Distinguished for his housing reforms and as a philanthropist.

Bagot, Hon. Charles, 1781–1843. Second son of 1st Lord Bagot. Diplomatist. An early admirer of Harriet. Married Hon. Mary Welles-ley-Pole 1806. Six children, of which one certainly appears to have been illegitimate. This 'bone of contention' was born in 1812.

Bagot, Hon. and Revd Richard 'Dick', 1782–1854. Third son of 1st Lord Bagot. Married Lady Harriet Villiers 1806. Later appointed Bishop of Oxford. They had eleven children.

Beaufort, Charlotte Duchess of, 1771–1854. Granville's sister. Married 6th Duke of Beaufort 1791. Harriet respected and felt affection for this entirely estimable sister-in-law but the tendency at Badminton was towards Evangelical piety, certainly where the female contingent was concerned – and there were eight daughters – though it seems to have imposed no restraints on the rakish, unsatisfactory heir, Lord Worcester.

Berry, Mary, 1763–1852. Unmarried. A close friend of Horace Walpole who bequeathed her Little Strawberry Hill. She was known for her famous salons in Curzon Street, for her well-informed mind and sharp tongue. In 1798 her edition of *Works of Horace Walpole* appeared which was not universally well received. She and her younger sister Agnes were known as 'the Berrino'.

Bessborough, Henrietta Countess of, 1761–1821. Harriet's aunt. Younger daughter of 1st Earl Spencer. Married 3rd Earl of Bessborough 1780. Not so beautiful as her sister, Duchess Georgiana, but more seductive. She had had lovers and many admirers, but Granville, by whom she had had two children, was the most loved, 'almost to Idolatory' (*sic*).

Boringdon, Viscountess, *see* Morley, Frances Countess of.

Brougham and Vaux, Henry, 1st Baron, 1778–1868. Whig MP.

Attorney General to Queen Caroline 1820. Lord Chancellor 1830–4. Amorously involved with Hon. Mrs George Lamb. Married 1819 granddaughter of Sir Robert Eden, Bt.

Byng, Hon. Frederick ('Poodle'), 1784–1871. Given the sobriquet by Canning for his curly hair. Fifth son of the 5th Viscount Torrington. Clerk in the Foreign Office 1804–39. Married Catherine Neville, his mother's maid. A wit and one of the dandies of society, towards the end of his life he was known as a 'Regency remnant'.

Canning, George, 1770–1827. Prime Minister 1827. Died at Chiswick House, lent to him by the Duke of Devonshire. Supposedly once the lover of Queen Caroline, he had absented himself abroad during her trial in 1820.

Canning, Harriet, *see* Clanricarde, Marchioness of

Carlisle, Frederick, 5th Earl of, 1748–1825. Married Lady Caroline Leveson Gower 1770, Granville's half-sister. His verses, written in earlier days, had been well regarded. In the Devonshire House set he was considered 'the most finished macaroni of his time'. Lived with his family and unmarried sister at Castle Howard.

Carlisle, Georgiana Countess of ('Dearest G'), 1783–1858. Harriet's elder sister and the recipient of these present letters. Eldest daughter of the 5th Duke of Devonshire. Married Viscount Morpeth, eldest son of 5th Earl of Carlisle 1801. A devoted wife and sister and mother of twelve children; a dutiful daughter-in-law. A prey to nerves and fanciful disorders, hers was a more gentle and less independent character than her sister's.

Cavendish, Lady George. Died 1836. Married Harriet's uncle, younger brother of the 5th Duke of Devonshire, 1782. She died one year after her husband which caused the 6th Duke to observe: 'Poor Aunt George, only one year of happiness.'

Clarendon, George Villiers, 4th Earl of, 1810–70. Entered Diplomatic Service as attaché. While Ambassador in Madrid formed an intimate connection with Countess de Montijo, whose daughter became Empress Eugénie, wife of Napoleon III. From Madrid he proposed marriage by letter to a widow, Lady Katharine Barham, whom he had met only very occasionally. This marriage, though lacking the rudiments of romance, proved an exceedingly happy one.

Clanricarde, Harriet Marchioness of, 1804–76. Daughter of George Canning. Married Marquess of Clanricarde 1825, having tried, unsuccessfully, for Lords Ashley and Gower.

Clanricarde, Ulick, 1st Marquess of, 1802–74. Married Harriet Canning 1825. Ambassador to St Petersburg 1838–41. He had a bad reputation for low company. In 1826 Lady Cowper thought 'the youth hardly presentable', lacking in manners and looking like an Irish chairman.

Clifford, Augustus (Admiral Sir), 1788–1877. Harriet's half-brother.

Illegitimate son of 5th Duke of Devonshire and Lady Elizabeth Foster.
Entered Navy 1800. Created baronet 1838. After the Duke's death, his
mother, with great vulgarity of mind, attempted unsuccessfully to get
him acknowledged as a Cavendish. He was recognisable by his
resemblance to his father.

Coigny, Marquise de, 1758–1832. Before the French Revolution
a friend of Queen Marie-Antoinette. Famous in Paris society for
her wit and sharp tongue. Friend of Duchess Georgiana while an
émigrée in London till 1801. Said to have married Montrond during
her exile.

Conyngham, Elizabeth Marchioness of. Died 1861. Married 1st Marquess, Lord Steward of the Household, 1794. Her ascendancy over
George IV was established in 1819. She was less attentive to concealing
her boredom with the King than to salting away the jewellery and
furniture he lavished upon her. Mme de Lieven considered that 'she did
not belong to the kind of society one invites to dinner'.

Cowper, Emily Countess of, 1787–1869. Daughter of 1st Viscount
Melbourne. Married 5th Earl Cowper 1805. In 1839, two years after his
death, she married Viscount Palmerston. Handsome and worldly, the
leading political hostess, she had great influence at Almack's Assembly
Rooms, admitting or excluding as she saw fit.

Devonshire, Elizabeth Duchess of, 1748–1824. Second wife of the 5th
Duke of Devonshire whom she married in 1809. Daughter of the 1st Earl
of Bristol and widow of T.J. Foster, by whom she had two sons. Lived at
Devonshire House as an intimate friend of Duchess Georgiana and
became mistress of the Duke who fathered two children on her.
Ambitious and a schemer. During her second widowhood she lived
mostly in Rome where she contributed to local excavations, particularly
on the Palatine and in the Forum. She was on close terms with Consalvi,
Cardinal and statesman.

Devonshire, Georgiana Duchess of, 1748–1806. Mother of Harriet.
Daughter of 1st Earl Spencer, married 5th Duke 1774. A ravishing
creature of charm and beauty who kissed the butcher to win a Whig
vote. Crippled by gambling debts and bad health. One illegitimate
daughter by 2nd Earl Grey.

Devonshire, William ('Canis'), 5th Duke of, 1748–1811. Father of
Harriet, Married Lady Georgiana Spencer 1774. Apathetic and indifferent to the claims of his family but devoted to his greyhound puppies –
one of the few topics on which he would expatiate.

Devonshire, William ('Hart'), 6th Duke of, 1790–1859. Brother of
Harriet. Marquess of Hartington until succeeding his father in 1811.
Remained a bachelor despite heavy flirtations with Princess Charlotte,
Hon. Margaret Mercer Elphinstone, Lady Hunloke, and others. His
asthma and deafness inclined him in youth to hypochondria but with

maturity came enthusiasm for enlarging his collections at Chatsworth and elsewhere, and extending and developing his estates. Generous and warm-hearted, he was a devoted brother and uncle.

Dudley, John William, 1st Earl of, 1781–1833. Tory Foreign Secretary 1827–8. Died in an asylum at Norwood where he had been committed a year earlier.

Elphinstone, Hon. Margaret Mercer, *see* Flahault, Comtesse de.

Flahault, Comte Charles de, 1785–1870. Reputedly the illegitimate son of Prince de Talleyrand. Married Hon. Margaret Mercer Elphinstone 1817. French Ambassador in London 1842–8. He had fathered a son (Duc de Morny) on Queen Hortense of Holland 1811.

Flahault, Comtesse de, Hon. Margaret Mercer Elphinstone ('Poor Dear'), Baroness Keith and Nairne in her own right, 1788–1867. Married Comte de Flahault 1817. She had been an intimate friend of Princess Charlotte, and as an heiress with a strong mind and ambitions she had hoped, without success, to marry the 6th Duke of Devonshire.

Fox, Hon. Mary. Died 1891. Daughter of Lord Holland. Married 3rd Baron Lilford 1830. In her mother's view her charm consisted in her *beauté du diable*. It seemed to Harriet that her repressed home life had done nothing to enhance her looks or her general attitude.

Gower, George Granville Leveson ('Govero'), Earl, 1786–1861. Later 2nd Duke of Sutherland. Eldest son of 2nd Marquess of Stafford, 1st Duke of Sutherland. Married Lady Harriet Howard, daughter of 6th Earl of Carlisle. MP 1806–33. As a young man he had been in love with Louisa Queen of Prussia, Princess Pauline Borghese, Lady Selina Meade, but was quickly captivated by the daughter of his first cousin. On 25 April 1823 the Duke of Devonshire gave a coming-out ball for his niece, Harriet Howard. Her mother's diary records: '29 April, Hope of Lord Gower. 1 May, Lord Gower's note. 2 May, Lord Gower proposed and was accepted.'

Granville, George Granville Leveson Gower, 1st Earl, 1773–1846. Third and youngest son of 1st Marquess of Stafford by his third marriage. Married Lady Harriet Cavendish 1809. MP for Staffordshire. Subsequently Ambassador to France. Created Viscount 1815, Earl 1833. Clever, handsome and selfish with a grave propensity for gambling; notably one of the best whist players of his day. For many years the lover of Lady Bessborough who bore him two children. After marriage he settled down as an exemplary husband.

Granville, Harriet ('Hary-o'), Countess, 1785–1862. Younger daughter of 5th Duke of Devonshire. Married Lord Granville Leveson Gower (later 1st Earl Granville) 1809. Accompanied him as Ambassadress to France in 1824. The writer of these present letters, she was known for her wit and intelligence.

Greville, Lady Charlotte. Died 1862. Daughter of 3rd Duke of Portland.

Married Charles Greville, father of the diarist 1793. A close friend of the Duke of Wellington.

Greville, Charles Cavendish Fulke ('Punch'), 1794–1865. Known principally for his celebrated *Memoirs*. Privy Purse to the Duke of York. Clerk to the Council.

Harrowby, Susan Countess of, 1772–1838. Granville's sister. Married 1st Earl of Harrowby 1795. An enthusiasm for life and an elegance of person ensured Harriet's attachment to her.

Hertford, Francis Charles, 3rd Marquess of, 1777–1842. Married Maria Fagniani, reputedly the illegitimate daughter of the 4th Duke of Queensberry ('Old Q') 1798. Notorious as Thackeray's model for the depraved Marquess of Steyne in *Vanity Fair*, he was also renowned for his collection of art treasures.

Holland, Elizabeth Lady, 1770–1845. Married Sir Godfrey Webster 1786. Divorced for adultery with Lord Holland with whom she eloped, and subsequently married in 1797, but not before a son was born to them. Another son and two daughters, born in wedlock, followed. For many years she was not received by the prudish members of society because of her divorce, but at Holland House in Kensington all who were most brilliant in the world of politics and letters were to be met there if not afraid of her caustic tongue and often downright ungraciousness. Her manner was brusque, her mind fiercely political; a Whig; a devotee of Bonaparte. She had been a close friend of Duchess Georgiana. Harriet did not really like her.

Holland, Henry Richard Vassall, 3rd Baron, 1773–1840. Nephew of Charles James Fox. Married Lady Webster 1797. A Whig, a martyr to gout, deeply loved by his friends. 'Toleration was his darling object', Lady Holland wrote after his death. 'Peace, amity and indulgence were the predominant feelings of his heart.' These sentiments are borne out in Harriet's letters.

Hunloke, Anne Lady. Married 1807 Sir Henry Hunloke, Bt., of Wingerworth Hall, Derbyshire, by whom she had a son and two daughters; widowed 1816. A jolly, loquacious, flirting widow of most uncertain age, to whom the Duke of Devonshire was unexpectedly and rather unsuitably attracted.

Jersey, Sarah ('Silence') Countess of, 1785–1867. Eldest daughter of 10th Earl of Westmorland. Married 5th Earl of Jersey at Gretna Green 1804. From her grandfather, Robert Child of Osterley Park, and from her mother she inherited great wealth derived from Child's Bank of which she held the chief interest. With black hair and pale complexion, the leader of London society, she was the chief patroness of Almack's, that temple of fashion in whose Assembly Rooms only the brilliant were countenanced. She seemed to be perpetually in motion and her tongue never still. Mme de Lieven remarked that she chattered so hard that she lost her voice. Represented as Zenobia in Disraeli's novel *Endymion*.

Lamb, Lady Caroline ('Caro William'), 1785–1828. Harriet's first cousin. Daughter of 3rd Earl of Bessborough. Married Hon. William Lamb 1805. Fell in love with and pursued Byron, creating the celebrated scandal. In 1816 she published *Glenarvon*, an autobiographical romance, which further estranged her from society. Her mind which had always been unsound now became unbalanced. She had a son, Augustus (1807–36), who was subject to fits, some of them violent; his development was retarded.

Lamb, Hon. Frederick, 1782–1853. Created Lord Beauvale 1839 and succeeded his brother as 3rd Viscount Melbourne 1848. Diplomatist. Married Countess Alexandrina Maltzahn 1842 after many years of scandalous love affairs. He was forty years her senior.

Lamb, Hon. George, 1784–1834. Youngest son of 1st Viscount Melbourne. The Prince of Wales was said to be his father. Married Caroline St Jules 1809. Good-humoured and intelligent, boorish, noisy like his brothers, but unlike them, impotent. MP. Translated poems of Catullus.

Lamb, Hon. Mrs George ('Caro George') 1785–18? Harriet's half-sister. Illegitimate daughter of 5th Duke of Devonshire and Lady Elizabeth Foster. Lived at Devonshire House as Caroline St Jules until her marriage to Hon. George Lamb 1809. Finding him impotent she turned for consolation to Brougham with whom she had a somewhat protracted and wavering affair. She was often to be encountered with her half-brother and half-sisters who were fond of her.

Lamb, Hon. William, 1779–1848. Though a putative son of Lord Egremont, heir of 1st Viscount Melbourne whom he succeeded in 1829. Married Lady Caroline Ponsonby 1805 to whom he showed remarkable patience and affection despite her delinquencies. Whig MP. As Prime Minister at Queen Victoria's accession he guided and advised her for several years.

Leveson Gower, Lord Granville, *see* Granville, Earl of.

Leveson Gower, Lord Francis, 1800–57. Second son of 2nd Marquess of Stafford, 1st Duke of Sutherland. Married Harriet Greville, sister of the diarist 1822. Adopted his grandmother's name of Egerton 1833. Created Earl of Ellesmere 1846. Inherited an enormous fortune from his great-uncle, 3rd and last Duke of Bridgewater.

Lieven, Dorothea Countess, Princess, 1785–1857. Daughter of German Baron von Benckendorff, she was brought up in the Tsarist court after her mother died, in the care of the Empress Marie Feodorowna. Married Russian Count (later Prince) Christopher Lieven 1800. Cosmopolitan in outlook and with a sharp brain, she had been trained in diplomacy from early years when her husband was accredited to Berlin as Ambassador.

In 1812 he was appointed Russian Ambassador to England, where they remained twenty-two years. Mme de Lieven was perhaps feared more than she was liked, an arch-intriguer as unscrupulous as she was unsparing in her reports of others. It was power, in particular the power of politics, which motivated her. With Metternich, her most celebrated lover (though there were others), she carried on a correspondence for eight years, feeding him, as well as the Russian court, with every turn and twist, every rumour or circumstance of the English Government. Gossip, for which she was avid, often wittily presented, was hurriedly relayed. But despite her strictures on the dreariness of life in England, of the climate, of the bores, she nonetheless vastly enjoyed her time in London. In 1834 her husband was recalled to Russia. Princess Lieven, as she then was, preferred to settle in Paris where she became the constant companion of Guizot, the French statesman. She died in Paris having survived her husband and her two sons. Her friendship for Harriet, though relatively sincere, was not returned in like strength, probably because Harriet could not be hoodwinked. The Granvilles' son, Frederick Leveson Gower, recorded that his mother 'did not really feel much affection for her'. His father delighted in her conversation.

Long, Catherine Tylney-. Died 1825. Granddaughter of 5th Earl of Plymouth. Married Lord Wellesley (later 4th Earl of Mornington) 1812. A very considerable heiress – the Duke of Clarence offered for her six times when in the search for a wife. To be 'the Mother of Kings' appears to have been no inducement.

Luttrell, Henry, 1765–1851. Natural son of 2nd Earl of Carhampton. Brilliant, witty, a dynamic figure in society and accomplished poet. Lady Holland took a less enthusiastic view: 'In a small coterie he is ditch water.' He and his close friend George Nugent (said to be his half brother) were known as 'the Albanians'.

Metternich, Prince Clemens, 1773–1859. Austrian statesman and Prime Minister. At one time the lover of Mme de Lieven; she corresponded with him, repeating political news and gossip.

Montrond, Comte Casimir, 1768–1843. Lifelong friend of Prince de Talleyrand whose *âme damné* he was said to be. A gambler, a roué, and generally dangerous.

Morley, Frances Countess of ('La Donna'). Died 1857. Married 1st Earl (previously Viscount Boringdon) as his second wife 1809. Her fund of high spirits and witty sayings made her universally popular.

Morpeth, Lady Georgiana, *see* Carlisle, Georgiana Countess of.

Norton, Mrs Caroline, 1808–77. Daughter of Thomas Sheridan and granddaughter of Richard Brinsley Sheridan. Married Hon. George Norton 1827 who unsuccessfully brought an action for adultery against Lord Melbourne. Separated from her husband 1836. Made a living as writer and poet. Distinguished for her beauty.

Nugent, George, Baron, 1788–1850. Younger son of 1st Marquess of Buckingham. Succeeded to his mother's Irish peerage 1813. Said to be a half-brother of Henry Luttrell – together they were known as 'the Albanians'. Lady Charlotte Bury dubbed him 'a fat fubsy man very like a white turkey cock, a good musician and sings correctly'.

Paxton, (Sir) Joseph, 1801–65. Manager of the Duke of Devonshire's estates in Derbyshire and employed at Chiswick House as ornamental and architectural gardener. His 300-foot-long conservatory at Chatsworth served as model for the Crystal Palace at the Great Exhibition in Hyde Park 1851. MP for Coventry 1854–65.

Pisaroni, Benedetta, 1793–1872. Italian contralto singer from Piacenza. Disfigured by smallpox and by an ungainly shape she was nevertheless acclaimed for the beauty of her voice.

Rawdon, Elizabeth, *see* Russell, Lady William.

Russell, Lady William 1793–1875. Married Lord William Russell, second son of 6th Duke of Bedford 1817. Gifted in languages and intellect, hers was a dominating and rather selfish character.

St Jules, Caroline, *see* Lamb, Hon. Mrs George.

Shelley, Frances Lady, 1787–1873. Married Sir John Shelley, Bt., a distant connection of Percy Bysshe Shelley 1807. His interests were centred on the gambling table and the Turf; he once won the Derby. Lady Shelley's *Diary* promotes her friendship with the Duke of Wellington.

Stafford, Elizabeth Marchioness of, *see* Sutherland, Elizabeth Duchess of.

Stafford, 2nd Marquess of, *see* Sutherland, 1st Duke of.

Stewart, George, 1804?–70. Illegitimate son of Lady Bessborough and Granville whom he looked upon as his guardian. Given his paternal grandmother's maiden name. Lived with the Granvilles, travelled abroad, and from 1824 became his father's secretary.

Stewart, Harriette, 1800–52. Illegitimate daughter of Lady Bessborough and Granville whom she looked upon as her guardian. Given her paternal grandmother's maiden name. From childhood she lived with the Granvilles. Married 1824 George, Lord Godolphin (8th Duke of Leeds 1859).

Sutherland, Elizabeth, Duchess of, 1765–1839. Countess of Sutherland in her own right and immensely rich. Married 2nd Marquess of Stafford 1785. Known as the Duchess-Countess when her husband became 1st Duke of Sutherland. Her high standard in society did little to sweeten her temper or moderate her dominating attitude. Harriet as a girl 'could not bear her', nor was she inclined to like her much better as a sister-in-law.

Sutherland, George Granville, 1st Duke of, 2nd Marquess of Stafford, 1758–1833. Granville's half-brother. Married Elizabeth Countess of Sutherland in her own right 1785. Responsible for the clearances in

Sutherland, bringing suffering as well as agricultural reforms. Owned a distinguished collection of pictures, part of which had come from Orléans House. 'A Leviathan of wealth', according to Charles Greville.

Villiers, Hon. George *see* Clarendon 4th Earl of.

Ward, Hon. John William, *see* Dudley, 1st Earl of.

Wrottesley, Lady Caroline. Died 1818. Sister of 5th Earl of Tankerville (better known as 'Little O', for Lord Ossulston – as he was before he succeeded – was small in stature). Married Sir John Wrottesley 1795, created Baron 1838.

Yarmouth, Richard, Earl of, 1800–7. Succeeded his father as 4th Marquess of Hertford 1842. Unmarried. Enormously rich and led a life of extravagance and dissipation. He left his fine collection, which included that of his father, to his natural son (Sir) Richard Wallace who also added to it. This now forms the Wallace Collection at Hertford House, London.

Index

Entries in bold type are included in the Biographical Index

Magennis, Mr, 239
Majocchi, Teodoro, 138
Marie-Amélie, Queen of France (1782–1866), 192, 238, 241, 271, 275
Mars, Mdlle (1779–1847), 79, 80, 263, 273
Maryborough, 1st Baron (1763–1845), and Katherine Lady (1760–1851), 178
Mecklenburg-Schwerin, Princess Hélène of, 271–2, 273
Melbourne, Elizabeth Viscountess (1752–1818), 51, 65, 66, 105, 109
Melbourne, 1st Viscount (1744–1828), 43, 187
Melbourne, 2nd Viscount, see Lamb, Hon. William
Melville, 2nd Viscount (1771–1851), 118
Mesnard, M. de, 76
Metternich, Prince (1773–1859), 76, 78, 80
Milbanke, Annabella, see Byron, Lady
Milon, L-J., 108
Montagu, Hon. Edward (1787–1847), 54, 134, 163, 166
Montesquieu, Comte de, 81
Montrond, Comte (1768–1843), 225
Montrose, 3rd Duke of (1755–1836), 176
Moore, Thomas (1779–1852), *Lalla Rookh*, 116
Morley, 1st Earl of ('Borino') (1772–1840), 70, 113, 114, 135, 141; at Saltram, 82ff, 172; Pains and Penalties, 142; and a false rumour, 167
Morley, Frances Countess of (1781–1857), 154, 155; character, 82, 165, 172; at Saltram, 85, 86, 172; in Paris, 114, 204
Morny, Comte de (1811–65), 96
Morpeth, Viscount, see Carlisle, 6th Earl
Morpeth, Georgiana Lady, see Carlisle, Countess of
Mount-Charles, Earl of (1795–1824), 155, 156

Napoleon I, Emperor, see Bonaparte
Nash, John (1752–1835), 137
Neumann, Baron von (1778–1851), 123
Ney, Marshal of France (1769–1815), 80, 81
Nicholas I, Emperor of Russia (1796–1855), 76
Noailles, Mme de, 79, 197, 217

Normanby, 1st Marquess of (1797–1863), 279
Norton, Hon. George (1800–75), 267, 268
Norton, Hon. Mrs George (Caroline) (1808–77), at Chatsworth, 230; and scandal, 267, 268, 269; *The Wife and Woman's Reward*, 266
Nugent, Baron (1788–1850), 53, 54, 84, 91, 145

O'Neill, Eliza (1791–1872), at Plymouth, 86–7; Belvidera, 66, 67, 68, 86; *Isabella*, 68; *Measure for Measure*, 97, *Romeo and Juliet*, 67
Orléans, Duc d', see Louis Philippe, King
Orléans, Duchesse d', see Marie-Amélie, Queen
Orléans, Ferdinand, Duc d' (1810–42), son of Louis Philippe, marriage, 271, 272, 278
Orsay, Comte d' (1801–52), 170
Osborne, Lady Francis (d. 1847), 185; character, 181, 183–4, 187, 188
Osborne, Lord Francis (1777–1850), 183, 186, 187, 188
Osborne, George (1802–72), love for Harriette and marriage, 183, 184–5, 187
Ossulston, Corisande Lady (1782–1865), 32
Ossulston, Lord ('little O') (1776–1859), 32
Otway, Thomas (1652–85), *Venice Preserv'd*, 66
Oxford, Jane Elizabeth Countess of (1772–1824), 19

Paget, Hon. Sir Arthur (1771–1840), and Lady Augusta, 135
Pahlen, Count (1778–1864), 166, 267
Pains and Penalties, Bill of, 136–48
Paisiello, Giovanni (1741–1816), 111
Paley, Ven. William (1743–1805), 23
Palmerston, 3rd Viscount (1784–1865), 250, 280; as Foreign Secretary, 264, 265; marriage, 280
Pasta, Giuditta (1798–1865), 216
Paxton, Joseph (1801–65), 265, 270, 288
Peel, Sir Robert (1788–1850), 264, 271
Pennant, Thomas (1726–98), 65
Périgord, Comtesse de, see Dino, Dorothea Duchesse de
Perry, Mr, surgeon, 94

Petersham, Viscount (1780–1851), 100
Pierrepont, Hon. Henry (1780–1851), 75, 100
Pigot, Major-General Sir George Bt., and wife, 35
Pisaroni, Benedetta (1793–1872), 220, 224–5
Planta, Joseph (1787–1847), 169
Polignac, Prince de (1780–1847), 228
Ponsonby, 2nd Baron (1772–1855), and Frances Lady (d. 1866), 56
Ponsonby, Hon. Frederick (1783–1837), 68, 69, 70, 76, 81
'Poodle', *see* Byng, Hon. Frederick
Portsmouth, 3rd Earl of (1767–1853), 141
Pozzo di Borgo, Count (1768–1842), 53, 78, 245
Prussia, King of, *see* Frederick William III
'Punch', *see* Greville, Charles

Raguse, Duchesse de, 113, 114
Rawdon, Elizabeth, *see* Russell, Lady William
Rawdon, Hon. Mrs John, 48, 115
Rhodes, Revd R., 285
Rivers, 4th Baron (1810–66), first impression of, 247; marriage, 248, 249
Rivers, Frances Dowager Lady (1785–1860), 255
Rivers, Susan Lady (1810–66), 77, 96, 175; birth, 41; appearance, 41, 57, 118, 241, 248–9, 250; to Paris, 107, 108, 114, and Switzerland, 114; adored by Harriet, 247; engagement and marriage, 248, 254; honeymoon, 254; her presentation, 255; childbirth and illness, 257–8
Rogers, Samuel (1763–1855), at Ampthill, 126, 132–3, 270
Rolla, dog, 30, 55
Romney, George (1734–1802), 28
Rossini, Gioachino (1792–1868), 166, 176, 177, 178
Rothschild, Baroness James de (1805–86), 192
Rowe, Nicholas (1674–1718), *The Fair Penitent*, 20
Royal Lodge, 137, 228
Russell, Lord John (1792–1878), 138, 229, 264, 265
Russell, Lady William (1793–1874), appearance, 48, 100, 115, 133, 134, 150, 244; marriage, 115; at Woburn, 150, 151, 152, 153; her gift to Harriet, 266
Russell, Lord William (1790–1846), 133, 151, 152, 244; marriage, 115
Russia, Emperor of, *see* Alexander I
Rutland, 5th Duke of (1778–1857), 79–80
Rutland, Elizabeth Duchess of (1780–1825), 25
Ryder, Dudley, *see* Sandon, Viscount
Ryder, Elizabeth (d. 1830), 30–1

Sagan, Duchesse de (d. 1839), 80, 82
St Helens, 1st Baron (1753–1839), 176
St Jules, Caroline, *see* Lamb, Hon. Mrs George
Sand, George (1804–76), *André*, 266
Sandon, Viscount (1798–1882), 29, 125, 129
Sandwich, Louisa Dowager Countess of (1781–1862), 177, 280
Sandwich, Mary Countess (1812–59), 278, 279
Saxe-Coburg-Kohary, Prince Ferdinand (1816–85), and Augustus (1818–85), 267
Schwarzenberg, Field-Marshal Prince (1771–1820), 81
Scott, John, editor (1783–1821), *Tour de France*, 91
Scott, Sir Walter (1771–1832), 65; *Heart of Midlothian*, 122; *Kenilworth*, 154
Seward, Anna ('Swan of Lichfield') (1747–1809), 47
Seymour, Lady George (d. 1848), 177
Shelley, Frances Lady (1787–1873), character and appearance, 56; and Wellington, 74, 75, 77, 78, 81
Shelley, Sir John, Bt., (1771–1852), 56, 74, 75, 137
Sheridan, Richard Brinsley (1751–1816), 20, 39, 82
Siddons, Sarah (1755–1831), 234
Sloane, Lady Gertrude (d. 1870), 167
Smith, Revd Sydney (1771–1845), 107, 209
Sneyd, Ralph, 90, 128, 166, 235, 291
Sneyd, Mrs, 45
Somerset, Lady Georgiana (d. 1865), 162
Somerset, Revd Plantagenet (1803–55), 164
Sophia, Princess (1777–1848), 139, 140

Soult, Marshal of France (1769–1851), 202

Southerne, Thomas (1659–1746), *Isabella*, 68

Souza, M. de, 112, 120

Spencer, Georgiana Dowager Countess (1737–1814), 12, 21, 24, 36, 39, 40, 64

Spencer, Lavinia Countess (1762–1831), 48

Spencer, William, 39, 57

Staël, Mme de (1766–1817), 98, 108, 109, 110, 111

Stafford, Elizabeth Marchioness of Stafford, *see* Sutherland, Duchess of

Stafford, 2nd Marquess of, *see* Sutherland, 1st Duke of

Stewart, George (?1804–70), parentage, 11; joins Granvilles, 49, and for sister's marriage, 185; character, 135; as Granville's secretary, 225

Stewart, Harriette (1800–52), 88; parentage, 11, 49, 54; joins Granvilles, 49, 50; appearance, 50, 87, 188; character, 51, 52, 149; endears herself to Harriet, 91; behaviour, 107, 125, 133; to Paris, 107, 108, 114, and Switzerland, 114; her ball, 128, 129, 130; dances at Saltram, 174; death of Lady Bessborough, 158, 161; her marital position, 166–7; love and marriage, 183, 184–5, 187, 188

Stewart, Lord (1778–1854), rivalry for Paris Embassy, 74, 76; reputation, 74, 75, 81; and Duchesse de Sagan, 80, 82

Strachan, Charlotte, 250

Stuart, Sir Charles, *see* Stuart de Rothesay, Baron

Stuart, Lady, 104

Stuart, Hon. Louisa (1818–91), 272

Stuart de Rothesay, 1st Baron (1779–1845), appearance, 67; characteristics, 67, 78, 95; as Ambassador, 73, 74, 75–6, 81, 183, and reappointment, 225, 227; marriage, 95, 259; behaviour, 104, 108, 109, 111–12, 113, 114, 240, 244, 272; recalled, 186, and departure, 188; raised to peerage, 225; return to Paris, 230, and remains there, 238

Stuart de Rothesay, Elizabeth Lady (1786–1867), marriage, 95, 259; appearance, 95, 107, 111, 193; behaviour, 104, 114, 240–1, 243; her popularity gauged, 109, 193; pecuni-

ary allowance, 189; as Ambassadress, 198–9, 204, 242; returns to Paris, 230, 272

Sutherland, 1st Duke of (1758–1833), 11, 32, 118, 230; portraits of, 27; characteristics, 42, 43; and clearances, 51, 106; quarrels with brother-in-law, 124; opposition to the Queen, 141, 144; repressed in spirit, 118, 166; health, 232; death, 256

Sutherland, Elizabeth Duchess of ('Duchess-Countess') (1765–1839), 66, 140, 146; portraits of, 27; character, 42, 64, 118, 119, 128; characteristics, 43, 106, 116–17; preoccupied with marital designs, 117, 166–7; and clearances, 51, 106; appearance, 53, 65, 106, 128; attitude to Lord Gower, 123–4; thoughts of poison, 124–5; good-humoured, 141, 230, 231; death, 277

Talbot, 2nd Earl (1777–1849), 35, 60, 106

Talbot, Frances Countess (1782–1819), 26, 44, 46, 50; appearance, 25; bilious, 59; on Woburn, 93; and Paris, 104

Talleyrand-Périgord, Comtesse Edmond de, *see* Dino, Duchesse de

Talleyrand-Périgord, Prince de (1754–1838), 81, 96, 266; as Ambassador, 77; appearance, 78, 237; travels with Harriet, 251–2, and calls upon her, 252

Talma, François Joseph (1763–1826), 80

Tavistock, Anna Maria Marchioness of (1783–1857), at Bolton Abbey, 60, and Chatsworth, 120, and Ampthill, 133; admiration for, 133; appearance, 150; character, 61

Tavistock, Marquess of (1788–1861), 120; at Bolton Abbey, 60, 61, 133

Thanet, 9th Earl of (1767–1828), 151–2

Thiers, Louis (1797–1877)), 289

Thomson, James, *Castle of Indolence*, 24

Tierney, George (1761–1830), 142

Times, The, 77

Tixal, 13, 48, 49, 50, 64, 87, 128, 135

Trelawny, Edward (1792–1881), 267, 268

Trimmer, Selina, 12, 24, 39, 40, 129

Tripp, General Baron, 57

Upton, Hon. Arthur (1777–1855), 20, 21, 22

Vernon, George (1785–1879)
Victoria, Princess, Queen (1819–1901), 117, 140, 287; marital conjectures for, 267; behaviour, 275, 277; appearance, 278, 279, 289; marriage, 280
Villiers, Hon. Mrs George (1775–1856), 37, 99, 103–4
Villiers, Theresa, daughter of Mrs George Villiers (1803–65), 150, 151, 204
Vyner, Henry (d. 1861), and Lady Mary (d. 1892), 291

Walewski, Comte (1810–68), 229
Waller, Thomas (1805–92), 239
Ward, Hon. John William, see Dudley, Earl of
Webster, Lady Frances (d. 1837), 77, 78–9
Wellesley, 1st Marquess (1760–1842), 141
Wellington, Catherine Duchess of (1772?–1831), 111, 129
Wellington, 1st Duke of, 50, 109, 176, 289; in Paris, 73, 74, 76, 111, 115; and Lady Shelley, 74, 78, and Lady Frances, 77, 78–9, and Lady Caroline Lamb, 80, 87–8, 112; wins Harriet's respect, 112; and Lady Charlotte Greville, 129; gifts offered to, 146; visits Wherstead, 153, 163, 167, 175–6; with King at Waterloo, 157; appointed Prime Minister, 225; resigns, 237
Westmorland, 10th Earl of (1759–1841), 192

Wherstead, 128–9, 134–5, 149; a day at, 143–4; Duke fails to visit, 165
William I, King of the Netherlands (1772–1844), 182
William IV, King, 129; at the theatre, 155, 156; suffers from gout, 176; succeeds, 236; death, 273
Willis, Dr Francis (1718–1807), and Dr John (1751–1835), 30
Wilmot, Robert (1784–1841), 125, 137, 144
Wilson, Harriette (1789–1846), 56, 250
Windsor Castle, 207, 228
Worcester, Georgiana Marchioness of (d. 1821), 150, 152
Worcester, Marquess of (1792–1853), 151, 164
Wortley, Lady Georgiana (1779–1856), 62; as Lady Wharncliffe, 289
Wortley, James (1776–1845), 62
Wrottesley, Lady Caroline (d. 1818), 33; and scandal, 44, 45
Wrottesley, Sir John (1771–1841), 45
Wyatville, Sir Jeffry, 228

Yarmouth, Earl of (1800–74), 253; behaviour, 248, 249–50
York, Duke of (1763–1827), 22; at Woburn, 150, 151–2; at the theatre, 155, 156; at Wherstead, 175, 176, 177; at the Pavilion, 177; death, 219–20
York, Vernon Harcourt, Archbishop of (1757–1847), 101, 141, 142, 144
Yorke, Lady Elizabeth, see Stuart de Rothesay, Elizabeth Lady